Stories We Pray

Insights into the Inner-Work of Jewish Worship

Joel Lurie Grishaver

ISBN 13 #978-1-934527-46-7

TORAH AURA PRODUCTIONS

4423 FRUITLAND AVENUE, LOS ANGELES, CA 90058

(800) BE-TORAH • (800) 238-6724 • (323) 585-7312 • FAX (323) 585-0327

E-MAIL <MISRAD@TORAHAURA.COM>
VISIT THE TORAH AURA WEBSITE AT WWW.TORAHAURA.COM

Manufactured in USA

TABLE OF CONTENTS

FOREWORD

I began collecting stories because Shlomo Carlebach told stories. For a long time I considered myself to be just a teacher who told stories. It took Peninnah Schram to convince me that I was a storyteller and Robbie Gringris to put me in a context in which I was regularly telling stories. Telling stories got me to collect stories. Torah Aura Productions gave me a context in which I was using my stories as curriculum. About ten years ago I began to see a pattern connecting *midrashim* to prayers. This book has grown out of my search for that pattern. Torah Aura gave me the space and the time for this quest. Much of this material originally was found for Torah Aura's *T'fillah* Curriculum.

Midrash doesn't understand truth the way that logic does. In it things can be simultaneously contradictory and true. Midrash works with the logic of the myth, and a myth is "a truth frozen in a story" (Robert Bly). Truth is different from history. In myth, two or more things are usually true at the same time; simultaneous ambivalent truth is the way of the world, and the way of midrash.

The Rabbis were not systematic writers; rather, they worked associatively. That means that it is impossible to find a midrash or *aggadah* for every prayer in the liturgy. But the Jewish tradition is larger than just the Rabbinic one. Often, not in shaping the liturgy, but in exploring it, folktales or H̲asidic stories dig to the heart of a prayer. In choosing the stories for this collection I was not always able to find the midrashic "origin" story. Sometimes I had to work backwards from other sources. All these stories have a Jewish context, sometimes evolving through Jewish folk literature, sometimes through original works of fiction, particularly by Yiddish writers or their American extensions between the 1930s and 1950s who were well schooled in Jewish forms and Jewish insights.

What can be said about this collection is that it has a preference for Rabbinic origin stories. Where these could not be found, other branches of Jewish literature were mined until a story that dug into the "inner work" of a prayer could be found. Just like the *Hallel* liturgy that has six or seven origin stories, this collection does not claim to be exhaustive, but it does claim to facilitate the work of looking into the *kavanah* (inner work) of many pieces of the Siddur.

All of the tellings in this book are original, even if none of the stories were. Often they are midrashic expansions of a single idea in order to contextualize it within the Jewish tradition. Other times, much longer forms were shortened to fit into the context. The wording is all mine; the origins are as well sourced as I can reconstruct them after ten years of work. Enjoy.

a person is incapable of a sudden confrontation with the Creator. The overwhelming experience of such awareness is just too awesome. Truth, the stark Truth, must be camouflaged. Only then can the soul gradually absorb it.

God, so to speak, is camouflaged in stories. These are the stories of Creation and of Adam and Eve. The stories of the Flood and of the Patriarchs. The stories of Jewish exile and redemption. God is hidden in all the stories of human history. And, in the as yet untold stories of each and every human being. His trials. Her tribulations. And their salvation.

At the Pesah seder we tell stories—*maggid*. We recount the stories of the exile in, and the redemption from, Egypt. These represent the collective stories of humankind. They typify the individual stories of each and every one of us. As we relate the details of these stories, we must relate to them. Be aroused by them. See the Hand of God in the stories of our own lives...

(Rabbi Nahman of Bratslav, *Likkutei Halakhot*, Nedarim 5:6-8)

INTRODUCTION: THE POWER OF NARRATIVE

Every prayer tells a story. Those stories are paths to understanding how to use their words for self-transformation and for connecting with God. This book is a collection of many of those stories.

CREEDOLOGY VERSES DRAMATURGY

We usually think of the Siddur, the Jewish prayerbook, as a carefully ordered and structured collection of words. We tend to study those words as texts, believing that their job is to teach us about God. In his collection of CDs, *The Hidden Poetry of the Jewish Prayerbook: The What, How, and Why of Jewish Liturgy* (Brookline: Our Learning Company, 2006), Reuven Kimelman suggests that each prayer is an argument. He teaches that those arguments are premises about God that we are supposed to come to believe. He suggests that the Jewish liturgy is a creedology, a series of ideas we work to believe deeply. Each repetition of those ideas is designed to reinforce and more deeply connect us to those beliefs. It is the spiritual equivalent of writing something fifty times on the blackboard. This is a good, traditional Jewish approach, most clearly rooted in Maimonides' work, where he lays out in his Thirteen Attributes of Faith an essence of Jewish belief that he believes is central to Jewish life. In his commentary on the *Mishnah* (*Sanhedrin*, chapter 10), Maimonides says that these elements of faith are "the fundamental truths of our religion and its very foundations." Kimelman and many others apply this Maimonidean process to the liturgy.

Taking nothing away from that thinking, I am committed to what I believe is an older, more reflection-oriented form of Jewish thinking. When the Rabbis, the compilers of the Siddur and Haggadah and the authors of the Talmud and the Midrash, try to explain prayers, they use stories. They tell an origin story, the story of the first time a prayer was said. This is much like the culture found in comic books (a mainly Jewish art form), where the superhero's origin explains his or her nature.

To understand this in the Siddur, let's take an example. *Hallel* is a collection of the six Psalms, 113-118, that are said on the three festivals of Pesah, Shavuot, and Sukkot; the new month except for *Tishrei*; Hanukkah (but not Purim); and *Yom ha-Atzma'ut* (Israel Independence Day) and *Yom Yerushalayim* (Jerusalem Day).

On the one hand, the tradition teaches that all of the Psalms were written by King David. Therefore, the midrash on Psalms teaches, "When David thought of how glad the children of Israel were when they went forth out of Egypt, he began to sing in praise of the Exodus from Egypt" (Psalm 114). In other words, memory of an historical event triggered a spontaneous act of prayer. The Talmud, however, gives us a second, contradictory and complementary origin of *Hallel* by saying, "*Hallel* was said by (a) Moses and Israel at the Reed Sea, (b) Joshua when the Canaanites threatened Israel, (c) Deborah and Barak before they faced Sisera, (d) Hezekiah when Jerusalem was attacked by Assyria, (e) Hananiah, Misha'el and Azariah when Nebuchadnezzar threatened them, and (f) Mordechai and Esther when Haman wanted to destroy the Jews" (*Pesahim* 117a). All six of these are Jewish victories. If taken literally, Israel created the *Hallel* at each of the biblical moments when they faced significant danger. In the Talmud (*Pesahim* 118a) we are told *Hallel* is said at times when Israel is in danger, and it is said when Israel is rescued. And, we can add, because of the David midrash, when we say *Hallel* we remember being in danger and we remember being rescued.

Creedology is a hybrid word that meshes "creed" (a list of required beliefs) with "theology" (the study of God). I don't know who coined it, but it has been used by such diverse thinkers as the poet Michael Pain and the Jewish writer Chaim Potok (in a 2002 interview with the magazine *Christianity Today*). It suggests that a liturgical repetition of a list of beliefs can lead to their internalization. This is one view of the role of liturgy.

Dramaturgy is a theater term used to talk about the craft of writing for the stage, the shaping of a story into a form that may be acted out. Dramaturgy is also a hybrid word that was first used sociologically by Erving Goffman in his 1959 book *The Presentation of Self in Everyday Life* (New York: Knopf Doubleday Publishing Group, 1959). He uses it as a way of applying the framework of theater to human interactions. He says that human relations are dependent upon time, place, and audience. He explains that the sense of self is a dramatic effect that comes from the scene being acted out. My teacher, Rabbi Haskell Bernat, used dramaturgy as a fusion of drama and liturgy, referencing both the sociological and the dramatic implications of the word. He used it, as I now use it, to describe the ability of the liturgy to be acted out in the heart. This is a different, more affective definition of the Jewish liturgical process.

THE RABBIS AND THE ACTOR'S STUDIO

When the Jewish liturgy was first created there was an order, but there was not a book. Or at least there were not very many copies of the book. To replace the sacrificial process, the Rabbis (after 70 C.E.) created a series of blessings that had set endings, sometimes set beginnings, and flexible middles. This created a process of prayer that was often improvisational, created out of personal expressions of predetermined theological themes. I called it "jazz"; Rabbi Bernat used to speak of it as the artistry involved in a "concerto grosso." The process was much like a Tour de France of blessing, with each stage beginning and ending at the same point, but with the individual participants moving in their own paths in their own ways. The existing structure of the Siddur, suggested in the Talmud, was specifically laid out by Rabbi Amram Gaon of Sura, Babylonia, in about 850 C.E. It was an answer to a question asked by the Spanish Jewish community. The Siddur was first printed in 1486 by the Soncino House in Italy. It was then that the Siddur began to become a text.

Jewish prayer has always been a dialogue between *keva* (fixed form) and *kavanah* (transformational insight). While we know that prayer involves "inner work," the question has long been "What is the nature of this inner work?" Many, like Kimelman, draw on Maimonides and see prayer as a creedology, a carefully crafted set of "exercises" that continually reinforce a set of beliefs. I believe that the Rabbis saw prayer as a set of theater games. To understand this we need to know just a little about method acting.

Developed by Konstantin Stanislavsky in collaboration with the playwright Anton Chekhov, "the method" is a way to create dramatic performances by having the actor match the psychological and emotional make up of the character. Rather than seeing acting as the mastery of a series of techniques (thirty-seven kinds of laughter, twelve ways of crying, twenty-two sobs, etc.), acting was defined as a kind of inner work. Popularized by the Group Theater in New York in the 1930s and advanced by such teachers as Lee Strasberg and Stella Adler, method acting was a form of radical empathy.

An actor created a "back story" for the character, imagining the full history of the character before and after the story arc of the play. The actor looked for the subtext (emotional impact) of each speech, then hunted for a "sense memory" or "affective memory" in his or her own life experience that most closely matched the emotional vector of the character in the play. In essence, the actor revealed his or her own inner self in order to reach and project the emotional experience of the character.

When the Rabbis who selected and ordered the prayer service tried to explain the process of prayer, they told stories. They picked moments when biblical characters had breakthroughs in their experience with God. They saw the liturgy as a collection and sequence of moments and experiences rather than of ideas. Our knowledge of the character in the Bible and in the Midrash became "the back story" that contextualized the prayer. The prayer became the speech, the words said by the character in that moment. The job of the person praying was to grasp the subtext of the prayer and find his or her own "affective memory" (sense memory) that most closely approximated the experience the character speaking the prayer was having. Thus in our own performance of this piece of liturgy we match our spiritual experiences with the experience of God being recalled in this archetypal moment. Rather than being a collection of Jewish beliefs about God, the Siddur becomes a reliving and recreation of key moments in the Jewish experience.

If we take our example of the *Hallel*, we become like David, looking back at the Exodus and remembering our own moments of being at risk and needing "a Power greater than ourselves to restore us." It is a way of learning how to ask for help internally and externally. And as we apply the matrix of the six examples of victory given in the Talmud, it is a celebration of moments of rescue. It is looking for moments of salvation that have come in response to our opening ourselves up to help. We are finding our own life experiences that converge with and testify to the truth of the Exodus, the rescue of the Jewish people in the time of Esther, and so on. The remembered Jewish experience triggers a reflection on our own experiences, and the two intertwine.

JEWISH PRAYER

Before we start to tour the Siddur, here are two stories about the nature of prayer.

THE SHEPHERD'S SONG

Every night King David would hang his harp over his bed. In the middle of the night the north wind would begin to blow. The wind would move the strings. Slowly a melody would emerge. When that happened, David would wake up and sing with his harp. He would add words and create his psalms. These were David's prayers. (Talmud, *Brakhot* 3b)

Rabbi Zusya was a Hasidic rabbi who lived in the 1700s. Once he was taking a walk in the country. He heard a shepherd playing a tune on a reed flute. He began to sing along. The melody grabbed him. He sang it to himself over and over. He sang it as he continued his walk. Suddenly he realized that this melody was a long-lost song of King David. At this moment David's song was freed from its exile. (Martin Buber, *Tales of the Hasidim, Early Masters*)

These two stories are interconnected, the second based on the first. The Talmudic passage is telling us that our prayers are a reaction to God's creations. When we pray, we combine our artistry with God's. The second story, the Hasidic story, tells us that an insight into God's world can be passed on from one person to another. It tells us something we already know: that music is a powerful part of the worship experience. The Siddur is the liberation of many melodies.

So here are the questions that take these texts and make them into inner work. First, "When does the world play you God's music?" "What in your life brings awe?" Second, "When do the songs of others bring you closer to God?" "How does the past build your future?" All this happens during Jewish prayer.

THE WORK OF THE HEART

Once Jews offered sacrifices in the Temple. These sacrifices were called **עֲבוֹדָה** *avodah*, work. When prayers replaced sacrifice, they were called **עֲבוֹדַת הַלֵּב** *avodat ha-lev*, the work of the heart. The secret to prayers bringing us closer to God and not just being words we say is **כַּוָּנָה** *kavanah. Kavanah* (usually translated as "intention") actually comes from a root that means aiming or pointing. One needs to learn how to read Hebrew prayers. One needs to learn how to understand prayers. And one needs to learn where to point one's heart while one is praying. Heart-pointing is how we do *avodat ha-lev.*

This is a story from the Baal Shem Tov, the first Hasidic teacher, about *kavanah*, heart-pointing.

There was a king who loved music. The king had a court musician who played beautifully. But after a while his playing got to be tired and bored. He got tired of playing the same thing over and over. Every time the king asked for his favorite song it had less and less life in it. The musician told the king, "I am having a hard time being excited about this song. I have played it too many times."

The king had an idea. He brought in a guest and asked the musician to play his favorite song especially for this guest. The playing was again wonderful. The guest made the difference. The music was again filled with feeling and meaning.

Every day the king brought in a different guest. Each day the musician played the same song with new excitement. When he played it for a new guest it became a new thing. But eventually the king ran out of new people to be guests. With no one new to hear it, the music became old and tired again.

The king thought and thought and came up with a new idea. He blindfolded the musician and told him a new guest was there to hear his playing. The musician imagined the guest, and his playing was again filled with spirit. The king did this every

> day and every day, the musician found the *kavanah* with which to play the king's favorite song. *(Shivhei ha-Besht, In Praise of the Baal Shem Tov)*

Saying a prayer with meaning is like trying to shoot an arrow at a target. The most important part of shooting an arrow is knowing how to aim. The same is true of praying. The Rabbis teach that the secret to praying is to imagine God actually listening to your words. Note that I use the word "imagine" God is listening rather than proclaiming that God is listening. A traditional Jew understands that "faith takes knowledge"; those of us who are more existential know that the liturgy takes "a willing suspension of disbelief" in order to enter its metaphors. Prayers are like a ladder that goes from where you are to God. We "point our hearts" and climb up to God on our prayers. Each prayer has a story. Each story is a path we follow in our heart that leads us to God.

One of the core problems with Jewish prayer is its קֶבַע *kevah*, its fixed nature. The rhythm of liturgy with little change is a challenge to most people's motivation. A sense of fatigue can emerge. That is the essence of this story by the Baal Shem Tov. Siddur fatigue is nothing new. Here's the lesson: Even when there is nothing new, we need to create something new. Rabbi Nahman of Bratzlav taught (and I once learned this from a talk by Shlomo Carlebach) that the greatest sin in the world is to do something for the second time. Just like the king, we can't always find new visitors, but like the musician, we can imagine them. Each "us" at our latest moment of prayer is different from the "us" that prayed previously. We need to look into the moment for the newness we can find in and bring to the Siddur this time, and the newness that we can take from the Siddur this time.

It is like walking a path we travel every day. That familiar walk gives us a chance to think and associate. A new path mandates that we pay attention to the route and not the place to which our mind/heart takes us.

הַשְׁכָּמַת-הַבֹּקֶר
WAKING RITUAL

Before the בִּרְכוֹת הַשַּׁחַר *Birkhot ha-Sha_h_ar*, the morning blessings, there is a "still in bed" acknowledgement of consciousness. These blessings are to be done by the individual, and even if transferred to the synagogue, they are designed to be said alone. On this list are *Modeh Ani*, the *tzitzit brakhot*, the *tefillin brakhot*, and a few other pieces.

מוֹדֶה אֲנִי *MODEH ANI*

מוֹדֶה אֲנִי *Modeh Ani* is a wake-up prayer. It is designed to be the first words that a Jew says upon awakening. Later it was added to the beginning of the morning service.

Modeh Ani

- thanks God for returning our soul.
- makes our connection to God our first thought of the day.
- reminds us that we can count on God.
- says that every day we get to start over.

Modeh Ani connects to part of the traditional prayers that we say at bedtime, which come from the books of Psalms. We ask God to take care of our soul while we sleep. We say, "Into Your hands I place my soul."

In the morning, we say *Modeh Ani*. It thanks God for watching over our soul and for returning it to us.

> Rabbi Helbo explained, "Every day God creates a new set of angels who sing a brand new song of praise to God. *Modeh Ani* tells us that every day we wake up to a new adventure, a new set of possibilities, and a new chance to connect to God." (*Lamentations Rabbah* 3:8)

THE SHOES THAT GOT TURNED AROUND

There was a girl. She was angry with her family. This was a long time ago—in a much safer time. This was far away in a little village in the woods.

This girl decided to run away from home. She threw everything she owned or wanted into a napkin; she tied the napkin to a stick. She put on her cloak, put the stick over her shoulder, and started walking. She walked all day, stopping only to take a little lunch out of the napkin. Then, as it got to be dark, she stopped again. She took a little supper out of the napkin and ate dinner. Then she got ready to go to sleep. She took off her shoes and pointed them in the direction she needed to go in the morning. Then she covered herself with the cloak, used a moss-covered tree trunk for a pillow, and went to sleep.

This is when the interesting part of the story takes place. Somehow the shoes were turned around. Maybe a trickster came along and turned them. Maybe an angel. Maybe an animal nudged them, or maybe the girl turned them in her sleep. We will never know.

In the morning the girl woke up. She ate the last of the food she had brought, tied the much lighter napkin onto the stick, put on her cloak, put on her shoes, and continued walking in the direction in which they pointed. She walked all day. She came to a village in the woods. It looked a lot like her village, but it was different. It was more colorful and more interesting. She walked down a street and saw a woman who looked a lot like her mother. The woman smiled at her and welcomed her in the way she wished her mother would. She came into the house and became part of this new family that was very much like her family but at the same time different. She felt very much at home because this new home was everything she wanted her home to be. And so she and her family lived happily ever after.

(This is a folktale I learned from Rabbi Ed Feinstein. The gender of the hero was changed to add some girls into the mix of these stories that tend to be male. The story is best known as a Chelm story.)

Once again we get the notion that a new perspective changes reality. This is another story saying the world changes when we rethink it. This is literally a story about starting a new day with a new vision. The message is simple and clear: When we say *Modeh Ani* we need to be like the "new angels," turning our shoes around, looking at our life, our world, our praise of God from a new vantage point.

EDUCATING THE SOUL

When God was hovering over the darkness, before God even said, "Let there be light," God created the human soul.

On the sixth day, when God was ready to make people, God sent the angel Gabriel to collect dirt from the four corners of the earth. Gabriel went all over the earth, but every time he tried to collect soil, the earth stopped him. She said, "I am not going to help you make people. People are going to fight wars. They are going to dump waste and make a mess. People are going to destroy me in all kinds of ways. I am not so crazy as to aid in my own destruction."

Gabriel came back to God and told of his failure. God went out alone to do the job. The earth could not refuse its Creator. God gathered red and black soil, white and brown clay, soil in every color from all kinds of places. God took the soil and shaped it into a person.

Next the Torah tried to stop God. She told God not to create people. She said, "People will lie and steal; they will murder and hurt each other. If you create them, then there was no point in creating me. People will break every rule that is found in me."

God said to the Torah, "That is why I am patient and merciful." Then God went to the place in Jerusalem where the Temple would be built. God went to the place in the Temple where the altar would be. On that altar Israel would one day offer sacrifices that asked for forgiveness for each of their mistakes. God took one spoonful of dirt and added it to the mud, saying, "I will take people also from the place of atonement so that they will survive."

God took the souls that would become Adam and Eve and showed them not only their life, but also the future of all their children. They saw history from beginning to end. They saw the places they would live and the place they would be buried. They saw the places where they did noble things and the places where they failed. When they understood that each thing they did could either help or hurt, when they understood that every action has a consequence, their souls were ready. God made sure that the wisdom would remain but the knowledge of the future would be gone. And so people were born.

God prepares every human soul in this same way. And every night the soul returns to God again to be given wisdom and

> to come very close to its Creator. Every single morning God returns our soul to us and we begin a brand new day. (This weaves together a number of midrashim, starting with *Genesis Rabbah* 1:4, 5:5, 8:3-5, *Midrash Alpha Beta d'Rabbi Akiba, Yalkut Shimoni, Bereshit,* chapter 5, *remez* 41, *Zohar Vayigash* 98a, and a number of other sources.

This intertwining of midrashim shows that people are born neither good nor bad but with the potential for holiness. God knew the risks involved in our creation and decided to go for it. To solve the problem, God gave us Torah. Every night when our soul returns to God we re-experience the process of creation, seeing like Adam our potential for good and bad, and getting the chance to know about our best possible future. In the morning, when our soul returns to our body, we get a new beginning with a renewed vision. *Modeh Ani*, often used with children who are too small to learn the full liturgy, makes each day a new beginning with new potential.

What are your Adam and/or Eve moments? When do you feel created? When is your morning a walk to the Garden?

בִּרְכוֹת הַשַּׁחַר
BIRKHOT HA-SHAHAR

בִּרְכוֹת הַשַּׁחַר BIRKHOT HA-SHAHAR

In the Talmud (*Brakhot* 60b) we are introduced to *Birkhot ha-Shahar*, the morning blessings. These are a series of *brakhot* that are designed to make the process of waking up a spiritual experience. Originally these prayers had no specific order and were designed to be said at home as a reaction to individual steps involved in waking up and getting ready for the day. These *brakhot* were a lot like home exercise equipment—a good idea but not put into practice very often. Eventually they were taken out of the home and put into the Siddur so they could be done in the synagogue. Even though the connection to the original actions was lost, it was better to have them said as a group than not said at all.

אֲשֶׁר יָצַר ASHER YATZAR

Asher Yatzar and the prayers that follow are part of the *Birkhot ha-Shahar*. *Asher Yatzar* started out as a prayer to say after going to the bathroom. It is a blessing that says "God designed my body perfectly. All the parts work perfectly. And when it breaks down, God (usually) makes healing possible." When said in the morning, *Asher Yatzar* makes us focus on physically waking up. It makes our own body the first connection we make every day with God.

אֱלֹהַי נְשָׁמָה ELOHAI NESHAMAH

The same Talmudic page (*Brakhot* 10a) suggests that *Asher Yatzar* parallels *Elohai Neshamah*, "The Soul which You breathe into me is pure." Where *Asher Yatzar* talks about physical awakening, *Elohai Neshamah* speaks of spiritual awakening. It tells two stories. First it recalls that God created people by blowing breath into them. Second, it says that sleep is a little like death and waking up is a little like being born again. It is as if the soul returns when we awake. One big idea in this prayer is that people are born "pure." This is the opposite of the Christian belief that people are created with "original sin."

בִּרְכוֹת הַתּוֹרָה *BIRKHOT HA-TORAH*

There is a third part to the morning blessings, a series of *Birkhot ha-Torah*, Torah blessings. There are three blessings: לַעֲסוֹק בְּדִבְרֵי תוֹרָה *la'Asok b'Divrei Torah*, to busy ourselves with Torah, הַמְלַמֵּד תּוֹרָה *ha-M'lamed Torah,* Who teaches Torah, and נוֹתֵן הַתּוֹרָה *Notein ha-Torah*, the same blessing said when we read Torah. There are three study texts: Numbers 6:24-26, the priestly blessings, *Mishnah Pe'ah* 1:1, אֵלּוּ דְבָרִים שֶׁאֵין לָהֶם שִׁעוּר *Eilu D'varim she-Ein lahem Shi'ur*, a piece of Mishnah that speaks of things whose reward is unlimited, and *Shabbat* 127a, is a piece of Gemara that goes into more depth with and expands *Notein ha-Torah*.

מַה טֹּבוּ *MAH TOVU*

מַה טֹּבוּ *Mah Tovu* was first created to be the prayer that a person says privately when walking into the sanctuary in the morning. Today it is often a song that is placed at the beginning of the service. It is a collection of five biblical verses that are put together. The first is Numbers 24:5, which tells the story of Bila'am.

The second sentence in *Mah Tovu* is

וַאֲנִי בְּרֹב חַסְדְּךָ אָבוֹא בֵיתֶךָ, אֶשְׁתַּחֲוֶה אֶל הֵיכַל קָדְשְׁךָ בְּיִרְאָתֶךָ.

Va'Ani b'Rov Hasdekha Avo Vetekha, Eshtahaveh El Hekhal Kodshekha b'Yiratekha.

AND I, IN THE "MUCHNESS" OF YOUR MERCY, COME TO YOUR HOUSE AND BOW TO YOUR HOLY HOUSE (originally "The Temple" but now suggesting the synagogue we are entering) (Psalms 5:8).

It has ten words. Often this verse is used to find out if there is a *minyan*. We say this sentence rather than counting with numbers.

Mah Tovu is a prayer that

- helps us turn from our outside lives to a prayer space.
- reminds us that while a synagogue is a holy place, we need to find a holy space inside us to have it make a difference.
- says we can be like Bila'am, changing from our anger and frustration into a time for blessing.

When we say the *Mah Tovu* we are getting ourselves ready to move from outside the sanctuary to inside it. We are making a change from the part of us that deals with problems and frustrations to the part of us that is ready to get close to God.

BILA'AM SAYS *MAH TOVU*

At the end of forty years in the wilderness, B'nai Israel was marching towards the land of Canaan. They wanted to follow the King's Highway, the major road that led through the country of Moab. Balak, the king of Moab, didn't want 600,000 homeless people walking through his country. Rather than use an army to stop them, he hired Bila'am. Bila'am was a wizard. He was supposed to stop the Families of Israel with a curse.

Balak sent messengers to Bila'am and offered him a room full of gold to curse Israel. Bila'am asked God for permission. God said "No." Bila'am therefore told the messengers, "No." They relayed the "No" to Balak, who sent them back with the offer of two rooms full of gold. Bila'am again asked God. God told him, "You can go, but don't say anything that I don't tell you to say."

Bila'am got up in the morning and saddled his donkey. He headed off to Balak. Three times God put an invisible angel with a sword in front of the donkey and drove it off the road. Each time Bila'am fell off. That didn't stop Bila'am either. He picked himself up and beat the ass with a stick. God then made the donkey talk to Bila'am. The donkey said, "Listen, you have been riding me for years. I have never acted like this before. Turn around and look." It was then that Bila'am saw the angel with the sword of fire that God had placed in the road. The angel told him, "Don't say anything that God doesn't tell you to say." Bila'am still went ahead with his mission.

When Bila'am came to the mountain overlooking the Israelite camp, he was ready to curse Israel. But something amazing happened. His words changed in his mouth. He looked out at the tents and the camp and got ready to say a curse, but it came out as the *Mah Tovu*—a blessing. (Numbers 22-23)

The moral of this story is simple: "Curses can be turned into blessings." When we enter the synagogue our head is often a jumble. We are filled with mixed feelings and mixed thoughts. The *Mah Tovu* moment is a moment of transformation. We enter the synagogue and we need to be turned toward blessings, just like Bila'am.

בִּרְכוֹת הַשַּׁחַר *BIRKHOT HA-SHAHAR*

בִּרְכוֹת הַשַּׁחַר *Birkhot ha-Shahar* is the name of a whole section of the morning service. It is also a set of (traditionally) fifteen *brakhot* that were first described in a passage in the Talmud. The Talmud doesn't give a fixed order for these blessings, but rather gives a series of events and reactions. For example, "When one opens one's eyes one should say 'Blessed is The One Who gives sight to the blind.'" We take the ordinary daily experience of opening our eyes for the first time in a morning, and, by adding a blessing, we make a God connection to that simple act. The blessing literally says, "God lets the blind see." Nice miracle. But there is a secondary meaning. In certain ways we are all blind. There are things we should see that we don't see. Using the first opening of the eyes to focus on a wider opening of our eyes in our life uses the process of waking up to create spiritual growth. So it is with each of the *brakhot*.

Rabbi Harold Schulweis, author of *For Those Who Can't Believe: Overcoming the Obstacles to Faith* (New York: Harper Collins, 1994), teaches that we should add the words "through me" to every prayer. When we praise God for "straightening out the bent over," we should be asking, "God, straighten out the bent over *through me*." Every time we praise God for doing something we are committing ourselves to the same action.

WAKING UP

A man woke up in confusion every morning. He never knew where he put things. He spent a lot of time every morning searching for the things he needed to put on. One night he had a brilliant idea. He made a list of where he put each thing. When he woke up in the morning he picked up the list. "Pants—bedpost." "Shoes—under the bed." "Socks—in the shoes." And so it went until he came to the end of the list, "Cap on the door knob." The system worked. The man was proud. But then he asked, "Where am I?" He looked down at the list and discovered that his name was missing from the list.

> He looked all over the room and couldn't find himself. After a while he gave up. Every night he used the list, but never again in the morning did he bother to look for himself. (This well-known Chelm tale is retold from *Chasidic Tales Retold* [New York: URJ Press,1967].)

This comic story makes it clear that this man needs *Birkhot ha-Shahar.* In these morning *brakhot* normal steps are lifted up to a series of connections to God. The *brakhah* connects an action and an insight. We put on a hat and re-enact "God crowns us with glory." We buckle a belt and re-enact "God girds us with strength." God is in my life. And with God in my life, I know who I am...I am someone who struggles to be all that God wants me to be.

אֲשֶׁר יָצַר *ASHER YATZAR*

Openings and holes. The obvious focus of this prayer is the engineering of the body by God, but there is a secondary focus. The prayer begins "Who created Humans with חָכְמָה *h̲okhmah*, wisdom." At the beginning of Genesis Rabbah we are told that "wisdom only means Torah." (1:1) Therefore, people were created with and for Torah. While the body is an amazing machine, its most amazing quality, the quality that makes it different from all the other living machines that the Creator engineered and evolved, is the capacity to reason. The fundamental purpose of that capacity is Torah. The body is great! It lets us learn and live Torah.

THE CREATION OF PEOPLE

There are three partners in the creation of a person: the Holy One, a father, and a mother. The father supplies the substance out of which are formed the child's bones, sinews, nails, the brain, and the white in his eye. The mother supplies the substance out of which is formed the skin, flesh, hair, blood, and the black of his eye. The Holy One gives the spirit and the breath, beauty of features, eyesight, the power of hearing and the ability to speak and to walk, understanding and discernment. When it is the time to depart from the world the Holy One takes away God's share and leaves the shares of his father and his mother with them. (*Niddah* 31a)

When God was ready to create Adam, God gathered dust from each of the four corners of the earth. God mixed it with water, made clay, and shaped the clay into the form of a human. While Adam was sleeping and not yet awake, God whispered into Adam's ear the secrets of creation and showed Adam the righteous of every generation. When Adam did come to life he had a vague memory of what God had told and shown him. That is why he dreamed of the

> world to come. And because the spark of God is in each of us, that is why we, too, dream of the best possible future. (Rashi on Genesis 2:7; *Genesis Rabbah* 8:1, 8:10)

The deeper lesson of *Asher Yatzar* is that God created not only our bodies but our souls. While *Elohai N'shamah* will deal specifically with God breathing the soul into humans, the point of these two stories is that the body, too, is a divine creation, holy, and a connection with God (not a source of evil). Much Greek thinking that entered into Christianity was a dichotomy between the body and the soul. It was body = evil, soul = good. The point of these two stories is to show (and for us to remember) that God created all of us—and that "us" is both body and soul. "Us" has potential for holiness. "Us" has the ability to redeem the world.

אֱלֹהַי נְשָׁמָה *ELOHAI N’SHAMAH*

This prayer is a dividing line between the religious movements. In its original form it connects sleeping to death, waking up to resurrection of the dead. Resurrection of the dead is a perfectly good Jewish idea. It is part of the same world view that includes the messiah and the world to come. The Pharisees and the Rabbis of the Talmud emphasized a belief in resurrection of the dead and the world to come—eternal life after death. Then came the Reform Movement, a commitment to science and a philosophy called logical positivism, and out went a lot of mythical ideas. Resurrection of the dead was edited out of the Reform prayerbook. The Messiah, seed of David, became the Messianic Era. And in this one editing, Judaism became confluent with the modern and the scientific. When the Conservative Movement broke away from the Reform Movement, the language came back. Resurrection of the dead, the Messiah and the world to come were to be understood as metaphors, not physical realities.

Then came the post-modern world and the rise of spirituality. Eventually the Reform Movement put resurrection of the dead back in limited contexts in its Siddur, and the use of “world to come” and “Messiah” became more acceptable. The Reconstructionist Movement made changes that allow for the original understanding but don’t impose them. This is a prayer in which all three movements have their own version.

More than two generations of most American Jews were raised without awareness that these were Jewish thoughts. Reform had done away with them and the Conservative Movement didn’t talk about them. Resurrection of the dead was seen as a Christian belief in Jesus’ life story. The basic Jewish idea that the soul has a journey that it makes is something we can now talk about. And that idea is at the foundation of this prayer.

THE STORY OF OUR SOUL

When Adam's body had been finished, a thousand spirits circled his body looking for a way in. All of them were kept out. Then God came and drove these other spirits away. None of them had the chance to become Adam's soul. God breathed the breath of life into Adam and people came to life. All souls were contained in Adam's soul. (Zohar 3:19a)

God keeps a tree of flowering souls in Paradise. There is an angel who guards this tree. This tree produces all the souls that have ever been or will ever be created. (*Sanhedrin* 98a, learned from Howard Schwartz in *Tree of Souls* [New York: Oxford Press, 2004])

When God was ready to breathe a soul into Adam, God paused. God said, "If I breathe the breath of life into his mouth, that mouth will be used to speak badly of other people. If I have it enter through the eyes, those eyes will sometimes see the worst in others. If I enter it through the ears, the ears will listen to slander and gossip. But if I enter it through the nostrils, their only job is to filter out the bad and let the good in. This way people will take in Torah." (*Midrash ha-Gadol* 1, 74)

These three midrashic pieces say very simply that God created the human soul. Each gives us a different story. The *Zohar* teaches that a human soul is different from other souls. The human soul comes directly from God—and the belief in other souls (like animals and trees, vampires and werewolves) is a fantasy. *Tree of Souls* suggests that each of our souls is unique (though if you read it carefully, you will notice that it suggests reincarnation, another long-lost Jewish belief). The third story suggests that the essence of our soul is the ability to tell the difference between good and evil. And the punch line is that this ability makes us ready to study Torah.

The basic story is that God gives us a soul. That soul gives us access to eternity (however we understand it). We should be thankful for this gift. The question: "How can you be in the moment when God actually gives you your soul?"

בִּרְכּוֹת הַתּוֹרָה *BIRKHOT HA-TORAH*

In the section called *Birkhot ha-Shahar* (the Morning Blessings) you will find a series of *brakhot* called *Birkhot ha-Tora*h (Torah Blessings). It is found in different places in different traditions. This difference in the order comes because the Talmud originally assigned these *brakhot* to be said in response to actions, and when they got transcribed into the Siddur different "orders" were chosen.

Rabbi Moses Isserles was the author of the *Mappah,* an Ashkenazic commentary on the *Shulhan Arukh,* the leading sourcebook for Jewish law that was written from a Sephardic point of view. Rabbi Isserles supported first *Asher Yatzar,* then *Elohai N'shamah*, and finally *Birkhot ha-Torah*. He teaches that first we awaken the body, then the soul, and finally the intellect.

In the Talmud (*Brakhot* 11b) there is an argument about which blessing should be used to talk about Torah in *Birkhot ha-Torah*.

> What *brakhah* is said before the study of the Torah?
>
> Rav Yehudah said in the name of Shmuel: "Blessed are You...Who has made us holy with Your mitzvot, and made it a mitzvah for us to study the Torah."
>
> Rav Yohanan used to conclude his blessing for the Torah this way: "Make pleasant, therefore, we beg of You, O Eternal our God, the words of Your Torah in our mouth and in the mouth of Your people, the Families of Israel...Blessed are You, O Eternal, Who teaches Torah to Your people Israel."
>
> Rav Hamnuna said: "Blessed are You...Who has chosen us from all the nations and given us Your Torah. Blessed are You, O Eternal, Who gives the Torah."
>
> Rav Hamnuna said: "This is the finest of *brakhot*. Therefore let us say all of them."

Today all three of these *brakhot* form the first part of *Birkhot ha-Torah*. They are followed by three texts to study. Because we have said *brakhot* over studying, they would be empty *brakhot* if we did not follow them with an action. Therefore, we turn to study a piece of Bible, a piece of Mishnah, and a piece of Gemara. This is based on *Kiddushin* 30a (another passage in the Talmud), which says "One should divide one's study time into one-third Bible, one-third Mishnah, and one-third Gemara" (Numbers 6:24-6, *Mishnah Pe'ah* 1:1, and *Shabbat* 127a).

THE FOX AND THE FISH

> Our Rabbis taught: Once the wicked government of Rome issued a law forbidding the Jews to study and practice the Torah. Pappus ben Yehudah came and found Rabbi Akiva publicly gathering Jews together and teaching them Torah. He said to him: "Akiva, are you not afraid of the government?" Akiva replied: "I will explain to you with a parable."
>
> A fox was once walking alongside a river. He saw fishes going in swarms from one place to another. He said to them: "From what are you fleeing?" They replied: "From the nets cast for us by people." He said to them: "Would you like to come up onto the dry land so that you and I can live together in the way that my ancestors lived with your ancestors?" They replied: "Are you the one that they call the cleverest of animals? You are not clever but foolish. If we are afraid in the element in which we live, how much more in the element in which we would die!" So it is with us.
>
> This is the story of the Jews. If we are at risk when we sit and study the Torah, of which it is written, "FOR IT IS YOUR LIFE AND THE LENGTH OF YOUR DAYS" (Deuteronomy 30:20), if we go and neglect the Torah, how much worse off we shall be!
>
> Soon afterward Rabbi Akiva was arrested and thrown into prison. (*Brakhot* 61b)

Debbie Friedman explains this story simply. "Torah for the Jews is like water for fish." This story is not a personal memory until we make it one. It is a very nice parable about the importance of Torah. It is not a story until we hear its question. It is asking us, "How is Torah your life?" Torah can be something to study. Torah can be a way of acting. Torah can be a world view. Torah can be all of the above and more. But one of the questions we need to answer to fit ourselves into the Jewish tradition is "How is Torah our life?" Other core questions are "What Torah story am I living? Am I slaving in Egypt? Am I dreaming of ladders? Are my sister and I in competition?" Each of us lives out Torah stories. Each of us focuses in on Torah truths. In one way or another we need to figure out "How is Torah our life-sustaining water?"

A PORTION IN THE WORLD TO COME

This is the story of a poor man who had a daughter who wanted to get married. The daughter was beautiful, and a good yeshiva student wanted to marry her. The problem was that the poor man could not afford a dowry, and the boy's parents were not able to help. The poor man prayed. It did no good. He went to his rabbi and asked for help in finding the two thousand rubles that the couple needed.

Rabbi Meir told the poor man that he, too, was poor. The rabbi reached into his pocket and pulled out a single ruble. Rabbi Meir said, "This is all I have, but I am sure it will help you find what you need." The poor man took the ruble. On his way home he met the richest man in town, the town miser. The poor man said to the miser, "I'll offer you one ruble for your portion in the world to come." The miser, who valued every ruble said, "Sure."

After that the miser's life fell apart. His wife wanted to leave him. His daughter's fiancé wanted to call off the wedding. People didn't want to do business with him. Everyone was scared of a person who had no portion in the world to come. The miser felt he had no choice. He tried to buy back his portion. He offered five, ten, and then twenty-five rubbles. The poor man continued to say, "No."

The two men wound up meeting with Rabbi Meir and asking him for a solution. He thought and thought and thought, and he told the miser that he would have to pay the poor man two thousand rubles. The miser agreed. Then said Rabbi Meir, "Now you've finally begun to earn a portion in the world to come." (This story is retold from a story told by Shlomo Carlebach)

We understand the truth of this story from the last sentence, "Now you've finally begun to earn a portion in the world to come." The world to come is something we have to earn.

The Talmud makes several things clear when it says "All Israel has a portion in the world to come" (*Sanhedrin* 90b). The commentaries make it clear that (a) non–Jews can earn a place, too: "The Mishnah's use of All Israel does not exclude righteous gentiles" (Maimonides). And (b) "The Mishnah's terminology "חֵלֶק לָעוֹלָם הַבָּא *Heilek la-Olam ha-Ba*" literally means a portion "toward" the *Olam ha-Ba* (world to come). This indicates that we gain *Olam ha-Ba* through working toward it by performing good deeds" (*Ru'ah Hayyim*).

The story's ending makes it clear that portions in the *Olam ha-Ba* can't be bought or sold. They have to be earned with actions. That is why Chaim Potok says, "Jewish tradition is a kind of deedology, rather than a creedology" ("Judaism Under the Secular Umbrella, 1978 interview with Chaim Potok." *Christianity Today*, July 200). God judges our actions, not our faith. This is why the final Torah blessing says "Who planted within us eternal life" and why the Talmud text (Sanhedrin 127a) that is part of the study section of *Birkhot ha-Torah* says "These are the things whose fruits a person eats in this world, but whose reward remains for that person in the world to come." We study these three pieces of Torah and ask: "What is my *Olam ha-Ba* score?" "How am I doing?" "What else can I do?" We all need to earn eternity! That is true if we believe that our memory remains in the hearts of those who loved us, and it is true if we believe in a life after life.

פְּסוּקֵי דְזִמְרָה
P'SUKEI D'ZIMRA

פְּסוּקֵי דְזִמְרָה *P'sukei d'Zimra* means "sentences of praise." It is mainly a collection of Psalms and other prayers of praise. The first part of the morning service, *Birkhot ha-Sha<u>h</u>ar*, was a home ritual, so originally *P'sukei d'Zimra* started the synagogue service. The Talmud explains it this way.

> Rabbi Shlomai taught: "One should always start a worship experience with praise of God, and afterwards one prays. From where do we learn this?
>
> From the example of Moses in Deuteronomy 3:23, where Moses introduces a prayer story, "I SOUGHT OUT GOD AT THAT TIME" and then starts with prayers he said. First, "ETERNAL, GOD, YOU HAVE SHOWN YOUR SERVANT YOUR GREATNESS AND YOUR MIGHTY HAND..." These are words of praise.
>
> Then Moses got down to praying and asking for what he wanted. Moses goes on, "LET ME GO OVER AND SEE THE GOOD LAND..."
>
> (*Brakhot* 32a)

The daily service was constructed using this pattern of first praise, then petition (asking for what we want or need). Making this clear, the next page of the Talmud tells us "Those who were serious would meditate for an hour before their prayers, or pray in order to get into the proper state of mind." This, too, is *P'sukei D'zimra*.

הַלֵּל *Hallel* is a collection of Psalms that is said on special occasions, some holidays, and festivals. Explaining *P'sukei d'Zimra*, we find this passage in the Talmud:

> Rabbi Yosi said, "Let my fate in this life and in the afterlife be with those who complete *Hallel* every day." A Master said,

> "One is not allowed to say *Hallel* every day." The Gemara then explains, "Daily *Hallel* is actually *P'sukei d'Zimra*." (*Shabbat* 118b)

P'sukei d'Zimra is a Psalm-cycle. It begins with *Barukh she-Amar* as a kind of opening *brakhah*. *Mizmor l'Todah* and *Yehi Kh'vod* complete the introduction.

Six Psalms, 145 (*Ashrei*) through 150 (*Halleluyah*), are the meat of the process. They contain unabashed thanksgiving for what God has done.

A number of other pieces area added for a conclusion that culminates with יִשְׁתַּבַּח *Yishtabah*, which serves as a closing *brakhah* for this Psalm-cycle.

בָּרוּךְ שֶׁאָמַר *BARUKH SHE-AMAR*

בָּרוּךְ שֶׁאָמַר *Barukh she-Amar,* "Blessed be the One Who said," is the beginning of *P'sukei d'Zimra*. It is made up of seven blessings that Rabbi Elie Munk (*World of Prayer,* Paris: Feldheim Inc., 1953) connects to seven names of God.

The traditional pattern is to stand, gather the צִיצִיּוֹת *tzitziyot* (fringes) in front of you, and begin a period of complete silence (other than the prayers) that goes until the end of the *Amidah*, the Standing Benedictions.

As the first prayer in the "real" service, these seven blessings are "dialing the phone number" and establishing contact with God.

THE PRAYER THAT FELL FROM HEAVEN

The angels have a job: singing praise to God. In heaven the praise of the angels can always be heard. They are a choir who are always singing the *Barekhu* and its response. When Moses went up to heaven and heard the angels singing the *Shema,* he stole the second sentence and brought it down to earth. The angels sing in shifts, just like in the Temple. The morning shift was the most important. It was so important that the angel who was wrestling with Jacob gave up the fight so that he could get back to heaven in time to sing his praises to God.

The angels often sang specific songs when something important happened to Israel. Many of these turned into prayers. Perhaps the most famous story about the angels singing is that God stopped them from joining Israel in song when the Reed Sea divided. God said, "No heavenly praise when My own soldiers (the Egyptians) are drowning."

It is remembered that in the time of the Second Temple a tablet fell from heaven. On it was discovered the text of the *Barukh she-Amar.* A second memory says that the men of the Great

> Assembly (a group older than the Rabbis) wrote the words down and added them to the service. (Pirkei d'Rabbi Eliezer, 4, *Genesis Rabbah* 78:1, *Sefer Heikhalot, Midrash Rabbah* 2, 36, Rashi on Genesis 32:27, *Megillah* 10b, *Mishnah B'rurah* section 51, The *Mordekhai* at the end of his commentary on *Pesahim*)

So here is what we know: We stand. We call God by name. We pray an ancient prayer that either dropped from heaven or was compiled by those who were there before there were Rabbis or elders. It is like the tones of a modem waiting for the matching tones to make a connection. Our heart is ready to speak. It doesn't matter if God is on the other end or if it is only ourselves, ready to listen to our own prayers. It could be both. The connection has been made. Hearts are linked. The angels are filling in the choral parts. Now is the time to pray.

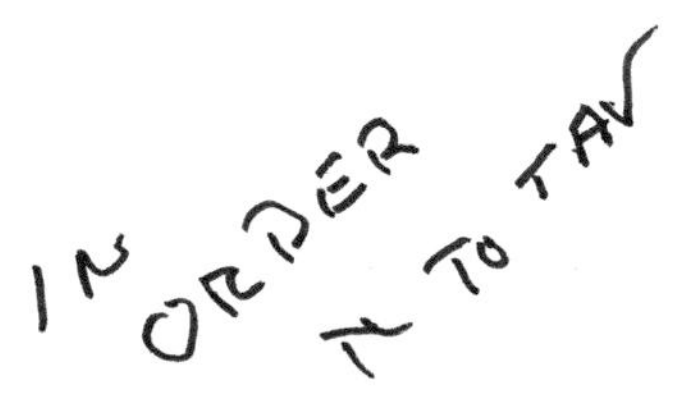

אַשְׁרֵי *ASHREI*

אַשְׁרֵי *Ashrei* is made of Psalm 145 and an introduction taken from other Psalms (84:5, 114:15).

Ashrei is an acrostic—that is an *alef*-to-*tav* (a–z) prayer. Its only surprise is that the נ *nun* (n) is missing.

Ashrei is said three times a day. It is said twice during morning services as part of the *P'sukei d'Zimra*, the verses of song, and again after the *T'fillah* (*Amidah*). It is said for a third time at the beginning of the *Minhah* (afternoon) service. When we say the *Ashrei* as part of the Torah service on Shabbat we are actually beginning the *Musaf* service (and replacing the weekday *Ashrei* that came after the *T'fillah*). We do not say *Ashrei* at evening services.

The Kabbalists explain why *Ashrei* is not said at night: "*Ashrei* is a prayer that thanks God for many things. The morning is a time when we feel really connected to our feelings of thanksgiving. As the day goes on our spirit is more directed toward just getting through the day. In the morning we say lots of prayers of thanksgiving at the beginning of the day. We have a long 'warm-up' for the service. In the afternoon these feelings are shrinking, and *Ashrei* is the only preparation for *Minhah*. By evening it is hard to find the *kavanah* (spiritual focus) for joyful prayers of thanks. We save up our thanks for the next morning and just about jump into the *Ma'ariv*, the evening service" (Rabbi Eli Munk, *The World of Prayer: Commentary and Translation of the Daily Prayers*. Jerusalem: Feldheim Publishers, 2007, pp. 195–6).

THE MISSING נ *NUN*

סוֹמֵךְ יי לְכָל־הַנֹּפְלִים, וְזוֹקֵף לְכָל־הַכְּפוּפִים.

Somekh Adonai l'Khol ha-Nof'lim v'Zokef l'Khol ha-K'fufim.

ADONAI LIFTS UP THE FALLEN AND STRAIGHTENS UP ALL WHO ARE BENT OVER.

Jews, especially Kabbalists, believe that Jewish words and Jewish letters have power. That makes the *Alef-Bet* very powerful. When we say *Ashre*i we are A–Z praising God. We are talking about everything.

In the Talmud we are told that anyone who says the *Ashrei* three times a day will earn a place in the *Olam ha-Ba* (the reality to come). To make this likely the Rabbis build it into daily services three times. In the Talmud they ask, "What makes this Psalm (and this prayer) so important that just by saying it enough one gets a great future?" The Talmud gives two answers:

1. Each line of this Psalm begins with a different letter of the Hebrew *Alef-Bet*—going from the first letter, *Alef,* to the last letter, *Tav.*
2. There is no verse for the Hebrew letter *Nun* in Ashrei. But that letter shows up in the ס *Samekh* line (the next letter) as part of the word נֹפְלִים *nof'lim* (fallen), when the Psalm says "God lifts up all the fallen." This teaches that when we follow God's example we will be lifted up, too. (*Brakhot* 4b)

Every time we talk about God we are talking about ourselves. That is a very simple extension of "BEING CREATED IN THE IMAGE OF GOD." If God lifts up the fallen and straightens the bent over, then we have both the capacity and the obligation to do the same. Every act of praise is also an act of self-direction. That is the power of the spark of God in each of us. But there is a second truth. In some way, just about all of us are bent over, fallen. We have some "fallen" part of our life that we are working on fixing. Not everyone who needs help is in the Sudan. We, too, can help and are in need of help. This prayer tells us that our life will be lifted up, maybe by God, or maybe by someone like us who also has a spark of God. And when this happens this, too, will be God's work.

THE *ALEF-BET* OF CREATION

God was ready to create the world. The letters of the *Alef-Bet* gathered around. Each wanted to be chosen as the beginning of the first word that God would speak to begin the process of creation.

First came ת *Tav*. It suggested that תּוֹרָה *Torah* would be the perfect first word. But God rejected ת *Tav,* saying, "You also end the word מֵת *met* (death)."

Next came שׁ *Shin* who tried "שָׂמֵחַ *same'ah* (happy)," but God countered with "שִׂנְאָה *sin'ah* (hatred)."

ר *Resh* said "רַחֲמִים *rahamim* (mercy)," but God said, "רַע *ra* (evil)."

So it went from letter to letter.

ג *Gimmel* suggested "גָּדוֹל *gadol* (big)." God replied, "גָּלוּת *galut* (exile)."

Finally ב *Bet* said "בָּרוּךְ *barukh*." God said, "Yes. I will use you to begin בְּרֵאשִׁית *B'reishit* (the first word in the Torah)."

Then God saw the א *Alef*. *Alef* had been silent. *Alef* never says anything. God said, "If only you had spoken up, I would have created the world through you. But to reward your humility I will begin the Ten Commandments with you. They begin with the words אָנֹכִי יי אֱלֹהֶיךָ *Anokhi Adonai Elohekha*." (Brakhot 4b)

The simple lesson first. Like the *Alef*, humility is good. The second lesson is that we are like the *Alef-Bet* with the power for good or bad. The way we are—is a question of what we choose. Like *Resh* we can be filled with *rahamim* (mercy) or *ra* (evil). We make that choice. But the big lesson is that like God, we are a whole *Alef-Bet* of possibilities. No one letter describes us. We are complex and need to work on a lot of parts. There are a lot of ways to be like God, to be who God wants us to be.

SHOWERING MERCY

The ט-verse in the אַשְׁרֵי says: "ADONAI IS GOOD TO ALL. GOD SHOWERS MERCY ON ALL GOD'S CREATIONS." The Midrash tells a story about it.

Once there was a drought. Rabbi Tanhuma told everyone to fast and say prayers of repentance. They had a mini-Yom Kippur, but still no rain came. Rabbi Tamhuma said to everyone, "If you have compassion for each other, then God will have compassion for you." The people of the town took him seriously and were better to each other.

The next day those people who were distributing food to the poor saw Mordechai. Mordechai was giving money to his ex-wife. Everyone assumed that he was cheating on his new wife by spending time with his ex-wife. They saw the money that changed hands as evidence of adultery. Rabbi Tanhuma sent for Mordechai. He asked him about what had been seen. Mordechai said, "I gave money to my former wife because she was not doing well. Her second husband died and she is now very poor. I listened to your words, had compassion on her, and helped her out."

Rabbi Tanhuma prayed, "Ruler of the Cosmos, just as this man who had no obligation to support this woman behaved compassionately toward her, You, the All-Compassionate One, should take care of Abraham, Sarah, Isaac, Rebekkah, Jacob, Leah, and Rachel's children, Your children."

It began to rain. (*Genesis Rabbah* 33)

This story echoes the *Nun* story. What we thank God for is what we need to become. God may like our prayers. God may enjoy the things we say, but what God really wants is for us to become our prayers. Compassionate is a good thing to be.

PSALM 150

Psalm 150 is the last psalm in the Book of Psalms and the last of six psalms that form the core of *P'sukei d'Zimra*. It is a culmination moment, the Jewish way of shouting, "Strike up the band." While most traditional commentaries focus on the opening and closing lines, the middle of the psalm, the part that praises God with lyre and drums, cymbals and probably an Eric Clapton guitar solo, is the part we remember. Here is where we channel the Levites singing and playing in the Temple. In your mind you get to hire your own musicians and singers. Where the psalm culminates "LET EVERY LIVING THING PRAISE THE ETERNAL," is where we find our stories.

CELEBRATION CREATES THE PSALMS

Adam (and Eve) get bad reputations with the tree thing, but the Midrash makes it clear that we don't understand them at all. When God asks of Adam: *"Ayeka,* WHERE ARE YOU?" (Gen. 3:9), we are told Adam is in the moment. Adam is admiring the glory of creation, composing and reciting psalms, and contemplating the majesty of God. Thus, when Adam is created and notices the world about him, he does the only thing a person can do: He breaks out in song. He devotes himself to praise of God and encourages all creatures to join him in praise. "Let us all see the creation that God has created." He is blown away; he begins to sing Psalm 93. And he is astonished in his heart. "THE ETERNAL IS RULER; GOD IS ROBED IN GRANDEUR...GOD IS GIRDED WITH STRENGTH. THE WORLD STANDS FIRM; IT CANNOT BE SHAKEN. YOUR THRONE STANDS FIRM FROM OF OLD; FROM ETERNITY YOU HAVE EXISTED..."

He then shouts and dances to "HOW GREAT ARE YOUR WORKS" (Psalms 104:24).

Adam is amazed. He sees the complex and simple beauty of the ocean and exclaims: "THE OCEAN SOUNDS, O ETERNAL, THE OCEAN SOUNDS ITS THUNDER, THE OCEAN SOUNDS ITS POUNDING

> AND ABOVE THE THUNDER OF THE MIGHTY WATERS, MORE MAJESTIC THAN THE BREAKERS OF THE SEA IS THE ETERNAL" (Psalm 93). Next comes "THE HEAVENS DECLARE THE GLORY OF GOD, THE SKY PROCLAIMS GOD'S HANDIWORK" (Psalms 19:1). When he hears all life he gets to Psalm 150. "ALL THAT BREATHES PRAISES THE ETERNAL" (Psalms 150:6). (Midrash Tanhuma, Pekudei 3 [end])

> Adam creates a sketch of the Psalms that David later fills in (*The Legends of the Jews* [Phildelphia: Jewish Publication Society, 1925, p.110, n.101 and p. 112, n.103. cites *Seder Rabbah d'B'reishit*, 7-8 and *Pirkei d'Rabbi Eliezer* 19]).

Adam and Eve aren't Neanderthals or Peking Man. They are spiritually sophisticated. They spend their life the way a person should: praying, resting on Shabbat, and studying the Torah of nature. Their universe is not one of cave paintings. Rather, it is a creation filled with God and with words to approximate the amazement. Joni Mitchell teaches us the lesson in her song "Woodstock," "We got to get ourself back to the Garden."

DAVID EXPERIENCES THIS PSALM

> "LET EVERY LIVING THING PRAISE GOD. HALLELUJAH!" (Psalms 150:6)

> When King David completed the last line of the last psalm, he bragged to God: "Creator of the Universe! Is there any creature in Your world that has sung praises to Your Name more than I have?" Suddenly a toad leaped up on a rock and croaked: "Don't let it go to your head, for I sing far more praises to God in a single day than you could in a lifetime!" (*Yalkut Shim'oni* on Psalm 150:6)

David, like us, is a work in progress. Here a frog teaches him Torah. Another day it will be a spider. He knows enough to say, "ALL LIVING THINGS PRAISE GOD," but he doesn't recognize the reality. He knows the abstraction, not the concrete reality. Ask yourself, "When does creation meaningfully croak to me?"

נִשְׁמַת כָּל־חַי *NISHMAT KOL HAI*

נִשְׁמַת כָּל־חַי *Nishmat Kol Hai* means "The souls of all the living." It is part of *P'sukei d'Zimra* only on Shabbat and festivals. It sits right between the recitation of the Song of the Sea (that is the song of praise that Israel sang after they crossed the Reed Sea) and the יִשְׁתַּבַּח *Yishtabah* that ends *Pirkei d'Zimra*.

The Talmud calls *Nishmat Kol Hai* בִּרְכַּת הַשִּׁיר *Birkat ha-Shir* (the Blessing of the Song) and connects it both to Passover and to prayers for rain. The reason given by the commentators for its "Shabbat only" status is the amount of concentration (*kavanah*) necessary for praying this prayer well. Shabbat (and festivals), where there is no work to get to, are the only times we can stretch out and do this prayer.

שׁוֹכֵן עַד *Shokhen Ad* is the last part of *Nishmat Kol Hai*. Buried in it is the name יִצְחָק *Yitzhak*. To some this suggests a connection to "Our Father Isaac," and to others it suggests that the authorship of this prayer has to be medieval because early liturgy writers didn't embed their names.

THE SKY OPENS

Sometimes the best things happen at the worst moments. Picture this: Isaac is bound and lying on the altar. His father has a knife in his hand. The best he can figure is that his life is all but over. One can assume that the moment is full of fear and anger, terror and frustration. But some Rabbis claim that it is a moment of clarity and vision. They have Isaac going willingly. Others say he reaches out his neck towards the blade. But there is one memory that is very different. Here Isaac looks over his father's shoulder. Isaac gets a look at the heavens opening—in whatever way you can say it, Isaac gets a look at the place God lives. Yes, God is everywhere. Yes, we can see God all the time—but in this moment Isaac gets a closer look. He sings, *"Nishmat kol Hai*—Every living thing blesses You."

Then comes the rest of the story: "Abraham, Abraham—don't hurt your son." There is the rescue and the ram. Abraham has what insight Abraham has. And Isaac, at the end, understands not fear, not God as dangerous, but the wonder of God, the God who deserves praise. He doesn't focus on the knife. He has looked over his father's shoulder into eternity. (*Kol Bo*)

This is a tough story. We are hearing it and scream at Abraham to stop. We are there yelling at Isaac "Run!" The last thing we expect is a moment of spiritual clarity, Isaac saying *"Nishmat Kol Hai..."* This story is a freeze frame. It is clarity—not emotional overload. All this is going on, and Isaac looks to heaven. He doesn't scream out for help. He doesn't plead. He rather has a deep vision. Literally, the heavens open. There is an eternal vision. In that moment, not as last words, not as a desperate prayer, but rather out of insight, Isaac says, "If you are alive, you need to praise God."

The question is when is your freeze frame? When do you have the break through? When does heaven open? When do you glimpse eternity? With that moment in mind, say *"Nishmat Kol Hai."*

THE RIGHT PERSON TO ASK FOR RAIN

Once there was a drought. The Rabbis learned in a dream that if a certain man would pray for rain, his prayers would be answered. So they sent for him. They asked him what he did for a living.

He said, "I am a donkey driver."

Shocked that God would accept a donkey driver's prayers while not accepting theirs, they asked, "Have you ever done an exceptionally good deed?"

He told them, "Once I rented a donkey to a woman who got on it and began to cry. When I went to comfort her, she explained that she was going to sell herself in order to raise the ransom money to free her husband, who was being held in an enemy prison. When we reached the city I sold my donkey and gave the money to her. I told her, 'Take this money, free your husband, and do not sin.'"

The Rabbis said, "You are the right person to voice our prayers."

The man prayed, and rain fell. (*Ta'anit Yerushalmi* 1:4, 64b)

A simple question: "Did saying *Nishmat Kol Hai* prepare the donkey driver to help the woman or did helping the woman prepare the man for saying *Nishmat Kol Hai*?" The harder question: "Have you ever done an exceptionally good deed?"

PRAYER FOR RAIN

When there was need for rain, the Rabbis would send the schoolchildren to Hanan. They would pull on his clothing and say, "Father, Father! Give us rain!" Then Hanan would pray, "Master of the Universe, please let it rain for the sake of the little children who cannot tell the difference between the Parent in Heaven who can give rain and the parent on earth who cannot." (*Ta'anit* 23b)

This story is rich with irony. Hanan, who didn't believe that his prayers could bring rain, prayed anyway. His lesson is that praying teaches us that we are not God. *Nishmat Kol Hai*, a prayer that praises God for being amazing, became a prayer for rain. Praising God teaches us how to ask.

יִשְׁתַּבַּח YISHTABAH

"(" This is an opening parenthesis. ")" This is a closing parenthesis. The service is both, with prayers that are "(" and prayers that are ")." Series of prayers start with a long blessing. A long blessing has a בָּרוּךְ *barukh* statement in the first sentence and in the last sentence. Series continue and end with short blessings. These have *barukh* statements only at the end. A series prayer can be () (Long-Short), or ())) (Long-Short-Short-Short). *P'sukei d'Zimra* is (————) (Long—a bunch of middle material—Short). It opens with *Barukh she'Amar* and ends with *Yishtabah*. What does all this teach us? That all the prayers in *P'sukei d'Zimra* are interconnected, part of a single flow. That is why we stopped talking between prayers back in *Barukh she-Amar.*

There are fifteen praises of God before the *barukh* in this prayer and fifteen afterward. The letter י *Yud* stands for 10. The letter ה *Hey* stands for 5. יה *Yud Hey* is God's name. It is also 15. Symbolically, *P'sukei d'Zimra* gets us to God.

STEPS TO GOD

In the Temple in Jerusalem there were fifteen steps that led from the ground floor up to the plaza where the holy work was done. Once a year, during Sukkot, the Levites sang and played music on these steps.

King David wrote 150 psalms. Fifteen of them are called שִׁיר הַמַּעֲלוֹת *Shir ha-Ma'alot,* Songs of Going Up. These fifteen psalms were sung by the pilgrims as they marched up to Jerusalem for the three pilgrimage festivals: Sukkot, Pesah, and Shavuot.

What exists on earth also exists in heaven. The Midrash teaches that God's throne has fifteen steps, too. First you visit the palace. Then you make it to the throne room. Once you are in the throne room it takes fifteen steps to get to God.

> When you call fifteen יה, God has a better chance of hearing because you are calling God's name. The Passover seder, too, has fifteen steps.
>
> *P'sukei d'Zimra* started with the prayer that fell from heaven. It ends with fifteen steps. It is a way to praise God, to get ready to talk to God, to ascend. Now we are ready for the real *avodah*, the foundational work of prayer.

The Talmud teaches us that "The pious used to pray for an hour before they would pray" (Brakhot 32b). In other words, the early spiritual masters knew that prayer took preparation. *P'sukei d'Zimra* is this preparation. A period of praising God made us like angels by starting with *Barukh she-Amar*, the prayer that fell from heaven; *Ashrei*, the *Alef-Bet* of prayer, continues the journey. On Shabbat we add *Nishmat Kol Hai*, Isaac seeing the heavens open. And we end with *Yishtabah*, our fifteen-step plan to ascend to being close to God. In our hour of preparation we move from earth to heaven.

זִמּוּן
ZIMMUN (THE INVITATION)

The חֲצִי קַדִּישׁ *Hatzi Kaddish* (morning and afternoon), which we will study later, and the בָּרְכוּ *Barekhu* sit in a kind of limbo between the warm-up materials and the formal beginning of the service, the *Shema* and her *Brakhot*. In many ways this is the gateway into the service.

בָּרְכוּ *BAREKHU*

The *Barekhu* is not the first prayer we say when we walk into a service, but it basically is the real start of the service. Before the *Barekhu* we say a number of prayers and meditations to get our hearts ready, a "warm-up." They are sort of like stretching exercises that players do before a game. The *Barekhu* is the "play ball" or the "kick-off" that begins the game. Up to now players can stretch and warm-up individually or in groups. Once the game has begun, they must act as a team.

The *Barekhu* is the way people in the synagogue become a congregation. It is the way that individuals become a prayer community. There are times for Jews to pray together.

The *Barekhu* is an invitation. It is a call and response. That means that the prayer leader asks a question and the congregation answers together. In answering they become a community.

The leader asks:

בָּרְכוּ אֶת־יי הַמְבֹרָךְ.

> *Barekhu et Adonai ha-M'vorakh.*
> Are you read to say *brakhot* (blessings) to God.

When everyone says,

בָּרוּךְ יי הַמְבֹרָךְ לְעוֹלָם וָעֶד.

> *Barukh Adonai ha-M'vorakh l'Olam va-Ed.*

The congregation is created and the community is formed. The answer means,

> Yes, God deserves *brakhot* forever and always.

This pattern of call and response as an invitation is used two other times in Jewish life. The exact same words are used to begin the blessings before the reading of the Torah. And very similar words (and the same pattern) are used to begin *Birkat ha-Mazon*, the blessings after eating that is said only when a community (at least three people) eats together.

The *Barekhu* is said only if there is a *minyan*, a group of at least ten people praying together.

THE FIRST HUMAN *BAREKHU*

On a mountain in Jerusalem all Jews used to gather to worship and to come close to God. Three times a year everyone would come to the Temple. At those times Jews felt they really belonged. At those moments God felt very close. Then it was over. The Babylonians conquered Jerusalem. The Temple was destroyed and left in ruins. The Jews were carried away as slaves, and the mountain where the Jews had gathered was empty. Israel was in exile.

It took seventy years to get permission to return. At first only a few Jews left their new homes and their new businesses and became pioneers. They began to rebuild the Land of Israel and to rebuild the Temple. It did not go well. There were many problems. Finally two new leaders came from Babylonia. They were Ezra and Ne_h_emiah. To bring people together they held an eight-day festival in the center of the unfinished Temple courtyard. For eight days, for the first time ever, the Torah was read from beginning to end.

At the beginning of this gathering, when everyone was standing in the unfinished courtyard waiting to see what would happen, the Levites came up on the stage. The Levites were the singers and musicians who led services in the Temple. They broke the silence by starting with words that were more or less the *Barekhu*. The people answered with their part. When this *Barekhu* ended, the exile was over. Israel was again one people. They again had a home. God was close. Then the Torah could be read. (*Ne_h_emiah* 8)

When the *Barekhu* is said, God is present. Just as God descended in a cloud over the Tabernacle, God joins a Jewish community at prayer. When we respond to the *Barekhu* we end our personal exile. Distances shrink. We are with our friends, with our community, with our people. It is as if we are back with Ezra—our community has been gathered. We are no longer alone.

THE POWER OF A *MINYAN*

The Midrash teaches that Abraham figured out that ten was the smallest number of people you could convene to make sure that prayers had a good chance of convincing God. He realized this when he was trying to save Sodom. He told God it was wrong to destroy the people if enough righteous people lived there. God agreed not to destroy the city if there were fifty good people. Then Abraham tried smaller numbers and stopped at ten (*Genesis Rabbah* 29:2). We've used ten since. Ten or more Jews praying together are a *minyan*.

The Hasidim understood the power of a *minyan* and told this story.

There was a blind Rebbe who was called the Seer of Lublin. The Seer could not see things through his eyes, but he saw in other ways. One of the students of the Seer was a man who lived in a town where there were no other Jews. One week a year he would leave his farm, ride almost two days on his horse, and then spend a week studying with, praying with, and being part of the Seer's community.

Once he rode into Lublin late on a Thursday afternoon. He went to put his horse away in the stable and found the Seer waiting for him. Almost magically, the blind Seer called him by name. The Seer said, "Go home." The man said, "But!" The Seer said, "Go home and get there before Shabbat starts." The man said, "But it is Thursday afternoon, and my farm is two days away." The Seer said, "Go," and the man had no choice. He got on his tired horse and rode through the night. Near morning he came to an inn.

The man said, "I am tired. My horse is tired. We will stop for food and water, and then we will rush on." In the inn were nine other Jews. They begged the man to stay with them and be the tenth person in their *minyan* for Shabbat. He explained that the Seer had told him to go home, so he said, "Sorry, but no." The man ate, drank, fell asleep, woke just before Shabbat, panicked about not getting home in time, and then realized that he was stuck.

It was an amazing Shabbat. When they sang together it was as if angels were singing with them. When they danced it was as if they were dancing in the air. When they studied together walls of fire surrounded them. As soon as Shabbat was over the man got back on his horse and rode through the night to get back to Lublin to apologize. When he got there the Seer was waiting. Again he was magically called by name. The Seer said, "You were supposed to die this Shabbat. That is why I wanted you home."

The man said, "I am still alive."

The Seer explained, "Sometimes a *minyan* has more power than a miracle-working rebbe." (Martin Buber, *Tales of the Hasidim, Later Masters*)

Together we are more than we are alone. When we come together as a *minyan* we have a louder voice. The community can accomplish more than the collected individuals alone. When we say the *Barekhu* we reflect on the meaning of "we."

AN ANGEL NAMED ISRAEL

Jacob wrestled with an angel named Israel. After a long night of fighting the angel told Jacob, "LET ME GO BECAUSE DAWN IS BREAKING" (Genesis 32:27). Why did the angel care about the dawn? Was he allergic to sun? No!

Jacob said to him, "I WILL NOT LET YOU GO UNLESS YOU BLESS ME!" Israel, the angel, blessed Jacob with his own name. Jacob became Israel.

The angel Israel returned to heaven, where he led the angels in their morning prayers. The angels' prayers began with Israel the angel leading the others in the *Barekhu*. (*Hekhalot* 4:29, *Zohar* II, 4b)

The angel Israel starts prayers in heaven. The *Barekhu*, the formal beginning of our services, echoes the angels' prayers in heaven. With each *Barekhu* we are challenged to be Israel. We are asked, "Can you wrestle with God and people and survive?" The Hebrew word for angel, מַלְאָךְ *mal'akh*, means "messenger." We are asked, by coming together, by being in community, "Are you ready to be God's messenger?"

שְׁמַע וּבִרְכוֹתֶיהָ
SHEMA U'VIRKHOTEHA

After the *Barekhu* we enter a part of the service called the *Shema and her Brakhot.*

This part of the service tells three big stories. These stories are the themes of three prayers. These prayers are wrapped around a collection of biblical texts, the *Shema.*

יוֹצֵר אוֹר *Yotzer Or* and מַעֲרִיב עֲרָבִים *Ma'ariv Aravim*

The first prayer is about creation. It reminds us that we are living in a world that God created. When we say the יוֹצֵר אוֹר *Yotzer Or* in the morning we are like Adam and Eve looking out in amazement at the world around us. It is filled with miracles. Each and every thing we can see, hear, taste, smell, and touch contains a trace of God. By looking at the creation we get to understand the Creator. We, too, are one of God's creations. This first *brakhah* celebrates everything that God made (and is still making). מַעֲרִיב עֲרָבִים *Ma'ariv Aravim* is the evening form of the creation *brakhah.*

אַהֲבָה רַבָּה *Ahavah Rabbah* and אַהֲבַת עוֹלָם *Ahavat Olam*

The *brakhah* אַהֲבָה רַבָּה *Ahavah Rabbah*/אַהֲבַת עוֹלָם *Ahavat Olam* is about revelation. "Revelation" is a big word for communication. It talks about the ways that God communicates wisdom to us. The big revelation moment was at Mt. Sinai, when God gave the Torah to Israel. But there are many other Mt. Sinai moments in our lives. There are many other ways we come to understand things that God wants us to understand. Some of them we figure out on our own by studying things, and some of them we learn from other people.

Sometimes, in some moments, we can almost hear God teaching us directly. This *brakhah* celebrates all of the Mt. Sinai moments in our lives.

גְאֻלָּה *G'ULAH*

The last *brakhah*, the גְאֻלָּה *G'ulah*, is about redemption. Redemption is being rescued. Redemption is also a dream about a perfect world, one with peace and freedom, safety and plenty. Jews remember the time when God took us out of Egypt as a redemption, and we believe that when people have finished working with God there will be a final redemption. This last *brakhah* remembers the redemption from Egypt and directs us toward an even bigger redemption in the future. This *brakhah* celebrates every time we have been freed from something that has enslaved us.

שְׁמַע *SHEMA*

In the middle of this section is the *Shema*. The *Shema* is one sentence that says that God is One. And the whole *Shema* is three paragraphs from all over the Torah that each say that God gave us all of the *mitzvot*. As a package, the blessings around the *Shema* tell us a history of the things that God has done: created the world, revealed the Torah, and liberated us from Egypt. When we put them together with the *Shema* we remember that we bring these memories to life and build redemption in the future by doing the *mitzvot*. The *mitzvot* teach us about God, help us become good people, and guide us to work together to make a better world.

עַרְבִית ARAVIT
(EVENING SERVICE)

מַעֲרִיב עֲרָבִים MA'ARIV ARAVIM

Jacob was coming home after twenty years. He was about to meet his brother Esau. Years before Jacob had tricked Esau into selling his birthright and had stolen his blessing. Now Esau was coming with a huge army. Jacob was scared. He went off alone and prayed to God. This was the first *Ma'ariv* service. When we pray the prayer *Ma'ariv Aravim* we are joining Jacob under the stars asking God for strength and for that which we need. (*Brakhot* 26b)

In the morning we say two prayers before the *Shema*. In the evening we also say two prayers before the *Shema*. The evening prayers parallel the morning prayers. In the morning we say *Yotzer Or*, a prayer that celebrates sunrise. In the evening the first blessing is *Ma'ariv Aravim*, a prayer that celebrates sunset.

מַעֲרִיב עֲרָבִים *Ma'ariv Aravim* has two meanings. It can mean "The One Who evenings the evening" or it can mean "The One Who mixes the mixtures." Sunset is a moment of both.

IT HAPPENED IN THE MIDDLE OF THE NIGHT

At the Passover seder the first song that we sing after the formal service is over, just before *Dayenu*, says "It happened in the middle of the night." This is from a teaching that the Exodus from Egypt began at night. When we remember that the Jews were liberated from Egypt we remember that many important Jewish events happened at night. We learn that God saved Abraham from both Avimelekh and Laban at night. We learn that Jacob escaped his wrestling match with the angel at night. The Israelites defeated the Canaanite army of Sisera at night. Nebuchadnezzar was defeated at night, and Daniel was rescued at night. Haman was stopped and defeated at night, too. And the Messiah will come at night as well. Night is the time of redemption. It is when we are saved.

Usually we are scared of the darkness because it is a time of no light. Usually we think of the night as a bad time, but the Midrash says that good things happen at night. It says "Rome was connected to the sun, Israel to the moon. During the day the sun wipes out the moon, but at night it can shine. When Rome sets, Israel has a chance to shine." In our life there are many bright and loud things that hide other things. Nighttime teaches us that God has "a still, small voice" and a hidden light. Night is a time when we can connect to God. (*Genesis Rabbah* 6:3)

This is not so much a story as a convergence of stories. Night has many feelings. The prayer is looking for one set of those "rememberings." We stare up into the sky and are scared and awed by the endless reaches of uncountable stars. That is a moment of creation. It is sitting quietly, alone, in the peace of night. Night can be many things, but it can bring us close to ourselves, close to our memories, and close to God. Night can be a time when we believe in the future. It can be a moment when we can realistically hope for a best possible future.

אַהֲבַת עוֹלָם AHAVAT OLAM

Jeremiah was a prophet who gave two messages. First he told Israel that God would destroy their country if they didn't go back to following the Torah. Then, when Babylonia destroyed Israel, he gave them a message of comfort. He told them that God still loved them. One of the things he said was, "THE ETERNAL APPEARED TO ME IN THE DISTANCE, SAYING, 'YES, I HAVE LOVED YOU WITH AN EVERLASTING LOVE, THEREFORE WITH LOVING-KINDNESS HAVE I DRAWN YOU.'" (*Jeremiah* 31:1–2) Even when God seems far away, we are still loved.

אַהֲבַת עוֹלָם *Ahavat Olam* is the second blessing before the *Shema* in the evening. It is a parallel to אַהֲבָה רַבָּה *Ahavah Rabbah* that is the second blessing before the *Shema* in the morning. It begins with Jeremiah's teaching of "everlasting love." This prayer teaches that the giving of Torah was a huge act of love. Torah teaches us a good way of living and helps us know who we are. Torah also helps us get close to God.

RACHEL AND AKIVA: A TORAH LOVE STORY

Rabbi Akiva was a poor and ignorant shepherd working for a rich man, Kalba Savua. Akiva was forty years old and had not studied a word of Torah. He did not even know a Hebrew letter. Rachel, Kalba Savua's daughter, fell in love with Akiva. She said to him, "If I am willing to marry you, will you go to a house of study?" Akiva answered, "Yes." So they were engaged in secret. When her father learned about it he drove her out of his house and cut her off. To get even she went and married Akiva. They were so poor that they had to sleep in straw. When Rabbi Akiva picked the straw from her hair, he would say, "If I had the means, I would give you a golden hair-piece, 'a Jerusalem of gold.'"

The prophet Elijah came disguised as a beggar and asked, "Please give me a bit of straw—my wife is about to give birth, and I have nothing for her to lie on." Rabbi Akiva gave him some of their limited bedding and said to his wife, "Look, this man doesn't even have the straw that we have!"

Soon Rachel told him, "Now is the time for you to go to learn Torah." He went and studied for twelve years. He had to start at the beginning. He went directly to a schoolhouse, and he and his son began reading from a child's tablet. Rabbi Akiva took hold of one end of the tablet, and his son took the other end. The teacher wrote down *alef* and *bet* for him, and he learned them; *alef* to *tav,* and he learned them; the book of Leviticus, and he learned it. He went on studying until he learned the whole Torah. At the end of twelve years he had become a leading scholar. He returned home, bringing with him twelve thousand disciples. The whole town went out to meet him. Rachel went out to meet him, too. When she came near him she fell upon her face and was about to kiss his feet. The disciples started to push her out of the way. Rabbi Akiva shouted at them, "Let her be—all I have and all that you have really belongs to her."

Her father fell upon his face before Rabbi Akiva. He gave Rabbi Akiva half of his wealth. Rabbi Akiva bought Rachel, his wife, a Jerusalem of Gold. (Avot de Rabbi Natan 6:12)

This is a wonderful story because it speaks of Torah as a love story. Many writers have spoken of the Torah as a love letter from God to Israel. *Ahavat Olam* speaks of God's eternal love for Israel. It ends (and so does the morning blessing *Ahavah Rabbah)* אוֹהֵב עַמּוֹ יִשְׂרָאֵל *Ohev Amo Yisrael,* the Lover of God's People, Israel. But what this story says is that there is Torah in the love between people. Love another, learn about God. The Torah of love is not only a relationship with the Divine, but the exploration of the connection between people. "What are your eternal loves?" "Who eternally loves you?"

שְׁמַע *SHEMA*

Shema stories will be found in *Shaharit* (page 77).

גְּאֻלָּה *G'ULAH*

The גְּאֻלָּה *G'ulah* is the first *brakhah* after the *Shema*. *G'ulah* means redemption. Inside the *G'ulah* is the מִי־כָמֹכָה *Mi Khamokha*, part of the Song of the Sea that the Israelites sang after the Reed Sea divided (Exodus 15:11). "WHO IS LIKE YOU AMONG THE GODS, ETERNAL. WHO IS LIKE YOU, GLORIOUS IN HOLINESS...." This passage is sung antiphonally (back and forth) between the service leader and the congregation. It is a reenactment of the moment when Moses and the Families of Israel sang the song, this way at the beginning of the Exodus.

Some commentator (I no longer remember who and can't find it) points out that this third blessing around the *Shema* is different. The first two *brakhot*, the one for creation and the one for revelation, end with a *brakhah* in the present tense. The *G'ulah* is in the past tense. In Hebrew the past tense easily becomes the future. Two things are said. First, that it is easy to say that God "brings evening" (causes the lights) and "loves Israel" because that is continually true. We put the *G'ulah* in the past tense because God has redeemed us in the past and we are waiting for God to do it in the future. We also put the *G'ulah* near the end of this series of blessings, hoping we can change it to the present tense by the time we finish.

Redemption is a big idea. It means being taken out of slavery. It means being free. It means every person having what every person needs. Redemption is the Jewish utopian vision, and we believe that in one way or another, using the Torah as a guide, we can transform creation into a redeemed world. That is the connection between the blessings surrounding the *Shema*.

THE BIRD OF HAPPINESS

There was a special light that shone when God created the world. It disappeared when Adam and Eve left the Garden. God took a piece of this light, put it in a crystal, and gave it to Adam and Eve to light the darkness. The crystal was passed from generation to generation. Noah used this *zohar* to light the inside of the Ark. It was passed from Abraham to Isaac to Jacob and made it to Solomon, who used it to light the inside of the Temple. When the Temple was destroyed it disappeared.

Aaron was a Jewish boy. He and his family were escaped slaves walking through a desert. One night Aaron had a dream of being lost in a sandstorm and being rescued by a large white bird. When he awoke he found a glowing crystal in his hand. He hung it from a leather thong around his neck. It glowed only when they were walking in the right direction. It led them to pools of water and oases filled with fruit. It led them to a great city that they learned was Jerusalem. They also learned that the king had died and the city needed a new one. To find the new king they released the Bird of Happiness. When it landed on Aaron's shoulder, the boy who had been a slave became the new king. It was the bird of his dream.

The people dressed him in robes and put a crown on his head. His family now lived in a palace. The crystal became a guide. It would glow when the right answer was yes. It would remain dark if the right answer was no. One hour a day Aaron sneaked away to a shack. He took off his royal garb and put on the rags he had worn as a slave. He wanted to remember from where he had come. (Iraqi Jewish folk tale. This telling is influenced by Howard Schwartz's telling)

In the Talmud and quoted in the Passover Haggadah we are told:

חַיָּב אָדָם לִרְאוֹת אֶת עַצְמוֹ כְּאִלּוּ הוּא יָצָא מִמִּצְרַיִם.

Hayyav adam lir'ot et atzmo k'Ilu hu yatza mi-Mitzrayim.

Every person is required to see him/herself as if he/she personally escaped from Egypt.

When we say the *G'ulah* we are like the boy returning to our slave clothes, remembering our origins, being committed to redeem others, and being ready to help perfect the world.

The *zohar,* the crystal in this story that comes from Noah's ark, stands for the light of Torah that guides the boy on the right path and helps him to make the right choices. Those choices and the memory of having been a slave, help him to create the best possible kingdom.

Virtually every Hasidic rebbe has taught: "Each of us has our own Egypt. Each of us needs to be freed from some enslavement." The deep questions of this story and of the *G'ulah* are "What is your enslavement?" and "How can God help you get free?"

הַשְׁכִּיבֵנוּ *HASHKIVEINU*

הַשְׁכִּיבֵנוּ *Hashkiveinu* is the odd *brakhah* out. The Mishnah (*Brakhot* 2:4) says that there are two blessings before the *Shema* in both the evening and the morning, and only one *brakhah* after the *Shema* in the morning. But the evening service includes two blessings after the *Shema*. *Hashkiveinu* is the extra evening *brakhah*. The question is: Why add an extra blessing in the evening? The Talmud (*Brakhot* 4a) makes it clear that *Hashkiveinu* is and isn't an extra *brakhah*. The Rabbis count this prayer as an extension of the *G'ulah*. They explain that night is scary enough that it takes an extra prayer for protection.

THE LAST NIGHT IN EGYPT

The story of *Hashkiveinu* is the story of a Torah verse. "AND YOU SHALL TAKE A BUNCH OF HYSSOP, AND DIP IT IN THE BLOOD, AND PAINT THE LINTEL AND THE TWO SIDE-POSTS WITH THE BLOOD; AND NONE OF YOU SHALL GO OUT OF THE DOOR OF HIS HOUSE UNTIL THE MORNING." (Exodus 12:22)

It was a night of terror. They had marked their doorways. They had set themselves out as different, as rebels. While the angel of death roamed Egypt, taking the firstborn of every household, they alone were safe. Why did they need to paint their doors with blood? Didn't God already know who was Jewish? Yes! God knew, but God needed them to choose to be Jewish, to paint their doors. They had held the first Passover seder, the seder in Egypt. They had eaten the Pesah̲ and used its blood as paint. They had spoken of their hopes of leaving Egypt and reaching a promised land. Now they were locked away. They did not know if the blood would work and keep the angel of death away. They didn't know if the Egyptians would seek revenge in a pogrom against their slaves. The night was dark. Outside were the shrieks of parents as they discovered the death of their firstborn. It was a very long night. And as they sat in the dark, behind their blood-stained doors, Israel prayed, "Cause us, Eternal, to lie down in peace and then stand us up, Our Ruler, to life." "Help me make it through the night" (Kris Kristofferson). (Nahal Eshkol, Beit Yosef on the Tur)

Hashkiveinu has us remember our last night in Egypt. We remember the fear. We remember asking God for help. We remember that we woke up safely and went on to freedom. We all have our own versions of that night. Our job is to connect our version to this prayer.

A SECOND *HASHKIVEINU* MEMORY: THE FIRST NIGHT IN THE WILDERNESS

The good news: They were out of Egypt. The bad news: They didn't know if Pharaoh would change his mind and bring them back. The good news: They were free. The bad news: They were in the wilderness. They were under the stars. All the food they had was the matzah they had brought with them. The future was really unclear. The Promised Land seemed too far away. It was dark. They gathered some wood and lit some fires. They huddled together, scared of wild animals, scared of the wilderness, and scared of the future. They needed sleep. It had been a long day. Tomorrow would be the same. Out of their fear and their faith they prayed. "Cause us, Eternal, to lie down in peace and then stand us up, Our Ruler, to life." "Whatever gets you through the night!" (John Lennon) (Learned by Joshua Mason-Barkin in childhood at some summer camp)

Once again we are in the dark. Night surrounds us. Our lives, our futures are at risk, and everything seems beyond our control. We turn to God, the only possible source of help, and ask God to help us make it through that long night. Apply this prayer to your memories of such long nights.

שַׁחֲרִית *SHAHARIT*
(MORNING SERVICE)

The Talmud says that Abraham established the practice of שַׁחֲרִית *Shaharit*, the Morning Prayer Service. The Rabbis learn it from Genesis 19.27: "ABRAHAM AROSE EARLY IN THE MORNING TO THE PLACE WHERE HE HAD STOOD BEFORE GOD." They explain that "stood" can only mean standing in prayer for the *Amidah*, the long silent blessing-chain in each of the daily services (*Brakhot* 26a). (By the way, Isaac gets credit for *Minhah*, the afternoon prayers.)

> Why does the Torah call attention to the fact that Abraham would stand as he prayed? This position indicates that the function of this morning prayer is to make a spiritual stand. We need inner fortitude to maintain the ethical level that we have struggled to attain. The constant pressures and conflicts of day-to-day life can chip away at our spiritual foundation. To counter these negative influences, the medium of prayer can help us by etching holy thoughts and sublime images deeply into the heart. Such a prayer at the start of the day helps protect us from the pitfalls of worldly temptations throughout the day. (Rabbi Chanan Marrison, *Gold from the Land of Israel: A New Light on the Weekly Torah Portion from the Writings of Rabbi Abraham Isaac HaKohen Kook*. Jerusalem: Urim Publications, 2006.)

יוֹצֵר אוֹר *YOTZER OR*

יוֹצֵר אוֹר *Yotzer Or* is

- the first of two *brakhot* before the *Shema* in the morning.
- a *brakhah* about the creation of light.
- a memory of the Garden of Eden.
- a look at good and evil in the world.
- a glance at a better future.

The traditional *Yotzer Or* is a long prayer that gets even longer on Shabbat. In the Reform Siddur (and in some other prayerbooks) a shorter version is used.

Yotzer Or is about light. Light means many things.

Light was the first thing that God created. Everything started with light. When we thank God for making the light we are also thanking God for all of creation.

When we speak of light and darkness we are also talking about good and evil. Black, darkness, stands for evil, the place where God seems to be missing. Light is the place where people are connected to God and do what is right.

Light also stands for learning and wisdom. When a person gains knowledge we call him or her "enlightened." For Jews, the Torah is the central wisdom that God wants people to have. We also say and sing "תּוֹרָה אוֹרָה *Torah Orah*," that the Torah is light.

At the end of this prayer is a sentence that is not in every prayerbook. It says, "אוֹר חָדָשׁ עַל צִיּוֹן תָּאִיר *Or Hadash al Tzion Ta'ir*"—"Shine a new light on Zion." This "new light" refers to a biblical mystery. God creates light on the first day of creation but does not create the sun, moon and stars until the fourth day. That means that there was some unusual light that shone for the first three days. One interpretation is that this is a special light that will come back when the world is finally ready for the Messiah or the Messianic Era. This is when people are finally ready to live the way God wants.

ADAM AND EVE'S FIRST SHABBAT

Adam and Eve were created on the first Friday, about an hour before sundown. In that one hour the two of them managed to fall in love, have an argument, eat the fruit from the one tree they were told to avoid, and get God really angry.

Just before candle lighting, just before Shabbat was ready to begin, God was prepared to kick them out of the Garden. Adam and Eve were really scared. When they had been created the sun was yellow and high in the sky. Now it was blood red and sinking towards the horizon. The warmth was vanishing from the world. Night was coming. And Adam and Eve knew that they had done wrong. Now they were terrified. God was punishing them. God was uncreating the world. Soon it would all be gone. They would be in darkness—in nothingness forever.

Just as God got ready to show them to the gates of the Garden, Shabbat stepped in and stopped God. She said, "You promised me that I would not be alone. Everyone else has a partner. Sunday has Monday. Tuesday has Wednesday. Thursday has Friday. Only I am alone. You promised me that I would have a partner. You promised me Israel. If you kick Adam and Eve out of the Garden before they spend a Shabbat, Israel will never know how wonderful it can be—they will never have a foretaste of the world to come. They will not partner with me. I will be too much effort with a reward they do not understand." God agreed and said, "Adam and Eve can spend this Shabbat in the Garden, but then they will have to leave."

As the sun continued to set God showed Adam and Eve how to light Shabbat candles. This was the first fire. They then walked together around the garden, God showing off all the things that had been created. God even introduced them to Shoshana, the macaw. Together they sat down and ate Shabbat dinner. God then told the two of them that everything would be fine. They were nervous. It had gotten very dark. The candles were burning out. Blackness was enveloping them. But God said, "Things will be okay." God settled them down, tucking them in to go to sleep. The Midrash even tells us, "God braided Eve's hair."

The two of them heard the words "Things will be okay," but they did not believe. They did not sleep at all. They tossed and turned all night. It was the longest night. I'll bet you know that kind of night, the kind where you do not sleep at all because your mind will not let go. They thought and thought about what they had done. They were lost in remembering how they had forgotten God's big command. They felt really bad about the way they had acted—about how, after everything God had done for them, they had let God down. The darkness surrounded them, and they thought it would never end.

Then suddenly the night seemed to lighten. Suddenly there was gray at the edges of the black. Slowly the black became gray and then moved toward purple. Finally the night was edged in blue as everything came into focus again. At last the corner of the sun sparked between two mountains, and Adam and Eve realized that the world had not been destroyed by their actions, that night would not go on forever. As they faced the new day, their new chance, they said together, "Praised are You...THE ONE WHO RADIATES LIGHT AND CREATES DARKNESS, THE ONE WHO MAKES PEACE AND EVEN CREATES EVIL." Later Isaiah would speak those same words (45:7). Even later the Rabbis who arranged the Siddur would use them as the prayer to greet the morning light because they knew that, in some way, every morning is like that first Shabbat morning that greeted Adam and Eve—a chance to start over. (This is a weaving of many midrashim from *Pirkei Avot*, *Midrash Rabbah*, *Leket*, and a Danny Siegel poem)

יוֹצֵר אוֹר *Yotzer Or.* The opening of this prayer comes from a lesson that the prophet Isaiah taught. Isaiah said that God says, "I AM THE ETERNAL AND THERE IS NO ONE ELSE. (1) I RADIATE LIGHT AND CREATE DARKNESS. (2) I MAKE PEACE AND CREATE EVIL." Isaiah thought that it was important to teach that God created evil as well as good.

Later, when the prayerbook was assembled, the Rabbis changed the words "created evil" to "creates all (including evil)." Their big concern was a Persian religion that believed in two gods, a good god and an evil god. People were reading the two sentences in this prayer as if each applied to a different god. By changing "evil" to "all" they leave no doubt that the One God created everything.

HIDDEN LIGHT

The Torah tells us that God created light on the first day. It also tells us that God created the sun, moon, and stars on the fourth day. For the first three days the world had a very strange kind of light—light that came directly from God.

The Talmud tells us that when one looked at things in this light, one could see from one side of forever to the other side of forever. When people started to do evil things, God hid this light away so that it would not be used in the wrong way. We are told that in the future righteous people will again get to use this light.

The Baal Shem Tov said that God hid this light in the Torah. (*Ein Yaakov*; Martin Buber, *Tales of the Hasidim*)

Hidden light is the central metaphor of Kabbalah, Jewish mysticism. It teaches (and we can learn) that Torah means many different kinds of learning. We can learn Torah everywhere. We can learn Torah from everyone. The sparks of hidden light are all over. Our job is to gather them and make sense of them. "Where have you found light lately?"

אַהֲבָה רַבָּה *AHAVAH RABBAH*

אַהֲבָה רַבָּה *Ahavah Rabbah* is

- the second of two *brakhot* before the *Shema* in the morning.
- a *brakhah* about God's love for Israel.
- a memory of Mount Sinai.
- a statement about the power of studying Torah.
- a look at the relationship between God and Israel that Torah creates.

The moment that most shaped the Jewish people happened at Mount Sinai.

It was at Mount Sinai that God gave us the gift of Torah. Torah showed us that God loves us, because in it God gave us the wisdom we need to live a good life.

The Torah has to be studied. It is filled not with simple words but with words we need to work on and work at. Many of the lessons in the Torah emerge only after careful study. We commit ourselves to working hard to understand the Torah because it is a love letter to us from God.

Torah makes us God's partner. When the Jews received the Torah they agreed to work with God to make the world into the best possible place. Torah is a book of directions for changing ourselves into the best people we can be and changing the world into the best place we all can make it. Torah creates a contract. When we accepted the Torah, we agreed to work with God to create a world of peace, justice, freedom, and prosperity.

אַהֲבָה רַבָּה *Ahavah Rabbah* talks about our relationship with God. It reminds us that the Torah was given at a moment when Israel and God were closest. And it reminds us that through the Torah we can have other moments of being close to God.

TWO MEMORIES OF SINAI

Sometimes different people remember the same event differently. Sometimes one person can remember the same thing in more than one way. Memory is like that. Sometimes we have more than one true memory of the same moment. The Jewish people have many different memories of receiving the Torah at Mt. Sinai.

Here is the first memory. The Torah is a very demanding book. It asks people to do many things that are not easy. It asks people to not do many things—and not all of those things are easy to stop yourself from doing. It is hard to be a Jew because the Torah expects a lot. God went to a lot of different people and asked them to accept the Torah. Each nation asked about the Torah, and God repeated one or two of its rules. Each time God described the Torah, the nation who heard about it politely said, "No, thank You!" There were things that the Torah asks you to do that they did not want to do. There were things that the Torah asks you not to do that they did not want to stop doing. Israel was God's last chance. Everyone else had said, "No, thank You!"

The Families of Israel were at Mt. Sinai. They, too, asked about the Torah. They, too, said, "No, Thank You." This time God was prepared. God lifted up the mountain and held it over their heads. It hung in the air like a huge open coffin. God said to Israel, "Do you want to accept My Torah, or do you want Me to put the mountain down?"

It was at that moment—with Mt. Sinai hanging in the air over their heads—that the Families of Israel said, "We will do it, and we will obey it." And that is how Israel accepted the Torah.
(*Shabbat* 88a, *Sifrei Deuteronomy* #343, *Pesikta Rabbati* 21, *Pirkei d'Rabbi Eliezer* 99b)

Rabbi Yehudah Aryeh Leib Alter, known as the *S'fat Emet*, taught, "Every person has their own piece of Torah." He explained, "The complete Torah was given to the Jewish people as a whole. However, each person has a personal teaching, his or her own Torah, inside. This is hidden within the soul. There is a piece of Torah that can be learned from every person."

The Torah involves choosing. It requires us to be a choosing people and a choosing person (Mordechai Kaplan). Torah comes with challenges and obligations. It says "no" to things we might want to do and "yes" to things we might not want to do. While it is a privilege and a gift, it can also be a pain. This first memory recognizes the difficulty of accepting the Torah. When we say אַהֲבָה רַבָּה *Ahavah Rabbah* we balance God the Police Officer with God the Parent bringing gifts to us. We understand that laws can be acts of love. Here we get to play out our own tensions between the difficulty in being a Jew and the privileges Judaism offers.

THE SECOND MEMORY

The second memory is different. Israel is at Mt. Sinai. God offers the Torah to Israel, and Israel wants it badly. They believe that it will be fun to celebrate all the holidays. They think it will be an honor to become God's partner, just as little children wait to play a game at a birthday party. Israel jumped up and down and hollered, "Choose me! Pick me!" God said to Israel, "Why should I pick you? The Torah is really valuable. Who will co-sign the promise that you will treat it well? Who will guarantee that you will not ruin it?"

Israel said, "Abraham, Sarah, Isaac, Rebekkah, Leah, Rachel, and Jacob will take responsibility."

God said, "Every one of them broke the Torah at some point and did something wrong. They are not the ones to protect My Torah."

Israel said, "How about the prophets? They all taught Your word."

God said, "They told you the right things to do, and you usually did not listen to them. If you won't list to them, how can I trust them to be responsible?"

Finally Israel had a big conference. They talked and talked. At last they said to God, "Our children will be the ones to take responsibility. They promise that they will study the Torah and take it into their hearts. They promise to make the future better."

> God thought about it and then said, "The Torah is yours."
>
> As God gave them the Torah the Families of Israel shouted out, "We will do it, and we will obey it." And that is how Israel accepted the Torah. (*Mikhilta d'Rabbi Shimon bar Yohai*)

This story emphasizes the other side of Torah. Here we have Torah the privilege. This is Torah the gift that keeps on giving. Why does God finally give the Torah to us? It is given because we promise to study it and to have our children learn it. Torah is not a prop; it is a process. We get to receive Torah and to keep Torah by actively devoting time to unpacking it to find its meaning. The questions this prayer asks are, "When did Torah last get inside of you?" "When did you last feel the love?"

A Mt. Sinai moment is a time when you suddenly learn a great truth. It is when you understand one of the things that God wants you to understand. Sometimes another person teaches you this lesson. Sometimes you learn from something that happens. Sometimes you just know. Describe one of your own Mt. Sinai moments.

שְׁמַע *SHEMA*

שְׁמַע SHEMA

The שְׁמַע *Shema* is probably the most important sentence in the whole Torah. It states the single most important Jewish idea—there is only One God.

The *Shema* is also a collection of three paragraphs of the Torah that come from three different places that were brought together to be the heart of the morning and evening service. The three-paragraph *Shema* got created because of a problem.

Originally, back in the time of the Temple, the Ten Commandments were said as part of the Temple service every day. It was a big performance—an acting out of being at Mt. Sinai. People began to take the Ten Commandments too seriously. They began to believe that they were the only important *mitzvot*. They would say "I am a good Jew, I do the big ten" and not bother with the other 603 mitzvot. The Rabbis of the Talmud knew that they had to make a change.

They found three passages in the Torah that all said כֹּל מִצְוֹתַי *kol mitzvotai* "ALL MY COMMANDMENTS." They replaced the Ten Commandments with ,this new collection of passages.

The first paragraph of the *Shema* said וּבְשָׁכְבְּךָ וּבְקוּמֶךָ *u'v'shokhb'kha u'v'kumekha,* "WHEN YOU LIE DOWN AND WHEN YOU RISE UP." The Rabbis learned from that verse and had the *Shema* said every morning and every evening. It became a wake-up prayer and a bedtime prayer—it became part of the morning service and the evening service.

The *Shema* is also the source of many other common Jewish practices. In it you can find the source of the *mezuzah* and the *tefillin*, of the *tallit* and of parents arranging for their children to study Torah.

The *Shema* teaches us that God is One. It then makes sure that we live that Oneness at every moment of the day, everywhere we go, with everyone one we meet, through everything we do.

THE HISTORY OF THE *SHEMA*

Once, when the Temple in Jerusalem was still the central place of Jewish worship, there was no *Shema*. The parts were indeed all in the Torah, but they had not yet been brought together and made into a prayer. Instead Jews used to use a different part of the Torah as a portion of their daily service. At first Jews used to say the Ten Commandments every day. Eventually the daily use of the Ten Commandments began to cause some major problems.

Jews believe that there are 613 different *mitzvot* in the Torah and that all of them are important. Some people (who weren't really following the Jewish tradition correctly anymore) began to argue: "The Ten Commandments are the only Jewish rules that are important, Because we say them every day, the others—which aren't said every day—can be forgotten." Following that line of thinking, Shabbat would still be a *mitzvah* because it is in the Ten Commandments, but Rosh ha-Shanah, Yom Kippur, and Pesa<u>h</u> wouldn't because they are found elsewhere in the Torah. Likewise, the Ten Commandments make not murdering and not stealing a *mitzvah*, but don't say a word about rape, assault, fraud, cheating, or a lot of other important ethical rules. (They are talked about in other places in the Torah.)

To keep people from thinking that there were only Ten Commandments, the officials who ran the Temple service dropped the Ten Commandments from the daily service and replaced it with a collection of passages named after the first word in the first text: *Shema*. (*Sukkot* 42a, *B'rakhot* 13b, Jerusalem Talmud)

The *Shema* is about many things. We usually connect the "One" in the *Shema* to the Oneness of God. We will get there. But, what is clear here is that the *Shema* is connected to the "Oneness" of the *mitzvot*. From this perspective, the full *Shema* leads us to ask, "What *mitzvot* am I good at?" and "What *mitzvot* need work?"

THE DEATH OF JACOB

All of the *Shema* is found in the Torah except for one sentence. The part where we say:

בָּרוּךְ שֵׁם כְּבוֹד מַלְכוּתוֹ לְעוֹלָם וָעֶד *Barukh Shem K'vod Malkhuto l'Olam va'ed* (Praised be the Name forever and beyond) is not in there. In many synagogues there is a tradition to whisper it every day but Yom Kippur.

In the Talmud and the Midrash we find three different true stories of the origin of the *Barukh Shem* sentence. Most of them also explain the whisper.

Jacob is old, in Egypt, and ready to die. Jacob has a second name; at least some of the time he is called Israel. Jacob gathers his children. He is on his deathbed. He tells his children, "I am afraid to die."

They answer, "There is no need to fear death, Father. God loves you."

Jacob answers, "I am not afraid of dying—I am afraid of leaving you in Egypt without me. Egypt is a land that believes in many gods. It carves statues of people out of sides of mountains and pretends that they are gods. I am afraid that when I am gone you will forget the one God, the God Who spoke to Abraham and Isaac and to me."

His children then answered together in a loud voice, "שְׁמַע יִשְׂרָאֵל *Shema Yisrael* (Listen, Dad), יי אֱלֹהֵינוּ *Adonai Eloheinu* (Adonai is our God). יי אֶחָד *Adonai Ehad* (only Adonai)."

Then, with his dying breath, Jacob answered, "בָּרוּךְ שֵׁם *Barukh Shem* (Praised be God), כְּבוֹד מַלְכוּתוֹ לְעוֹלָם וָעֶד *K'vod Malkhuto l'Olam va'ed* (Whose glorious empire will last forever)."

When we say the *Shema* and whisper the *Barukh Shem* we are acting out this story. (*Pesahim* 56a)

This time the "One" in the *Shema* has a different meaning. Here we are talking about the continuity between generations. As much as there may be tensions between generations, as much as their music and fashions and aesthetics may be different, there are some things that must be shared. There is a "oneness" between the generations when it comes to values and commitments. This story gets us to look into our parents' and our children's eyes and say, "There are the things that are 'One' between us."

MOSES STEALS THE SHEMA

Moses went up to heaven to get the Torah. All around him were gathered the angels. They were carrying signs and yelling, "Keep the Torah! Don't let it go!"

Moses took off his *tallit katan,* the little *tallit* he wore under his robe, and tied it onto his staff. He shouted, "Truce!" Four angels came forward to talk to him, Michael, Gavriel, Uzziel, and Raphael. Moses said, "Let me ask three questions, and then you can make a choice to let me have the Torah, or I will just go home and bother you no more." They said, "We can handle three questions."

Moses asked, "Who here has ever been disrespectful to his parents? Please raise your hand if the answer is yes." No angel raised a hand. In fact, every one of them held his own hand down. They said, "We are angels—we don't have parents." (For Jews, angels came from God. They never had parents.)

Then Moses asked, "Who has ever stolen something? Please should out 'Me.'" The angels were silent. They put their hands over their mouths, and through their fingers they said, "We are angels—we don't steal."

Finally Moses asked, "Who here has ever murdered someone? Please take a step forward." Every angel took a step back. Every angel except one. One stood still. All of the angels said, "We're angels—we don't murder."

Then Moses shouted, "Don't you get it?! You don't need the Torah—we do. Torah isn't for those who already do what God wants. Torah is for those of us who need to learn how to be more like God in our actions." The angels agreed. They shouted, "Give the Torah to Moses!" and carried him around on their shoulders.

Next, the one angel who had not moved, the Angel of Death, came to him and whispered three words, "*Tzedakah* (charity), *T'shuvah* (repentance), and *T'fillah* (prayer). These are the ways to keep me away."

Just before he left heaven, Moses heard music in the background. He realized that Gavriel and some of the angels were always filling heaven with songs of praise. One of the songs they were singing over and over went, "בָּרוּךְ שֵׁם כְּבוֹד מַלְכוּתוֹ לְעוֹלָם וָעֶד *Barukh Shem K'vod Malkhuto l'Olam va'ed.*" Moses stole the angels' song and brought it back to earth along with the Torah.

We now sing the angels' song, *"Barukh Shem,"* as part of the *Shema* everyday. We whisper it because it was stolen. We say it out loud on Yom Kippur. That is the day on which we have done *tzedakah, t'fillah,* and *t'shuvah.* It is the one time when we are not guilty of being disrespectful to parents, or stealing, or murdering. It is the one time that we are as holy as angels. (*Deuteronomy Rabbah* 2:36)

Once again we have a story of how the *Barukh Shem K'vod* was added to the *Shema*, but this time we also learn why the *Shema* is said out loud on Yom Kippur. However, this story gives us a second way to think about the *Shema*. This time the "Oneness" of the *Shema* has us think about the law that the Torah brings, the ethics and the values. It sets us up for a oneness of behavior, of treating all people as if they are siblings—all created in the shared image of God. When we live this story, we look at our behavior, we think about honoring parents, not stealing, and not murdering, and all the other Torah values. We ask, "Are we living up to the *Shema*?"

THE *SHEMA* REBUILDS THE TEMPLE

Sometimes a whole story can be told in a sentence. The Temple was the place where the Jewish people came close to God. Three times a year every Jew would come up to Jerusalem, up to the Temple. The Temple was a very big place. But it was not actually big enough to fit the whole Jewish people. On those days, we are told, the Temple would stretch to make sure that there was room for everyone.

Here is a one-sentence story. Everywhere else in the world Jews answered a prayer with "Amen." In the Temple the people answered, *"Barukh Shem K'vod Malkhuto l'Olam va'ed."*

Amen means "Me, too." It is a way of saying "I believe what he or she said." When you say "Amen" God gives you credit for saying the prayer another person said. When the Rabbis added the *Barukh Shem* to the *Shema,* they made this one prayer a time when every Jew was again in the Temple. When we say *Barukh Shem* we know that we are One People connected to the One God. (*Ta'anit* 16b)

Here is another one-sentence story. When we say the *Shema* through the eyes of this one-line story all of Israel is again whole, we are "One."

Latifa Kropf told this story. A boy comes to his teacher, and starts to cry. She asks him what is wrong, and he explains that he has been praying and praying for the Temple to be rebuilt. He is upset that his prayers have not worked; the Temple remains broken. He says, "God doesn't answer me." The teacher asks the boy to close his eyes. She says, "Imagine that the Temple has become whole." The boy closes his eyes, and slowly a great smile fills his face. Finally he opens his eyes and says, "Teacher, I saw it—I really saw it—the Temple whole." The teacher smiles at him and says, "Your prayers were answered." (This story was e-mailed to me by Laitifa Kropf in response to the previous *Shema* story)

This story reveals the inner work involved in using the *Shema* to make the Temple whole again. It doesn't matter how you feel about the Temple. You can agree with Maimonides (*Mishneh Torah*, Laws of Sacrifice 7.1) that the Temple is to be remembered and not rebuilt. Rebuilding the Temple in our minds is not committing ourselves to return to sacrifice. It is a symbolic way of reuniting the Jewish people. When was the last time you experienced the Jewish people as "One"?

וְאָהַבְתָּ *V'AHAVTA*

The וְאָהַבְתָּ *v'Ahavta* is either part of the first paragraph of the *Shema* or the prayer that comes after the *Shema*. It depends on how your *Siddur* is organized and how you think about it.

The *v'Ahavta* comes from the Book of Deuteronomy, chapter 6, verse 5. The verse before this one is the sentence that begins *Shema Yisrael*.

In some synagogues the *v'Ahavta* is considered to be a prayer on its own. In other synagogues it is considered to be the rest of the first paragraph of the *Shema*. Either way, these are the words that are said after the *Shema* and that tell us how to live the idea that God is One.

The prayer before the *Shema* was *Ahavah Rabbah*.

It told us

- God loves us.
- God gave us Torah as a gift.
- by studying Torah we get closer to God.
- by studying and living Torah we make the world a better place.

The *v'Ahavta* continues this idea.

It teaches us that

- we should love God.
- the way to show our love is by studying and living Torah.
- *mitzvot* are the way we live Torah.
- there are *mitzvot* we can do at all times of the day (every day).
- there are *mitzvot* we can do anywhere and everywhere we go.
- some Jewish things we do help us to remember the *mitzvot*.
- teaching Torah to our children is a very important *mitzvah*.

Some synagogues say three paragraphs of the *Shema* in their service; some say only one. Those who say only one take the last line of the third paragraph and put it onto the ending of the *v'Ahavta*. This is the part that tells us that by doing the *mitzvot* we become *kadosh*, holy.

THE DEATH OF RABBI AKIVA

The Roman government wanted to get even with the Jews for the rebellion led by Bar Kokhba. They made a rule forbidding the Jews to study and practice the Torah. Pappus ben Judah found Rabbi Akiva holding public Torah lessons. Pappus asked Rabbi Akiva, "Aren't you afraid of the government?" Rabbi Akiva answered with the parable of the fox and the fish. He ended it saying, "If we are afraid to sit and study the Torah, how afraid should we be to stop studying Torah!"

Rabbi Akiva was arrested and thrown into prison. When he was taken out to be executed it was time to say the *Shema*. The executioners were combing his flesh with iron combs, yet there was a smile on his face. His students asked, "Why the smile?" He said, "All my life I have been bothered by this Torah verse 'With all thy soul' (Deuteronomy 6:5), which I have interpreted as: 'Even if God takes your soul.' But I said, 'When shall I have a chance to fulfill that mitzvah? Now I have a chance to do it.'" He stretched out the *Shema*'s last word, אֶחָד *Eḇad* ("one"), until he died as he finished saying it. It was his last breath. *(Brakhot* 61b)

The second sentence in the *Shema* says:

וְאָהַבְתָּ אֵת יי אֱלֹהֶיךָ בְּכָל-לְבָבְךָ וּבְכָל-נַפְשְׁךָ וּבְכָל-מְאֹדֶךָ.

V'ahavta et Adonai Elohekha b'Khol-l'Vavkha, u'v'Khol-Nafshekha, u'v'Khol-M'odekha.

And you shall love the Eternal, Your God, with (a) all your heart, with (b) all your soul, and with (c) all your resources.

The Rabbis believed that the Bible is like a telegram. REMEMBER TELEGRAMS? STOP. They believed that each word counted, that God—the Perfect Communicator—would use no extra words. They asked, why God needed three clauses when God could have just said, "Love God completely." Their answer was that each clause taught a different aspect of loving God. The Rabbi Akiva story became the classic example of loving God with our soul. It means doing the right thing, even if it risks our lives to do what is just and right. It is a heroic and extreme form of loving God completely. The question left by this story is "How do I love God with my heart? With my soul? With my resources?"

צִיצִית *TZITZIT*

The third paragraph of the *Shema* speaks about the *tzitzit*, the fringes on the ends of a *tallit*. The Rabbis made it a *mitzvah* for a person to always wear a four-sided garment, often known as a "small *tallit*," that is often worn under a shirt. The story below uses this fact.

Traditional practice has us gather the four fringes on our *tallit* or *tallit katan* (a.k.a. *tzitzit*) and kiss them each of the three times the word *tzitzit* is mentioned in the third paragraph.

THE SEVEN BEDS

This story is from the Talmud, but it is PG-13.

Rabbi Nathan said, "There is not a single *mitzvah* in the Torah, even the most minor, whose reward is not enjoyed in this world. As to its reward in the future world, I do not know how great it is. Learn this from the *mitzvah* of *tzitzit*."

Once there was a man who was very careful about his *tzizit*. He heard of a certain working woman in one of the towns by the sea who accepted four hundred gold denars for her hire. He sent her four hundred gold denars and made a date with her. When the day arrived he came and waited at her door. When he came in she prepared for him seven beds, six of silver and one of gold; and between one bed and the next there were ladders of silver, but the last was of gold. She then went up to the top bed and lay down upon it naked. He went up after her. As he climbed he took off his clothing. All of a sudden his *tzitzit* struck him across the face. He fell down and sat upon the ground. She joined him and said, "By the Roman capitol, I will not leave you alone until you tell me what fault you saw in me." He said, "By the Temple, never have I seen a woman as beautiful as you are. But there is one *mitzvah* that the Eternal our God has commanded us. It is called *tzitzit*, and God said about it, 'I AM THE ETERNAL YOUR GOD.' Now these four *tzitzit* appeared to me as four witnesses, reminding me how I should act."

> She said, "I will not leave you until you tell me your name, the name of your town, the name of your teacher, the name of the school in which you study the Torah."
>
> He wrote all this down and handed it to her. Next she divided her estate into three parts—one third for the government, one third to be distributed among the poor, and one third she took with her in her hand. The seven beds she kept. She then came to the school of Rabbi Hiyya and said to him, "Master, teach me how to become a Jew."
>
> He said, "My daughter, perhaps you have set your eyes on one of the students?" She took out the student's note and handed it to the rabbi. He said, "Go and enjoy your acquisition."
>
> The seven beds that she had spread for him in sin she now spread out for him in joy. "This is the reward of *mitzvot* in this world; and as for its reward in the future world, I know not how great it is." (*Menahot* 44a)

In the third paragraph of the *Shema* the Torah says "AND DON'T STRAY AND GO WHORING AFTER YOUR HEART AND AFTER YOUR EYES" (Numbers 15:39). I guarantee you that your prayerbook doesn't use the word "whore," but that's what the Hebrew actually says. This parable from the Talmud knows that text and builds its story around it. It understands that there are places where our desires overwhelm our knowledge of right and wrong. We all do things that we know we shouldn't. The story, like this paragraph of the *Shema*, understands this and says that the Torah and the *tzitziyot* can be tools to help us stop ourselves in those moments. The questions: "When do we behave in ways we wish we hadn't?" "What acts as your prevention?"

מִי־כָמֹכָה *MI KHAMOKHA/* גְּאֻלָּה *G'ULAH*

The מִי־כָמֹכָה *Mi Khamokha* is

- a sentence out of a poem in the Torah.
- part of the song that Israel sang when they crossed the Reed Sea.
- part of the *brakhah* that comes after the *Shema* in both the morning and the evening.
- a reminder that God has helped us and God will help us.

When the Families of Israel escaped from Egypt, the Egyptians chased them and caught them at the Reed Sea. (Reed Sea is what the Hebrew actually says. Red Sea is a typo). God worked a miracle, and the sea divided. Israel made it safely across on dry land. When the Egyptians tried to follow, the sea closed up and they drowned. Once they were safely on the other side (or maybe even before), Israel launched into song. The song they sang, the Song of the Sea, includes *Mi Khamokha*.

The third *brakhah* connected to the *Shema*, the one that comes after the *Shema*, is called the גְּאֻלָּה *G'ulah*. *G'ulah* means redemption. Redemption is a combination of rescuing and setting free. God redeemed us from Egyptian slavery. That is why this *brakhah* ends by saying:

בָּרוּךְ אַתָּה יי גָּאַל יִשְׂרָאֵל

Barukh Attah Adonai Ga'al Yisrael.
Blessed be You, Adonai, the One who redeemed Israel.

When we say the *Mi Khamokha* (and the rest of the *G'ulah*)

- we remember being rescued from Egypt.
- we say that God will always be there for us.
- we know that God will ultimately help us redeem the whole world.

Moses and the Families of Israel sang the Song of the Sea responsively. That is exactly the way we pray the *Mi Khamokha*. The leader sings a line, and then we respond. Praying the *Mi Khamokha* is reliving the Exodus. It is remembering being redeemed by God.

THE GOLEM

The first word in the *G'ulah* prayer in the evening is אֱמֶת *Emet.* The first prayer in the *G'ulah* prayer in the morning also begins with *Emet. Emet* means truth. This is an *Emet* story.

The Jews of Prague were in lots of danger. Some of the non–Jews in the town were telling lies about them and getting other people angry. There was danger of a riot against the Jews. This kind of riot is called a pogrom.

The Chief Rabbi of Prague was Judah Lowe. He was a great scholar—and he was a student of the *Kabbalah,* the mysteries of the Torah. One night he took his best student and his assistant down to the riverbank. They spent hours shaping a man out of river mud. Rabbi Lowe said prayers. He put a piece of paper with the secret 72-letter name of God into the mud man's mouth. He also traced three letters on his forehead. The first letter of the *Alef-Bet,* an א *Alef.* The middle letter, a מ *Mem*. The last letter, a ת *Tav*. The three letters spelled one of God's names, אֱמֶת *Emet.* Slowly the mud-man came alive. He became Joseph Golem, who was like a person but was extra strong and could not talk.

The Golem protected Prague. He stopped many people who were trying to frame the Jews by planting false evidence in the ghetto. The Golem protected Jews from those who would attack them. And in the end the Golem showed the world who the real liars were.

When the danger had passed the Golem lay down and again became mud when Rabbi Lowe erased the letter א *Alef.* The remaining two letters spelled מֵת *Met,* the Hebrew word for death. (Czech folk tale based in Biblical and Talmudic origins)

The *G'ulah* involves acting out the song that Moses and Israel sang at the Reed Sea. It is a celebration of God the Redeemer. It says that the God who liberated us in the past will redeem us in the future. Both the morning and evening versions of the *G'ulah* begin with overlapping the word *Emet* with the last word in the *Shema*. While we are going to end with a once and future miracle, we begin with truth. This story of the Golem (that probably goes back to Rabbi Elijah of a real place called

Chelm) teaches us that truth contains the power of life and death. We enter into our discussion declaring the ending, the utopian evolution of human existence, to be a truth. We ask, "When have we been liberated?" "How do we stand in need of liberation?" "What moments make liberation our story?"

MEET MIRIAM

After the Families of Israel crossed the sea, two song leaders led them in song. One was Moses and the other was Miriam. Miriam was Moses' older sister, the one who watched over him when he was in the Nile in the basket made out of bulrushes. Miriam was a prophetess, the one who predicted that Moses would lead Israel out of Egypt.

In the wilderness Israel was kept alive by two things. One was the manna that fell from heaven that Moses arranged with God. The other was Miriam's well, a well that moved from place to place and made sure that Israel always had water. Miriam's well is found in the Midrash.

For forty years the Families-of Israel had three leaders, Moses, Moses' brother Aaron, and Miriam.

When Miriam started to sing, all the women picked up drums and began to sing and dance with her. The Midrash asks an interesting question. "Where did the drums come from?" The Midrash answers its own question by saying "The women had faith. They believed that God would indeed liberate them from Egypt. They also knew that when God liberated them they would have to thank and praise God. They brought the drums as an act of faith. They had already planned that celebration."

(*Targum Micah* 6:4. *Hullin* 92a, *Mekhilta de-Rabbi Ishmael, Sotah* 11:1, *Ta'anit* 9[a], *Numbers Rabbah* 1:2, Exodus 15:20–21, Rashi ad loc)

Debbie Friedman's "Miriam's Song" is a snapshot of the moment at the Reed Sea where Miriam led the women in song and dance. It underlines the placement of Miriam as a major Jewish hero, but it doesn't tell the full story. Miriam of the Midrash plays more scenes, does more for the people, and becomes an archetype of female leadership. She is the source of water. Water is not only life, but a Jewish symbol of Torah.

But, most powerful is Rashi's statement about the women bringing drums out of faith. When things seemed hopeless they believed. The מִי-כָמֹכָה *Mi Khamokha* viewed through this story asks, "What do you do when things seem hopeless?" "How do you find faith?"

NAHSHON'S LEAP OF FAITH

Here is one of many stories about the first time the *Mi Khamokha* was said.

> Israel was trapped at the banks of the Reed Sea. The Egyptian army was coming, and there was nowhere to run. Everyone was in a panic. No one knew how to swim well enough. It was a mob scene. God was supposed to rescue them, but nothing was happening. One man, Nahshon ben Aminadav from the tribe of Judah, figured out the answer. He found himself a little space, backed up, and took a running leap toward the sea. He jumped way out into the water, but he never got wet. When his toe got to a place where it should have touched the water, the sea divided under him and he landed on dry land. Israel could then march forward into the dry sea bed.
> (*Sotah* 37a; *Numbers Rabbah* 13:7)

Here is another story about faith and miracles. The idea here is that one person can make a difference. Even if everyone else is afraid to act, the actions of Nahshon change the world. We all are afraid, and we all want to be that one person.

There is a folktale (that sometimes passes as a *midrash*) that God and a person are walking along a beach. The person looks back at the footsteps and notices that sometimes there is one set and sometimes two. The person asks God, "Why did You abandon me?" God answers, "The places with only one set of footprints are the places where I carried you." This *midrash* teaches that miracles only happen when we participate. "When have you helped miracles happen?"

My friend Rabbi Phil Warmflash has his own version of this *midrash*. Phil says that a circle of people are standing at the edge of the Reed Sea. Each was afraid to go into the water. Each tried to push someone else into the water. Eventually one man fell in by accident, and then the sea divided. Each of us can be called on to be the leader, even against our will, and the miracles still happen.

THE WOMEN HOLD HANDS

Here is another memory of how the Reed Sea divided. Every tribe wanted to be the first to enter the water. Each tribe wanted the bragging rights, so they prevented every other tribe from getting wet. It looked like a huge rugby game with everyone pushing and holding each other back. While the men were busy struggling, the women looked at each other. They nodded and stepped back a little. They started to take each other's hands and work their way around the men. They counted together, and on three all of the women-of-Israel (and a lot of the children) stepped into the sea at once. The second that they entered, the sea divided. When that happened, the men stopped struggling with each other and all of Israel began to cross. (*Sotah* 36b-37a; the portion about the women was passed to me as an oral tradition but it is rooted in *Sotah* 11b)

This gender-based tale suggests that miracles happen when people work together rather than struggle for control. We need to ask ourselves, "When are we like the men, pushing to be first?" and "When are we like the women, holding hands and working together?"

SAYING *KHAF* WITH A MOUTH FULL OF WATER

Here is another memory of the first time that Israel said the *Mi Khamokha*.

To understand this story you need to look at the words of the *Mi Khamokha*. It says:

מִי־כָמֹכָה בָּאֵלִם יי, מִי כָּמֹכָה נֶאְדָּר בַּקֹּדֶשׁ...

Mi Khamokha ba-Eilim, Adonai, Mi Kamokha Ne'edar ba-Kodesh...

It is כָמֹכָה *Khamokha* with a כ *Kha* the first time. It is כָּמֹכָה *Kamokha* with a כּ *Ka* the second time. This story explains the change.

Israel entered the Reed Sea singing together. When they sang *Mi Khamokha* the water was up to their ankles. The word *ba'-Eylim* came as they moved forward and the water reached their waists. By *Adonai* the water was at their chest.

They were getting nervous, and so they slowed their singing down. When they sang the second *Mi* the water was up to their necks. Still they pushed on and sang *Kamokha*. When they said *Kamokha* the water was over their heads. The word should have been *Khamokha* but it came out as *Kamokha* because you can't say a *kha* when your mouth is full of water. Only when they were in over their heads did God divide the sea. (Learned orally from Rabbi Shlomo Carlebach, based on *Exodus Rabbah* 21:10)

In the midrash about Nahshon we learn that one person of faith can make a difference. Here we learn that it was the whole nation trusting God that brought the miracle of the Reed Sea. We learn the lesson that we have to go as far as we can go on our own before God will step in and help, or before that extra little something that we didn't know was in us carries us through. We ask, "When have we had to do more than we thought we could?" "When have we succeeded?"

PREACHING TO THE CHOIR

The *Mi Khamokhah* praises God for rescuing Israel and for punishing the Egyptian army. It was sung on the banks of the Reed Sea. In the Midrash we learn that the destruction of the Egyptians bothered God. We are told that while Israel sang God's praise on earth, the angels were joining in up in heaven. God said to them, "Stop singing! My children are drowning." (*Megillah* 10b, *Exodus Rabbah* 23:7)

This famous *midrash* raises a question: "Why was it okay for the Families of Israel to praise God for drowning the Egyptians and not okay for the angels to join them?" The traditional answer to this question is not satisfying: "The Families of Israel directly experienced the miracle, and the angels did not." I prefer to think: "The angels should have known better." The key lesson, and it can be learned easily here, is that victories are better when no one else is hurt. We don't celebrate the death of others.

A second lesson: I was once in Des Moines teaching families. I asked them to come up with an answer to the Rashi question about "Where did the women get the drums?" One eleven-year-old, who had learned the midrash about God stopping the angels said, "The angels started a heavy metal band. The band began to play and praise God. God stopped them and threw their drums out of heaven. The women picked them up and used those drums."

One could not leave the stopping the angels story out of a collection of origin stories. It is one of the most famous. It forces us to ask, "Do we celebrate at the expense of others?"

עֲמִידָה AMIDAH

עֲמִידָה *AMIDAH*

The *brakhot* of the *Amidah* is the place where Jews do most of their deepest prayer work. It is a string of *brakhot* that are linked to form the heart of the morning, afternoon, evening, and extra (*Mussaf*) services. During the week the *Amidah* is made up of nineteen *brakhot*. On Shabbat there are seven.

Different communities pray the *Amidah* in different ways. Originally everyone stood, faced towards Jerusalem, took three steps forward, put their feet together, and said all the prayers in the *Amidah* silently without interruption. In the morning, afternoon, and *Mussaf* (extra) service the prayer leader then repeated the *Amidah* out loud. This did not happen in the evening. That is still the traditional pattern, but today many synagogues say or sing part of the *Amidah* out loud together and do not have a repetition.

The Talmud teaches a history of the *Amidah*:

- Each of these prayers was originally sung by the angels when something important happened on earth.
- Later the prophets gathered these songs into a collection of prayers.
- After the Temple was destroyed by the Romans in 70 C.E., the Rabbis collected these prayers and organized them into a service used to replace the sacrifices that took place in the Temple.
- Where once the Temple was the place that connected all Jews to each other and to God, now, everywhere in the world, all Jews are connected by the path to God created by the *brakhot* in the *Amidah*.

This string of prayers has three names. Each name teaches us something.

- עֲמִידָה *Amidah* means "standing." This name reminds us that this prayer is said standing (in a whisper, with our feet together). This "standing" is a way of being like the angels, acting out the story of Hannah, and physically showing our connection to God.

- שְׁמוֹנָה עֶשְׂרֵה *Sh'monah Esrei* means "the eighteen." Originally the *Amidah* had eighteen *brakhot*. Today there are nineteen. One was added for the protection of Israel from enemies. The number eighteen teaches many different lessons about how to get close to God. Various rabbis have researched and found various things that come only eighteen times. They include God's name in the *Shema*, sentences that have Abraham, Isaac, and Jacob together in the Torah, and eighteen specific prayers that are said by individuals in the Torah. Finally, we learn that there are eighteen joints in the spine. Together these things teach that we should connect to God through prayer, the way our ancestors did. God supported them, and God supports us, just as our spine does.
- הַתְּפִלָּה *Ha-T'fillah* means "the Prayer." Its root, פלל, has two different meanings. The root can mean to "check out". It means that one part of prayer is doing a "self-check," finding out how we are doing as God's partner. Another meaning is "to ask for." The *T'fillah* is the part of the service in which we ask God for the things we need.

Rav Kook, the first Chief Rabbi of Israel, taught, "The *Amidah* is where we learn what is really important in life. It teaches us the difference between the things we need and the things we just want. The *Amidah* is our time to ask God for the things we really need."

HOW TO DANCE THE *AMIDAH*

We begin the *Amidah* by standing up, facing Jerusalem, taking three steps forward, and then standing with our feet together. Some of the prayers we may sing together, but if we don't, they are said in a whisper, loud enough to be heard by your own ears—but by no one else.

Each of these "dance steps" has us acting out a different story.

When we **stand up** we are like Abraham. Abraham was the first person to figure out that there was only one God. In the Talmud (*Brakhot* 26b) we learn that he invented the morning service. He got up every morning and stood before the God he knew was there.

When we **face Jerusalem** we are like King Solomon (1 Kings 8:44–48) creating a house where God can be our neighbor. When we face toward

Jerusalem we are recreating our pilgrimage to the Temple, where sacrifices united all Jews. Now, three times a day, the *Amidah* creates the same connections.

When we **take three steps forward** we are like Moses. Moses went up Mount Sinai to come close to God. The Torah tells us that there was "DARKNESS, A CLOUD, AND THICK FOG" between Moses and the top of the mountain (Deuteronomy 4:11). God was hidden, and Moses had to work to get close. The three steps are our "darkness, cloud, and fog." They remind us that we, too, have to work to feel close to God. (Often people take three steps back in order to take three steps forward.)

The Baal Shem Tov explained these three steps by saying, "When a child is learning to walk, a parent takes three steps back and stands with open arms, giving the child room to learn. Like a parent, God takes three steps back from us to give us the room we need. To begin the *Amidah* we take those three steps back to God."

When **we whisper** we are like H̱annah. You will learn the story of H̱annah later, but she was a woman who needed God's help. She whispered when she prayed, and God answered her. Rabbi Levi Yitzẖak taught, "We whisper to remind ourselves that God is always close. We have no need to yell."

When we **stand with our feet together** we are like angels. In the Bible we learn that angels who are close to God's throne stand with their feet together (Ezekiel 1:7). When we ask God for the things we need, we stand like one of those angels.

THE WEEKDAY *AMIDAH* IS MADE UP OF NINETEEN *BRAKHOT*

PRAISE

The first three *brakhot* praise God. Here is a small piece of each of these:

1. בָּרוּךְ אַתָּה יי אֱלֹהֵינוּ וֵאלֹהֵי אֲבוֹתֵינוּ וְאִמּוֹתֵינוּ
בָּרוּךְ אַתָּה יי מָגֵן אַבְרָהָם.

Barukh Attah Adonai Eloheinu v'Elohei Avoteinu v'Imoteinu…Barukh Attah Adonai Magen Avraham…

Praised are You, Adonai, our God and God of our fathers and mothers…Blessed be You, Adonai, the Shield of Abraham…

2. אַתָּה גִּבּוֹר לְעוֹלָם אֲדֹנָי מְחַיֵּה מֵתִים/הַכֹּל אַתָּה...
בָּרוּךְ אַתָּה יי מְחַיֵּה הַמֵּתִים/הַכֹּל.[1]

Attah Gibor l'olam Adonai M'hayeh Metim/ha-Kol Attah Rav L'hoshi'ah...Barukh Attah Adonai M'hayeh ha-Metim/ha-Kol.

You are mighty Adonai, You give life to all/the dead. Blessed be You, Adonai, the One Who gives life to the dead/all.

3. אַתָּה קָדוֹשׁ וְשִׁמְךָ קָדוֹשׁ וּקְדוֹשִׁים בְּכָל־יוֹם יְהַלְלוּךָ סֶּלָה...
בָּרוּךְ אַתָּה יי הָאֵל הַקָּדוֹשׁ.

Attah Kadosh v'Shimkha Kadosh u-K'doshim b'khol Yom y'hal'lukha Selah... Barukh Attah Adonai ha-El ha-Kadosh.

You are Holy and Your name is Holy...Blessed be You, Adonai the Holy God.

PETITION

The next thirteen *brakhot* are a shopping list—asking God for the things we need.

4. אַתָּה חוֹנֵן לְאָדָם דַּעַת...בָּרוּךְ אַתָּה יי חוֹנֵן הַדָּעַת.

Attah Honen l'Adam Da'at...Barukh Attah Adonai Honen ha-Da'at.

You favor people with knowledge... Blessed be You, Adonai, the One Who makes a gift of knowledge.

5. הֲשִׁיבֵנוּ אָבִינוּ לְתוֹרָתֶךָ...בָּרוּךְ אַתָּה יי הָרוֹצֶה בִּתְשׁוּבָה.

Hashiveinu Avinu l'Toratekha...Barukh Attah Adonai ha-Rotzeh bi-T'shuvah.

Return us, Our Parent, to Your Torah... Blessed be You, Adonai, the One Who wants repentance.

6. סְלַח לָנוּ אָבִינוּ כִּי חָטָאנוּ...בָּרוּךְ אַתָּה יי חַנּוּן הַמַּרְבֶּה לִסְלֹחַ.

S'lah lanu Avinu ki Hatanu...Barukh Attah Adonai Hanun ha-Ma'rbeh li-s'lo'ah.

Forgive us, Our Parent, because we miss the mark... Blessed be You, Adonai, the One Who multiplies opportunities to be forgiven.

---

[1]Reform Jews read this prayer one way; traditional Jews read it another.

7. רְאֵה נָא בְעָנְיֵנוּ וְרִיבָה רִיבֵנוּ וּגְאָלֵנוּ מְהֵרָה לְמַעַן שְׁמֶךָ...
בָּרוּךְ אַתָּה יי גּוֹאֵל יִשְׂרָאֵל.

R'eih na v'anyenu v'rivah rivenu u'g'aleinu m'herah l'ma'an Sh'mekha...Barukh Attah Adonai Go'el Yisrael.

See our suffering and make problems for those who cause us problems, and redeem us quickly... Blessed be You, Adonai, the One Who redeems Israel.

8. רְפָאֵנוּ יי וְנֵרָפֵא...בָּרוּךְ אַתָּה יי רוֹפֵא חוֹלֵי עַמּוֹ יִשְׂרָאֵל.

R'fa'enu Adonai v'Nerafei...Barukh Attah Adondai Rofei Holei Amo Yisrael.

Heal us, Adonai, and we will be healed... Blessed be You, Adonai, the One Who heals the sick of Israel.

9. בָּרֵךְ עָלֵינוּ יי אֱלֹהֵינוּ אֶת-הַשָּׁנָה הַזֹּאת...בָּרוּךְ אַתָּה יי מְבָרֵךְ הַשָּׁנִים.

Barekh aleinu Adonai Eloheinu et ha-Shanah ha-Zot...Barukh Attah Adonai m'varekh ha-Shanim.

Adonai, our God, bless this year...Blessed be You, Adonai, the One Who blesses the years.

10. תְּקַע בְּשׁוֹפָר גָּדוֹל לְחֵרוּתֵנוּ וְשָׂא נֵס לְקַבֵּץ גָּלֻיּוֹתֵינוּ...
בָּרוּךְ אַתָּה יי מְקַבֵּץ נִדְחֵי עַמּוֹ יִשְׂרָאֵל.

T'ka b'Shofar Gadol l'Herutenu v'Sa Nes l'Kabetz Galuyoteinu...Barukh Attah Adonai m'Kabetz Nidhei Amo Yisrael.

Sound the big shofar for our freedom and lift up a flag to signal the ingathering of the exiles...Blessed be You, Adonai, the One Who gathers the exiles of Israel.

11. הָשִׁיבָה שׁוֹפְטֵינוּ כְּבָרִאשׁוֹנָה...בָּרוּךְ אַתָּה יי מֶלֶךְ אֹהֵב צְדָקָה וּמִשְׁפָּט.

Hashivah Shofteinu k'varishonah...Barukh Attah Adonai Melekh Ohev Tz'dakah u'Mishpat.

Return our judges...Blessed be You, Adonai, the Ruler Who loves righteousness and justice.

12. וְלַמַּלְשִׁינִים אַל תְּהִי תִקְוָה...בָּרוּךְ אַתָּה יי שֹׁבֵר אֹיְבִים וּמַכְנִיעַ זֵדִים.

v'La'Malshinim Al T'hi Tikvah...Barukh Attah Adonai Shover Oy'vim u'Makh'niah Zedim.

And for the informers don't let there be hope... Blessed be You, Adonai, the One Who shatters the enemies and oppresses the wicked.

13. עַל הַצַּדִּיקִים וְעַל הַחֲסִידִים...בָּרוּךְ אַתָּה יי מִשְׁעָן וּמִבְטָח לַצַּדִּיקִים.

Al ha-Tzaddikim v'al ha-Hasidim…Barukh Attah Adonai Mish'an u'Mivtah l'Tzaddikim.

For the righteous and for the pious… Blessed are You, Adonai, the One Who supports and the One Who is the-trust of the righteous.

14. וְלִירוּשָׁלַיִם עִירְךָ בְּרַחֲמִים תָּשׁוּב...בָּרוּךְ אַתָּה יי בּוֹנֵה יְרוּשָׁלָיִם.

V'liY'rushalayim Irekha b'Rahamim Tashuv…Barukh Attah Adonai Boneh Y'rushalayim.

And to Jerusalem Your City, return in mercy…Blessed be You, Adonai, the One Who builds Jerusalem.

15. אֶת־צֶמַח דָּוִד עַבְדְּךָ מְהֵרָה תַצְמִיחַ...בָּרוּךְ אַתָּה יי מַצְמִיחַ קֶרֶן יְשׁוּעָה.

Et Tzemah David Avdekha M'herah Tatzkmi'ah…Barukh Attah Adonai matzmi'ah Keren Y'shu'ah.

The seed of David, Your servant, quickly plant…Blessed be You, Adonai, The One Who plants the horn of salvation.

16. שְׁמַע קוֹלֵנוּ יי אֱלֹהֵינוּ...בָּרוּךְ אַתָּה יי שׁוֹמֵעַ תְּפִלָּה.

Sh'ma Koleinu Adonai Eloheinu…Barukh Attah Adonai Shome'a T'fillah.

Hear our voice, Adonai, our God…Blessed be You, Adonai, the One Who hears prayers.

THANKSGIVING

The last three *brakhot* in the *Amidah* thank God for all the blessings we have received.

*17. רְצֵה יי אֱלֹהֵינוּ בְּעַמְּךָ יִשְׂרָאֵל וּבִתְפִלָּתָם...
בָּרוּךְ אַתָּה יי הַמַּחֲזִיר שְׁכִינָתוֹ לְצִיּוֹן.

R'tzei Adonai Eloheinu b'Am'kha Yisrael u'vi-T'fillatam…Barukh Attah Adonai ha-Mahazir Sh'khinato l'Tziyon.

Adonai, our God, want Your people Israel and their prayers…Blessed are You, Adonai, the One Who returns God's neighborly aspect to Zion.

18. מוֹדִים אֲנַחְנוּ לָךְ שָׁאַתָּה הוּא יי אֱלֹהֵינוּ...
בָּרוּךְ אַתָּה יי הַטּוֹב שִׁמְךָ וּלְךָ נָאֶה לְהוֹדוֹת.

Modim Anakhnu Lakh she-Attah Hu Adonai Eloheinu...Barukh Attah Adonai ha-Tov Shim'kha u'L'kha Na'eh l'Hodot.

We give thanks to You, Who are the One, Adonai, our God...Blessed are You, Adonai, the Good One is Your Name and it is beautiful to thank You.

19. שִׂים שָׁלוֹם טוֹבָה וּבְרָכָה חֵן וָחֶסֶד וְרַחֲמִים...
בָּרוּךְ אַתָּה יי הַמְבָרֵךְ אֶת-עַמּוֹ יִשְׂרָאֵל בַּשָּׁלוֹם

Sim Shalom Tovah u'Vrakhah Hen va-Hesed v'Rahamim...Barukh Attah Adonai haM'varekh et Amo Yisrael ba-Shalom.

Give peace, goodness, and blessing, niceness, lovingkindness, and mercy...Blessed be You, Adonai, the One Who blesses Israel with peace.

ON SHABBAT

The thirteen *brakhot* of petition are removed, and in their place comes a short blessing about Shabbat. Included are:

שַׁבָּת: וְשָׁמְרוּ בְנֵי יִשְׂרָאֵל אֶת-הַשַּׁבָּת...בָּרוּךְ אַתָּה יי מְקַדֵּשׁ הַשַּׁבָּת.

V'Sham'ru V'nei Yisrael et ha-Shabbat...Barukh Attah Adonai m'Kadesh ha-Shabbat.

The Families of Israel shall keep Shabbat... Praised are You, Adonai, the One Who makes holy the Shabbat.

Praise, petition, and thanksgiving: The Midrash explains this three part structure with this image. Imagine someone going before a ruler in order to make a request. It would not be good to start with a list of requests. Rather, the person would begin, "The world is better because of this ruler. The world is better because this ruler is a fair judge..." The entire audience would then join that person in praising the ruler. After that start would be the time for requests. The *Amidah* is set up in the same way—first praise, then requests (*Sifrei*, Deuteronomy 343).

The praise *brakhot* resemble a servant praising a boss. **The petition *brakhot*** resemble a servant who asks a boss for a favor. **The thanksgiving *brakhot*** resemble a servant who has gotten the favor for which he has asked (*Brakhot* 34a).

The middle *brakhot* are removed on Shabbat: In order to make a "true petition" one must feel a sense of sadness, hurt, and desperation. In a petition we are asking God to help us meet a need we cannot meet alone (see the story of Hannah). Shabbat is supposed to be a happy time, a celebration. Shabbat is not a time for us to dwell on the saddest parts of our life.

HANNAH'S PRAYER

Hannah was an unhappy woman. She lived in the time of the Judges. This was between the time that Joshua led the Families of Israel back into the Land of Israel and the time King David made them into a real nation.

Hannah had a problem. She had a husband named Elkanah, but he was not the problem. He loved her a lot. Elkanah had a second wife named Penninah. Penninah was part of the problem. She had children, while Hannah had none. Even though Penninah had given birth to his children, Hannah was still Elkanah's favorite wife. To get even, Penninah picked on Hannah a lot. She was good at making Hannah feel bad about not having children. Her feelings about not being a mother were Hannah's biggest problem.

The worst time for her was the time once a year when the whole family went to Shiloh. The Mishkan (Tabernacle) was stationed here, and the family would go there to celebrate. Elkanah would go and stand in line and bring back the portions of the sacrifice for the whole family. He gave Hannah her one portion. He gave Penninah a whole stack of portions for her and children. For Hannah the pile of portions was the scoreboard of her failure. She got only her single portion, and that made her feel alone. When Penninah got lots of portions, Hannah felt that made Penninah a success.

One of those nights in Shiloh Hannah went for a walk. She was wandering close to the Mishkan and praying to God. She was speaking very softly. Her lips were moving, but no one else could hear her words. Hannah was begging God for a child. Eli was the High Priest. He ran the sacrifices and the

> Mishkan. He saw this woman wandering by herself, talking to herself, close to the Mishkan, and he thought she was drunk. He yelled at her for not respecting a holy place. Hannah answered him, "I have not had one drop to drink. I am just a woman who is מָרַת נֶפֶשׁ, *marat nefesh*." In most translations this will read "very sad" or "very bitter." But the Hebrew actually means "I have horseradish in my soul." Just like when you eat too much horseradish and your whole head turns red—it is too much for you—Hannah's sadness and hurt were too much for her. She explained that she had turned to God for help. Eli heard her and understood. He said, "May God answer your prayers." God did. Hannah gave birth to Samuel, who was a very famous judge and prophet.

The Rabbis of the Talmud studied her story and made her the model for the *Amidah*. We stand and whisper our prayers the way she stood and whispered her prayers. We try to have *marat nefesh* (horseradish in our souls), needing what we pray for and knowing that only God can help us.

אֲדֹנָי שְׂפָתַי תִּפְתָּח
ADONAI S'FATAI TIFTAH

These words are a warm-up. They come from a poem written by King David (Psalm 51:17). We will learn that story. It came from a moment when King David was having a lot of trouble knowing how to pray. David wrote those words and spoke them to God as a way of beginning his prayer, and we do the same.

Levi Yitzhak of Berdichev explained that in the days when the *Amidah* was first created, these words were not part of it. He taught, "In those days people knew how to point their hearts and feel close to God." In our day we have added this introduction "as a prayer that we may be ready to pray."

When God created Adam and Eve, God breathed into them the spirit of speech (*Targum*, Genesis 2:7). Words are the things that make people different. Words are our special gift. This prayer takes us back to the first people and asks God to help us use our words.

The Rabbis teach that two things make it hard for us to sincerely pray the *Amidah*.

- We don't feel that we are good enough to deserve God's help. We are afraid that things we have done wrong will bother God too much. We are afraid that God won't help us.
- We are afraid to admit that we need help. To pray the *Amidah* we have to admit that we have problems we cannot fix on our own.

The Talmud teaches us that God gave us the power to speak so that we could say we are sorry and so that we could ask for what we need. אֲדֹנָי שְׂפָתַי תִּפְתָּח *Adonai S'fatai Tiftah* helps us remember this.

KING DAVID SINGS THE BLUES

It was the worst moment in King David's life (so far). It started one day when he went out on the roof of the palace and saw a really beautiful woman sunbathing. Immediately he fell in love with her. It didn't matter that she was married to someone else. David had to be with her even though it was wrong. He could not get her out of his head. This was a moment when "I want it" was stronger than "I know this is wrong." David chose the wrong thing.

The woman's name was Batsheva, and her husband was one of David's soldiers. Even though she was married, David started spending time with her. Soon he had to have her for his own. David wrote to one of his generals. He had Batsheva's husband put in the lead in every battle—in the place with the most danger. When he was killed, David took Batsheva as a wife.

Nathan was a prophet in David's court. One day he came to him with a story about a rich man with many sheep who stole a poor man's only sheep. David listened and felt bad. He said, "The rich man deserves to die." Nathan pointed to David and said, "You are that man." Then he said, "God is now very angry with you."

David suddenly realized how wrong he had been. He was really sorry. There was no way that he could bring Batsheva's husband back and make things right. He didn't know how to fix things. He also was afraid that God would never forgive him. There was now a huge space between him and God—a big black hole. There was horseradish in his soul, too. It was then that he sat down and wrote a poem, a prayer to God.

David began: אֲדֹנָי שְׂפָתַי תִּפְתָּח וּפִי יַגִּיד תְּהִלָּתֶךָ *Adonai S'fatai Tiftah uFi Yagid T'hillatekha*. He said, "God, I don't know how to begin. Words will not come. I want to talk to You, but I don't know what to say. I don't feel worthy." His prayer began, "ETERNAL, IF YOU WILL OPEN MY LIPS AND HELP ME BEGIN, THEN MY TONGUE WILL FIND A WAY TO PRAY TO YOU." (II Samuel 11–12, Psalms 15:17, *Midrash Tehillim* ad loc)

We all have times when we feel like David. Doing the wrong thing puts us in exile. We are in exile from our friends, and we are in exile from God. It is hard to trust in God when we know that God is or should be angry with us. In a sense, we are even in exile from our best self. We start our *Amidah* with David's words. We are looking to start over, to close the distance between us and others, between us and God. We ask God to give us a push downhill, to "OPEN OUR MOUTHS," and we promise to do the rest.

אָבוֹת וְאִמָּהוֹת *AVOT V'IMAHOT*

אָבוֹת וְאִמָּהוֹת *AVOT V'IMAHOT*

The אָבוֹת וְאִמָּהוֹת *Avot v'Imahot* is the first prayer in the *Amidah*. Rabbi Simlai taught in the Talmud, "One must always start the *Amidah* with praise of God before one asks anything of God" (*Brakhot* 32a).

- The *Avot v'Imahot* is the first of three "praise" *brakhot* that begin the *Amidah*.
- The big idea of this prayer is *z'khut avot* (the merit of our ancestors). This means that we ask God to take care of us because our ancestors were good people who had good relationships with God.
- The Rabbis who organized the Siddur explained their choice of the *Avot v'Imahot* as the first prayer because of a Torah story about Moses.

> When Israel sinned with the Golden Calf, God was ready to destroy them. Moses stood and prayed to the Holy One to try to change God's mind. None of his prayers worked until he said, "Do it for the sake of Abraham, Isaac, and Israel, Your servants." It was those words that got God to forgive Israel. Therefore, we begin our *Amidah* by that same reminder to God. (*Mehilta, Bo* 13:3, Shabbat 30a)

Originally this prayer was just about the *Avot*, the "fathers," Avraham, Yitzhak, and Ya'akov. Like many things in Judaism, it was "man"-centered. Today many synagogues, and most non–Orthodox synagogues, have added the *Imahot*, "the mothers, Sarah, Rivkah, Leah and Rahel. This came as part of a growing understanding that all of us need women's stories, too.

> Nahmanides, a famous biblical commentator, taught: "This prayer only works if we remind ourselves of their lives and make a commitment to take their values and make them part of our lives." Why would doing that be a good thing?

Why does this prayer begin with אֱלֹהֵינוּ *Eloheinu* and then say אֱלֹהֵי אֲבוֹתֵינוּ *Elohei Avoteinu*? To teach us that one should not just believe in God because one's family did, but because of one's own search and one's own discovery. (*Otzar ha-T'fillot*)

Why does the prayer repeat אֱלֹהֵי *Elohei* for each mother and father? It is probably based on Exodus 3:15, which says, "THIS IS WHAT YOU SHOULD SAY TO THE FAMILIES OF ISRAEL, 'THE ETERNAL, GOD OF YOUR ANCESTORS, THE GOD OF ABRAHAM, THE GOD OF ISAAC, AND THE GOD OF JACOB, HAS SENT ME TO YOU.'" We can learn from this that each of the *Avot* had a different relationship with God. Each had a different faith. (Rabbi Zev Ya'avetz)

CHOREOGRAPHY

We bend our knees and bow on the opening and closing *Barukh* sentences of this *brakhah*. Remember, one meaning of *barukh* is "bending a knee." *Sefer Abudarham*, a major commentary on the Siddur, teaches that we are supposed to bend like a *lulav*, separating each of the joints in our spine. Remember, one reason that the *Amidah* is called The Eighteen is because of the eighteen joints in the spine.

Bowing symbolizes a sense of humility. Arrogance keeps people from connecting. Egotism creates distance between you and God (*Brakhot* 34a). This same passage in the Talmud forbids bowing at more than the *Avot v'Imahot* and at the *Modim*, because trying to look too humble is an act of pride.

The *Shulhan Arukh* (*Orakh Hayyim* 113.7) teaches that we should bend our whole body as if we were falling down, but stand up straight before we reach God's name (יי). This reminds us that God is the One Who keeps us from falling.

GOD AND THE *AVOT* AND *IMAHOT*

ABRAHAM—גָּדוֹל *GADOL*

גָּדוֹל *Gadol* means big. We learn from the Midrash that Abraham was the first person to believe in one God. He discovered God through looking at the world. Abraham then spent his life welcoming strangers and treating all people as if they were created in God's image. He was big on doing *hesed* (acts of loving kindness). He also spent his time spreading the knowledge that there was only One God. In the Bible we are told that Abraham was "GOD'S FRIEND" (Isaiah 41:8) and that God was the "SHIELD OF ABRAHAM" (Genesis 15:1). The founding relationship with God is "big."

ISAAC—גִּבּוֹר *GIBBOR*

גִּבּוֹר *Gibbor* means strong or hero. Isaac's big moment in the Torah is a very difficult and scary story (Genesis 22). God told Abraham to bring Isaac up a mountain "as a sacrifice." Abraham followed orders and brought him up "as a sacrifice." God stopped the whole thing before Isaac "became" a sacrifice. The Midrash praises Isaac for not rebelling and going along with this "test." They said that he had *g'vurah* (self-control and self-discipline). In the Torah we learn a secret from Isaac. God is called *Pa<u>h</u>ad Yitzhak* (the Fear of Isaac). Sometimes God can scare us. Isaac acted as a hero.

JACOB—נוֹרָא *NORA*

נוֹרָא *Nora* means awesome. Jacob had two major experiences of God in his life. When he left home he had a dream of angels going up and down on a ladder. He said, "HOW AWESOME IS THIS PLACE" (Genesis 27:17). Later Jacob wrestled with a stranger who changed his name to *Yisrael* (the One Who wrestles with God). In between, he started a huge family that grew into the twelve tribes, the Nation of Israel. The Rabbis said that Jacob served God through *tiferet* (truth and beauty). In the Bible we learn that God was *Avir Ya'akov* (The Mighty One of Jacob).

The *Avot v'Imahot* quotes Moses and calls God הַגָּדוֹל *ha-Gadol,* הַגִּבּוֹר *ha-Gibbor,* וְהַנּוֹרָא *v'ha-Nora*. In the Zohar we are taught that Avraham experienced God as *ha-Godol*, Yitzhak experienced God as *ha-Gibbor,* and Ya'akov knew God as *ha-Nora*.

Because we come from the generation that has added the אִמָּהוֹת *Imahot* to the *Amidah*, we have work to do to learn about them and discover the examples they set for us.

SARAH

Sarah was Abraham's partner and a prophetess. She shared the work of welcoming strangers and spreading the knowledge of the One God. She was "the mother of souls" (*Genesis Rabbah* 12:8). Sarah's big thing was laughter. When God first told her that she was to have a child, she laughed in a bitter, angry way. She did not believe it was possible for an old woman to give birth (*Genesis* 18:12). When Sarah gave birth to Isaac, her laughter changed. It became the laughter of joy. Sarah gives God credit, saying, "God has made laughter for me" (*Genesis* 21:6). Sarah let God help her heal her sadness and bitterness.

REBEKKAH

Rebekkah was picked to be Isaac's bride because she shared many values with Abraham. Hospitality—care for others—was a big part of her life. When she herself was unable to have a child, she turned to God in sincere prayer. When twins were fighting in her womb she asked, "If this is so, why do I exist?" Rather than just being a passive bride, she saw to it that Jacob and not Esau became the future of the Jewish people. Rabbi Beth Singer writes, "Rebekkah is clear-sighted, smart, humble, courageous, loyal, loving, and above all else, spiritually connected and clear regarding her life's purpose...She invites each of us to open our eyes to God's presence, to pray for awareness that our lives have meaning, and to direct our actions to...be God's partners in the continual work of creation" (*The Women's Torah Commentary*).

LEAH & RACHEL

Leah was the older sister, the one with "weak eyes," the quiet one. Jacob is tricked into marrying her, but she is the one who gives him many, many children. Rachel was the beautiful sister, the one whom everyone notices. She is the one Jacob first meets and loves. He works fourteen years in order to marry her.

Leah and Rachel together teach us a very important lesson—sisterhood. Even though they were in competition, even though sharing meant that they would each have less, these two women took care of each other. We learn in a midrash (*Lamentations Rabbah* 24) that Rachel helped Leah trick Jacob rather than revealing the plot. We learn in another *midrash* that Leah prayed for Rachel to have a child, even though it would mean competition for her children (*Midrash ha-Gadol*). In the book of Ruth we are told "May the Eternal make the woman who is coming into your house like Rachel and Leah, who together built up the house of Israel."

One of the Patriarchs or Matriarchs will become your personal favorite. All of them will speak to some aspect of your being. Our job is to learn about them and see how they become models for our lives. They are archetypes, possibilities for our lives. The idea is that as we study the Patriarchs and Matriarchs we ask, "Is that me?" "Could that be me?"

THE MISSING MOTHER

Abraham's mother was called Amat'la-i, the daughter of Karnibo, but you can't find her story in the Torah. You have to look for her in the Talmud and the Midrash.

> Nimrod was the wicked king who built the tower of Babel. Like all wicked kings he wanted people to believe that he was a god. Nimrod learned from an astrologer that soon a male child would be born who would grow up and teach everyone that Nimrod was not a god. That did not make Nimrod happy. He ordered the midwives of his empire to make sure that all male babies died. At the same time he offered a prize for every girl that was born. Nimrod built a huge palace and made all of the pregnant women in his realm live there. He pretended to take care of them, but this gave him a chance to make sure that no boys survived.
>
> Amat'la-i was married to Terah, the idol maker. He was a member of Nimrod's court. Amat'la-i hid the fact that she was pregnant. She knew that if Terah knew, he would turn her in, hoping for a reward. When it was time for her to give birth she went out to the wilderness. Abram (who would become Abraham) was born in a cave. His mother blessed him with three blessings: "May God be with you. May God never fail you. May God never leave you." Then she left him.
>
> Here is where the miracles start. Baby Abram sucked his thumb, and out came milk. This milk was amazing food. Ten days after his birth Abram was big enough and strong enough to stand up and walk out of the cave. He looked at the world and the way that nature works. He became the first person to figure out that One God had created everything. He prayed to that One God, saying, "I believe in You." Then, for the first time, he heard God's voice saying, "And I believe in you."

> Amat'la-i felt sick about having abandoned her child. She ran back to the cave and found it empty. While she was sitting at its entrance sobbing, a child, not a newborn, came up to her and said, "Why are you crying?" She explained, and he said, "Mother, don't you recognize me?" She hugged him, and he explained to her about the One God. Abraham's mother, the one who risked her life to give him life, became his first student. (Based on material in Louis Ginzberg, *The Legends of the Jews*)

The secret to this story is that Abram's mother, not Abram, was the first monotheist. When she prays for his safety, she prays to One God. Judaism started because she allowed her son to teach her what he already knew. It is through her that Abraham becomes the teacher of the One God. The story underlines that women's relationships with God are as important as men's. While the prayer started out with only the *Avot* standing with us, the truth is that we need the *Imahot* as well, surrounding us when we pray the *Amidah*.

THE POWER OF READING A BIOGRAPHY

In modern Hebrew there is a word *protectzia*. It is slang and comes from the English word "protection." When you need something done and you call in a favor based on a connection (especially a family connection) it is called *protectzia*. It is easy to think that starting the *Amidah* with Abraham, Sarah, Isaac, Rebekkah, Jacob, Leah, and Rachel is an attempt to do the same thing. This story teaches another understanding of *Z'khut Avot* (the influence of our ancestors).

> One day a stranger walked into the yeshiva and sat and listened to the lecture given by the Rosh Yeshiva, the head of the school. After the lesson the stranger, dressed like a successful businessman, stood in the back. After the students had gone, he walked up to the Rosh Yeshiva and smiled. The rabbi asked, "Do I know you?"
>
> The stranger responded, "Don't you recognize me? I was your *ḥevruta*, your study partner, when we were in yeshiva thirty years ago."
>
> The Rosh Yeshiva looked at him closely, turning back the years. He then said, "Of course I remember you. You changed

> my life. You were the one who taught me how to learn. You gave me the tools to become who I am today."
>
> The old friend suddenly looked sad. The Rosh Yeshiva asked, "What's wrong?" The friend said, "I was just thinking about how I wasted my own potential. I had a real talent for learning and teaching, and yet I never followed through. Why did you grow into a great rabbi while I just drifted away?"
>
> The rabbi answered, "Do you remember that biography of the Gaon of Vilna that was on the reading room table? When you read it your face was shinning, and you said, 'That man was just amazing.' When I read it I said to myself, 'I am going to be as like him as I can manage.' That, my friend, was the only difference."
>
> Rabbi Yitzchak Sender told this story and taught, "*Z'khut Avot* is not just acknowledging the greatness of our ancestors, but taking up the challenge they offer and attempting to emulate them." *(The Commentator's Siddur)*

This story is here to tell us how we should treat the biographies of our ancestors. We should not only learn about them, but find our own way to be like them.

ABRAHAM WAS A HERO

A war was going on in Canaan. It had nothing to do with Abraham. Four local kings were fighting five other local kings. Abraham (who was still Abram) was camped in the trees at Mamre when a refugee from the war staggered into camp. The refugee told him that Abraham's nephew Lot, who lived in Sodom, had been taken prisoner. The four kings had raided Sodom and Gomorrah, robbed all the wealth, and run away. Abraham gathered an army from the people in his camp. He chased the four kings into the north of Canaan. His army caught them and defeated them. Abraham rescued Lot and gathered up all of the possessions that had been stolen. He returned everything to the original owners. He kept nothing for himself. He gave nothing to his army. Melchizedek, king of Salem, threw a party. He gave Abraham (still Abram) a blessing. He said, "Blessed be Abram of *El Elyon* (God on High), Creator of heaven and earth." Abraham then blessed God with words that would later become part of the Psalms: "YOU, GOD, ARE A SHIELD ABOUT ME...I HAVE NO FEAR OF THE MANY FORCES THAT SURROUND ME" (Psalms 3:4-7). At that moment the angels in heaven started to sing, "בָּרוּךְ אַתָּה יי מָגֵן אַבְרָהָם *Barukh Attah Adonai Magen Avraham*—Praised are You, Eternal, Shield of Abraham." (Genesis 14, *Pirkei d'Rabbi Eliezer* 27)

This story could be called "Abraham does social action," because while he rescues Lot, he is also concerned with the neighborhood. What we find here is a biblical connection that links Abraham to the deed, adds the word "shield", and then expands with the angels singing. It asks us: "How do we fit into our community?" "Are we good neighbors?" "What do we do with Abraham's shield?"

SHIELD OF ABRAHAM

Once Abram (who would grow up to become Abraham) discovered that there was only One God, he could not stop spreading the news. His father, Terah, was an idol maker. Abram worked hard to convince his father's customers that the idols they wanted to buy were of no use.

A powerful man came in and asked for a powerful idol. Abram asked, "How old are you?" The man answered, "I have lived seventy years." Abram asked him, "Then why do you want to bow down before a piece of stone that was carved only a few days ago?" The man left.

One day Abram smashed all the idols in his father's store except for one. He put a stick in that idol's hand and told his father, "This idol got in a fight with the other idols and broke them." Terah yelled at his own son, "Are you making fun of me? They are stone—they cannot do anything!" Abram answered, "Father, learn from your own words."

Terah took his son and handed him over to Nimrod, the wicked local king. Nimrod challenged him: "Don't you know that I am god, the ruler of the Universe." Abram said to him, "Then tomorrow please make the sun rise in the west and set in the

> east." Nimrod stared at him in anger. Abram then said to him, "You are no god. You are just the son of Cush. You could not keep your father from dying—and eventually you will die, too."
>
> Nimrod had Abram taken away. He was put to work as a slave. The project Abram was working on was the Tower of Babel. This was Nimrod's attempt to reach heaven. Workers on the tower were trained to care more about the bricks than about other workers. Abram started a slave revolt. He taught everyone that there was only One God, that people should care about each other, and that no tower could reach God. Eventually God mixed up the languages of the workers, and Abram escaped.
>
> Abram went back home and continued teaching people that Nimrod was not god, because there was only One God. Nimrod had him arrested again. He was taken into the center of the city, tied hand and foot, and placed on a huge bonfire. The fire burned and burned, but Abram was protected. Nimrod grabbed his sword and his shield. The shield was a triangle with the point at the bottom. It stood for "Everything Comes to Me." Abram called for a sword and shield. His shield was also a triangle. Its point was at the top and meant "Everything Comes from God." The two of them began to fight on the bonfire. It was hot. At one point they banged their shields together, and they fused. Abram pulled back, and he now had a shield with six points. Nimrod fled and Abram was safe. That six-pointed shield was first *Magen Avraham*; only later did it become *Magen David*. At that moment the angels sang "בָּרוּךְ אַתָּה יי מָגֵן אַבְרָהָם *Barukh Attah Adonai Magen Avraham* (Praised are You, Eternal, Shield of Abraham)." (*Genesis Rabbah* 38:13, *Pirkei d'Rabbi Eliezer* 24, Rabbi Shlomo Carlebach, and other sources)

This is one of the few stories told in the Siddur in which the heroic comes out. Abraham is pure Errol Flynn. He outwits people, he wins a sword fight, and he drives away a wicked king. The phrase "Shield of Abraham" is transformed from someone who needs help to someone who provides help. Abraham becomes a model of not only faith, but strength. We ask, "When do I need to stand up for truth?" And we ask, "How is God my shield and my strength?"

HELPING SARAH/REMEMBERING SARAH

Some synagogues end the *Avot v'Imahot* with וְעֶזְרַת שָׂרָה *v'Ezrat Sarah,* (The One Who Aids Sarah). Others use וּפוֹקֵד שָׂרָה *u'Foked Sarah* (The One Who Remembers Sarah).

In the Midrash a rabbi named Resh Lakish teaches, "The *Avot* and *Imahot* are chariots" (*Genesis Rabbah* 47:6). This idea is explained by saying that our prayers can ride on them and reach God.

Resh Lakish also taught (in the days when this prayer included only the *Avot*) that while the prayer begins with all of the *Avot*, it ends with only *Avraham* to fulfill a promise that God made. When Abraham agreed to leave home and follow God, God made him five promises. The first was "YOU SHALL BE A BLESSING" (Genesis 12:12). *Magen Avraham* is his blessing (*Pesahim* 117b).

When the *Imahot* were added to this blessing Sarah got to share the final slot. Some siddurim talk about *Ezrat Sarah* (the God Who helped Sarah). Many now use *Poked Sarah* (the God Who remembered Sarah). This is based on Genesis 21:1. It says, "THE ETERNAL VISITED/REMEMBERED SARAH AS GOD HAD SAID, AND THE ETERNAL DID FOR SARAH AS GOD HAD PROMISED." The same root, *poked,* is used to tell what God did for the Jewish people when they were slaves in Egypt. "AND THE PEOPLE BELIEVED WHEN THEY HEARD THAT THE ETERNAL HAD REMEMBERED/VISITED THE PEOPLE OF ISRAEL AND HAD SEEN THEIR AFFLICTION, AND THEY BOWED THEIR HEADS AND WORSHIPED" (*Exodus* 4:31).

No matter which phrase we use to end the addition of the *Imahot*, what we need to know is that we are adding a different kind of relationship with God. While Abraham gets us protected, Sarah gets God to make a personal difference in her life. We ask, "When does God help me? When does God remember me?"

SARAH'S TENT

Sarah had a tent of her own. Every time the family made camp, Sarah's tent was set up first. Abraham taught about the One God to men, while Sarah was the women's teacher. Abraham's tent had doors on all four sides so that everyone who was looking for hospitality could easily find his way in. Sarah's tent was where Shabbat was created. Every week Sarah baked h̲allah. The smell of the h̲allah lasted from week to week. It was always in the tent. Every week Sarah lit Shabbat candles. The Shabbat lights burned from one Shabbat until the next set were kindled. The tent always smelled of h̲allah. It was always a place of light.

The *Shekhinah* is the part of God that gets close to people. It is the part that can be our neighbor. God was comfortable with Sarah and her tent. God liked the smell and the light and the peace of Shabbat. The *Shekhinah* would come down in a cloud and rest on Sarah's tent.

When Sarah died her tent grew dark; the smell of h̲allah began to fade. Isaac was sad. He refused to see anyone. Abraham sent his servant back to Padan Aram, the old country, to find a wife for Isaac. He picked Rebekkah. When Rebekkah rode into camp, she and Isaac saw each other and fell in love immediately. Isaac took Rebekkah into his mother's tent. Rebekkah baked h̲allah, and then she lit Shabbat candles. The tent smelled of h̲allah again. The tent was filled with light again. The *Shekhinah* came back. Isaac found comfort after his mother's death.

Years passed. God was hiding in the seventh heaven and crying. Israel had rejected the commandments. They had made a golden calf. All God's dreams were shattered like the tablets. God needed a way to start over. God needed a new beginning. Then God remembered Sarah's tent. God told Abraham to have Israel built a tent and to place within it twelve loaves of braided bread and a light that never went out. The tent would smell like h̲allah. It would always be a place of light. And God promised that God would come down and be a neighbor just as God had done at Sarah's tent. (*Genesis Rabbah* 60:16) (The story grew from a comment in Tamar Frankiel's book *The Voice of Sarah*, in which she teaches that Sarah is the prototype of the High Priest. Then there was an article by Danny and Cheryl Landes that talked about both Rebekkah and Isaac as abused children who comfort each other. This set me on the creation of a much larger version of this story, weaving together many more pieces of Midrash.)

The story, drawn from many sources, says that among Sarah's skills was the creation of a healing presence. It not only tells another one of the missing stories of our Mothers, but leads us to think about healing presences in our life. Sarah offers a very different kind of shield.

RACHEL ENDS THE EXILE

God is angry at the Families of Israel. God says that Israel will never be forgiven and will never be allowed to return to the Land of Israel. Abraham, Isaac, Jacob, and Moses leave their graves, and each tries to convince God to forgive the Jewish people. God remains fixed. Nothing changes God's mind—the Exile in Babylon will be forever. Even Jeremiah, the prophet of the Exile, cannot change God's mind.

Abraham said to The Holy-One-Who-is-to-Be-Blessed: "Ruler of the Universe, How could you exile my children and have the Temple destroyed? It stands on the very place where I offered my son Isaac as a burnt-offering to You."

The Holy-One-Who-is-to-Be-Blessed responded: "Your children sinned and broke the whole of the Torah."

Isaac spoke next: "Master of the Universe, when my father said to me: GOD WILL SEE A LAMB FOR A BURNT OFFERING—MY SON (*Genesis* 22:8), and I knew that I would be killed, I raised no objections, I didn't interfere with his ability to complete Your command. I let myself be bound and placed on the altar and even stretched out my own neck beneath the knife. Won't You remember my sacrifice and have mercy on my children?"

God did not respond.

Jacob spoke next: "Master of the Universe, didn't I stay for twenty years in Laban's house to try to build this family? And when I left his house, the evil Esau met me and tried to kill my children—and I risked my own life to save them. Now they have been delivered into the hands of their enemies like sheep to the slaughter after I raised them...and put up with the pain that raising children causes. For most of my life, I put up with a lot of trouble for their sake. Now won't You remember all this, and for my sake, forgive them."

God did not respond.

God was sad about the punishment given to *B'nai Yisrael* (just as parents are sad when their children need punishing). Moses was asked to comfort God.

Moses said: "Master of the Universe, did I not serve as a faithful shepherd to Israel for forty years? I ran before them the way a person leads a horse through the desert. When the time came for them to enter the Promised Land You issued a verdict against me that my bones should fall in the wilderness. This is just what they mean when they say 'I get no benefit from my master's good fortune, but I have to suffer from his bad luck.'"

God did not respond.

Finally Rachel appeared and spoke to The Holy One.

"Master of the World, You know that Your servant Jacob loved me very much and worked for my father for me for seven years. When those seven years were completed and the time for our marriage had come, my father planned to secretly substitute my sister for me. It was very hard for me, because I knew the plot, and I told my future husband. I gave him a sign, a way to tell the difference between me and my sister, so that my father could not make the exchange. After that I changed my mind. I held back my own desire and had empathy for my sister—that she should not be publicly shamed. On the night they switched my sister for me I taught her all the signs that I had worked out with my husband so that he would think she was Rachel. More than that, I went beneath the bed upon which he lay with my sister, and when they spoke to one another she remained silent and I spoke all the replies so that he would not recognize my sister's voice.

"I did her a kindness and was not jealous of her and did not expose her to shame. I am only a creature of flesh and blood, made out of dust and ashes. If I could get over being jealous of my rival, then You, The Ruler Who Lives Forever, the One Who is Merciful, should be able to get over Your jealousy of idolatry (which isn't even a real competitor) and stop the exile of my children and end their slaughter by the sword and prevent their enemies from doing with them as they wish."

Immediately the mercy of The Holy One Who Is to Be Blessed was stirred. God said: "For your sake, Rachel, I will restore Israel to their place." (*Lamentations Rabbah*, Proem 24)

Sometimes matriarchs can do things that patriarchs can't. "Who is in your pantheon of matriarchs?"

גְּבוּרוֹת *G'VUROT*

The גְּבוּרוֹת *G'vurot* is:

- The second of the three praise *brakhot* that begin the *Amidah*.
- A prayer that the Talmud names two different ways:
- It is called the *G'vurot* (the "power "prayer) (*Megillah* 17b). That makes it a prayer that talks about God's power through describing some of the good things that God does for people.
- It is also called מְחַיֵּה הַמֵּתִים *M'hayeh ha-Metim* (The One Who Gives Life to the Dead) (*Brakhot* 33a). It is a prayer that traditionally centers on the idea that God is stronger than death.

The *G'vurot* is a place where some modern Jews have changed the Siddur. In a number of siddurim the phrase מְחַיֵּה הַמֵּתִים *M'hiyeih ha-Metim* (The One Who Gives Life to the Dead) is replaced by מְחַיֵּה הַכֹּל *M'hayeih ha-Kol* (The One Who Gives Life to All) or מְחַיֵּה כָּל חַי *M'hayeih Kol Hai* (The One Who Gives and Renews Life).

This *brakhah* is built around the language of Psalm 146. There we are told that God:

- keeps faith forever.
- arranges justice.
- feeds the hungry.
- sets prisoners free.
- lifts up the fallen.

In the *Iyyun ha-T'fillah*, a commentary on the Siddur, we are taught, "This prayer shows that while people often use their strength to defeat and conquer others, God uses power in the opposite way."

In the same way that the *Avot v'Imahot*, the first prayer in the *Amidah*, tells the story of Avraham's (and Sarah's) experiences of God, the *G'vurot* grows out of stories of *Yitzhak* and *Rivkah* (and a *Yosef* story, too).

THE PRAYER FOR RAIN

From the last day of Sukkot until first day of Pesah we add the words מַשִּׁיב הָרוּחַ וּמוֹרִיד הַגָּשֶׁם *Mashiv ha-Ru'ah u-Morid ha-Gashem* to the *G'vurot*.

Some Jews add the phrase מוֹרִיד הַטָּל *Morid ha-Tal* during the times that *Mashiv ha-Ruah̲* is not said.

In the *Tur* (O.H. 114), a legal code, the connection between the *G'vurot* and the prayer for rain is explained. "Just as the resurrection of the dead will bring the dead back to life, so the rain brings the world back to life."

In the Talmud (*Ta'anit* 2a) Rabbi Abahu said, "Rain is a bigger miracle than resurrection of the dead because the rain falls for everyone, whereas only the good will be resurrected."

We will talk more about resurrection of the dead later, but here the idea is simple. If you live in Israel, California, or similar climate, rain only comes a few months a year. That which is virtually desert becomes green. It is an easy way to see life starting over again. It is a kind of creation. We get a firsthand experience of God giving life. The question: "Where do you see renewal?"

THE ORIGINS OF THE גְּבוּרוֹת *G'VUROT*

Most of the prayers in the Siddur were assembled out of biblical images. Each time we find a source it gives us another story to connect.

אַתָּה גִּבּוֹר *Attah Gibbor* (You are mighty): Moses, asking forgiveness for the Golden Calf, called God *Gadol, Gibbor,* and *Nora*.

מְכַלְכֵּל חַיִּים חֶסֶד *Mikhalkel H̲ayyim b'H̲esed* (cultivating/sustaining life in kindness): We learn that Yosef did the same thing (with the root כלכל): "YOSEF SUSTAINED HIS FATHER AND HIS FAMILY WITH FOOD" (*Genesis* 47:12).

סוֹמֵךְ נוֹפְלִים...וּמְקַיֵּם אֱמוּנָתוֹ *Somekh Noflim*...*U'M'kayyem Emunato* (Lifts up the fallen...and establishes faith): In Psalm 146 we read about God, "(GOD) KEEPS FAITH FOREVER, SECURES JUSTICE FOR THOSE WHO HAVE BEEN WRONGED, GIVES FOOD TO THE HUNGRY. THE ETERNAL SETS PRISONERS FREE...THE ETERNAL LIFTS UP THOSE THAT ARE FALLEN."

לִישֵׁנֵי עָפָר *Lishenei Afar*: In the book of Daniel (12:2) we find this prayer: "(MAY) MANY OF THOSE WHO SLEEP IN THE DUST AWAKE—SOME TO ETERNAL LIFE, SOME TO PUNISHMENT." It speaks of judgment after death.

IDEA OF *TEH̲IYYAT HA-METIM*

There are many different Jewish ideas of what happens after you die. Among them are:

- The good that people do lives on.
- People live on in memories.
- The soul returns to God.
- People's souls are reborn as another person (reincarnation).
- There is a place, like heaven, the Garden of Eden, where people go as a reward.
- There is a place, sort of like "the other place," called *Gehennah*, where everyone goes at first (for less than a year) to "burn off their sins" but where bad people stay.
- All good people will have their souls returned to their bodies, and they will live again.

GIVING LIFE TO THE DEAD

This is the way that one midrash retells the hardest story in the Torah.

> God told Abraham to bring his son up "as an offering." Abraham tried some delaying tactics, but they did not work.
>
> He got up the next morning and saddled a donkey. The donkey was one of the miraculous things that God created in the last hour before the first Shabbat. This was the same donkey that Moses would use to take his wife and sons to Egypt. This was also the donkey that the Messiah will use to ride into Jerusalem.
>
> Three days later they reached the mountain. They saw a pillar of fire rising from the mountaintop—a clear indication that the *Shekhinah,* the neighborly part of God, was waiting there. They went up to the top of the mountain. God showed them a place where an altar had been built. It was where Cain and Abel had offered their sacrifices. It was where Noah and his family had offered sacrifices. Abraham rebuilt this altar.
>
> Isaac said to his father, "Please bind me hand and foot so that I do not flinch. Help me to follow the command to 'HONOR YOUR FATHER.'" God watched as Abraham was binding with all his heart and Isaac was bound with all his heart. The angels cried.

> Abraham picked up the knife to kill his son. He touched the blade to Isaac's neck, and Isaac's soul fled. He was as good as dead. When the angels cried to Abraham, "LAY NOT YOUR HANDS UPON THE BOY," Isaac's soul returned. He stood up and said, "בָּרוּךְ אַתָּה יי מְחַיֵּה הַמֵּתִים *Barukh Attah Adonai M'hayyei ha-Metim* (Praised are You, Eternal, Who gives life to the dead)." He said it not only about himself, but because he now understood that all people will have an afterlife.
>
> Abraham sacrificed a ram on this altar and not his son. This ram was another one of the miraculous things created in the last hour before the first Shabbat. God turned it into a promise of a better future. Its ashes were used to mark the altar in the Temple. Its sinews would become the strings on King David's harp. Its skin became Elijah's belt. Its horns became the *shofarot* that will announce the coming of the Messiah. The angels sang, "*Barukh Attah Adonai M'hayyei ha-Metim.*" (*Pirkei d'Rabbi Eliezer* 31)

The idea of resurrection of the dead has been seen as Christian. But Christians got it from Jewish thinking. It was a central tenant of Rabbinic thinking and a boundary issue for the Pharisees. It is a perfectly good Jewish idea that in a scientific era is better understood as a metaphor than as a physical reality. When we accept this simple understanding, each of our lives comes with moments of renewal. We all have moments of rebirth.

REBEKKAH IS LIKE GOD

This *brakhah* lists some of the mighty things that God does—lifting up the fallen, healing the sick, freeing the captive, etc. These are all acts of *G'milut Hasadim,* "deeds of lovingkindness." The Talmud makes it clear that God does *G'milut Hasadim*. Rabbi Simlai taught that the Torah begins and ends with *G'milut Hasadim*. It begins with God clothing the naked, Adam and Eve. It ends with God burying the dead, Moses (*Sotah* 14b).

A story about Rebekkah shows that people can do the same. The Midrash describes what Eliezer saw when he realized that she was the perfect bride for Isaac.

Eliezer saw a beautiful woman coming toward the well with a jug on her shoulder. She first stopped beside a crying child. The child had cut his foot on a sharp stone. She washed and bound the wound and told the child, "Do not worry—this will soon heal." Then a half-blind woman came to the well to draw water. Rebekkah helped her carry the full pitcher of water home. When Rebekkah returned, Eliezer asked her to draw a little water for him. (From Rashi on *Genesis* 24:10)

JOSEPH THE TZADDIK

This story begins with a father who favors one son over his other sons. Joseph, the favorite son, begins to have dreams in which everyone bows down to him. He is a child who says "me" all the time. His brothers begin to hate him for his dreams and for his special treatment.

One day Jacob, the father, asks Joseph to go out to the pasture where the other brothers are watching the sheep. Joseph happily agrees. Maybe he doesn't realize how much his brothers hate him. Maybe he doesn't believe that anything bad could happen to him. Or maybe he just wants to make his father happy. Whatever the reason, it is a trip that changes Joseph's life—and that of his whole family.

Joseph's brothers capture him, throw him in a pit, tell his father that he is dead, and sell him as a slave. Joseph winds up in Potiphar's house in Egypt. Here Joseph becomes responsible. He cares about doing a good job. Joseph becomes a successful head of Potiphar's household. The problem comes when Potiphar's wife wants to cheat on her husband. She is beautiful. They could get away with it. But he refuses her, saying, "I have to be loyal to my master." The Midrash says, "He was ready to cheat, but he heard his father's voice."

Even though he says, "No," Joseph winds up in jail. There he makes a point of learning the language of everyone else in jail. The Torah makes a point of telling us that "God was with Joseph in jail." The Midrash explains that Joseph lived with the knowledge that there was one God Who demanded that people act with justice and kindness. Joseph becomes a leader in jail, too.

In jail Joseph explains some dreams. This gets him the chance to explain Pharaoh's dreams. These dreams wind up meaning seven years of plenty and then seven years of famine. Joseph winds up in charge of Egypt, and everyone loves him. They do bow down, just as in his childhood dreams.

When the famine comes, Joseph makes sure that there is food for everyone—no favoritism. There is food for every Egyptian and food for strangers from other countries who come in need. Joseph could charge oodles of money for the food, but he is fair and just in his pricing. The Midrash tells us that he personally went and spoke to all who needed food in their own language, using the languages he learned in jail.

When his brothers come down to Egypt Joseph has the power to get even with them. Instead of revenge, he does two things. First, he helps them understand what they did that was wrong. This understanding is a gift. Then he makes sure that his family has food, safety, and a good place to live. He forgives and helps. In the tradition Joseph, the child who started out saying "me," all the time, is called *Yoseph ha-tzaddik*, Joseph the Righteous Person.

Joseph lived the *G'vurot*. He did the *G'milut Hasadim* thing. He lived up to the image of God in the *G'vurot*. We get two questions: "When do I need God's help?" and "When can God do the things God does to help people through me?"

קְדוּשָׁה *K'DUSHAH*

The קְדוּשָׁה *K'dushah* is understood to be the angels' prayer. For some Jews, angels are very real. For other Jews, angels are a metaphor—a way of describing a special state of holiness, a special sense of closeness to God.

The *K'dushah* is:

- the third praise *brakhah* that begins the *Amidah*.
- said silently in some settings and then repeated out loud as a congregation, and just said out loud by the congregation in others.
- a dialogue, a back-and-forth singing or reading between the congregation and the service leader.
- a prayer about *k'dushah* (holiness).

There are many different texts to the *K'dushah*. It is traditional to say it more than once during the morning service. It is traditional to change its form between Shabbat and weekday services and to change its form at different times of day. What each of these forms has in common is the central idea that God is holy.

There is a *mitzvah* called *Kiddush ha-Shem*. It means "making God's name holy," and that means giving God a great reputation. Sometimes *Kiddush ha-Shem* means martyrdom. That is dying for a good cause because God's rules and God's values are sometimes worth giving up one's life for. But *Kiddush ha-Shem* can also mean living in such a way that God becomes real and holy through your actions.

We learn in the Torah that we are supposed to be holy because God is Holy (*Leviticus* 19:2), and that the Jewish people are supposed to be a Holy Nation (*Exodus* 19:6). The *Zohar* makes it even clearer when it teaches "We fill the earth with holiness through doing *mitzvot*."

The *K'dushah* is built out of the stories of Isaiah, Ezekiel, and Jacob.

The *Amidah* begins with three *brakhot*: the *Avot*, the *G'vurot*, and the *K'dushah*. These prayers all praise God—and each teaches us about a different experience of God. The *Avot* is connected to Abraham, the *G'vurot* to Isaac, and the *K'dushah* to Jacob. It is about his ability to see *emet*, the truth (*Sefer ha-Eshkol, Shibbolei ha-Leket*).

"Holy" is a hard word to explain.

In the Midrash we are told that when God tells us in the Torah, "YOU SHALL BE *KEDOSHIM*" (Leviticus 19:2), it really means "You shall be separate or different" (*Sifrei* on Leviticus 19).

Rashi, a medieval commentator, explains that being separate means separating one's self from one's animal urges. God is saying, "I have planted a spark of My *K'dushah* in you, and that gives you the power to resist the *Yetzer ha-Ra* (the temptation to do wrong)."

In the Midrash we are told, "God says, 'When you honor Me with your sense of justice, My *K'dushah* lives with you. If you guard two things, justice and ethical actions, I will redeem you with a complete redemption'" (*Deuteronomy Rabbah* 5:7).

JACOB VISITS THE PLACE

Makom is the Hebrew word for place. *Ha-Makom*, "The Place," is also a name for God.

Jacob left home, came to a place, and made camp. Using a rock for a pillow, he went to sleep and dreamed. In this *makom* he met *ha-Makom*. The Midrash teaches, "Why is God called 'The Place'? Because in every place where there are righteous people God is there." Jacob learned that every *makom* can be a place to discover *ha-Makom*.

In his dream Jacob saw a ladder. Its feet were on the ground. Its head was in heaven. Angels were going up and down on the ladder. At the very top of the ladder Jacob saw "The Gates of Compassion" just below God's throne. When he awoke Jacob said, "This place is the Gate of Heaven. This is the place where the gates of heaven open to hear prayers. Here will be *Bet El*, the House of God." Then Jacob said, "God is made holy through righteousness."

The angels answered and sang "בָּרוּךְ אַתָּה יי הָאֵל הַקָּדוֹשׁ *Barukh Attah Adonai ha-El ha-Kadosh* (Blessed be You, the Holy God)."

This was the first time the words that end the *K'dushah* were used (Genesis 28:10-22, *Pirkei d'Rabbi Eliezer* 35).

SOME THINGS TO KNOW ABOUT ANGELS

- Two different Hebrew words are used for "angel" in the Bible. One is מַלְאָךְ *Mal'akh*, which means "messenger." *Mal'akhim* (messengers) can either be heavenly creatures or humans doing holy work. The other word is אֱלֹהִים *Elohim*. It usually means "gods" but can also mean "God" (referring to "The One God").
- In the Bible there are other heavenly creatures, seraphim and cherubim, that are definitely not people and do have wings.
- In the Jewish tradition, angels are not dead people. Traditionally, when Jews die they go back to the Garden of Eden (and not up into heaven) and wait for the *Olam ha-Ba* (The World to Come).
- We learn in the Talmud that most angels exist to do only one job and then they disappear. Some angels—those with names—are *Mal'akhei ha-Sharet* (ministering angels) who continue to exist to do specific jobs. *Mikha'el, Gavri'el, Uri'el*, and *R'fa'el*, as well as the Angel of Death, are such angels.
- The *Zohar* teaches that angels are "a portion of God's strength." It is as if God rips off a small piece of God and sends it off to do a specific job.
- The Midrash, the Talmud, and the literature that follows are filled with stories about angels and stories that use angels. One big angel job is to carry people's prayers up to heaven. Another is to sing and provide human history with a sound track.
- Maimonides wrote that angels are just a metaphor for God's influence in the world. He did not believe in praying to angels or that they actually exist in a physical form (*Guide For the Perplexed*, 2:6, 1:49).

HOW TO DANCE THE *K'DUSHAH*

When the *K'dushah* is said silently, it is just part of the *Amidah*. When the *K'dushah* is said out loud with the community, it comes with three rules.

(a) It must be started with an invitation. This means that the service leader invites the group to say the prayer, just like the *Barekhu*. We do this because the prophet Isaiah tells of seeing angels calling one to the other (Isaiah 6:3).

(b) It must be said with a *minyan* (a community of at least ten). This is also like the *Barekhu*. We do this because of a teaching in Leviticus in which God says, "MAKE ME *KADOSH* IN A COMMUNITY OF ISRAEL" (Isaiah 22:32).

(c) We must stand because Ehud, a judge, stood when he delivered a message from God (Judges 3:20). We stand with our feet together, because angels stand as if they have one leg (Ezekiel 1:7). And we bounce three times when we say "קָדוֹשׁ קָדוֹשׁ קָדוֹשׁ *Kadosh, Kadosh, Kadosh*" in order to be like the angels who fluttered around (Isaiah 6:3), to show the lifting of the spirit (*Shulhan Arukh, Orakh Hayyim* 104:7), and to show that after we do all we can, we are carried by God (Rav Kook).

CALLING ONE TO THE OTHER: ISAIAH'S STORY

Isaiah was a prophet. He told the following story.

I was in the Temple and looked, and I saw God sitting on a throne. Seraphim (angels) were all around serving God. Each one had six wings. Two wings covered their face. Two covered their legs. Two were used to fly. They called to each other:

קָדוֹשׁ קָדוֹשׁ קָדוֹשׁ יי צְבָאוֹת מְלֹא כָל־הָאָרֶץ כְּבוֹדוֹ.

Kadosh Kadosh Kadosh Adonai Tzeva-ot m'lo Kol ha-Aretz K'vodo.

Holy Holy Holy is the Eternal of Hosts, the whole world is filled with God's glory.

The Temple filled with smoke, and I thought I was doomed. I said to myself, "I am not worthy. My lips are unclean."

One seraph flew over to me with a hot coal, touched it to my lips, and said, "Your sin is now cleaned away." Then I heard God speak and say, "Who shall I send to do My work?" I answered, "Send me." This is when I became a prophet (From Isaiah 6:1-9).

Every time the service has us sing antiphonally, we are acting out a biblical moment. Here we act out Isaiah's call from God. The *K'dushah* is the high point in the service. It is here that we recall getting closest to God. The idea is that Isaiah moved from the lower Temple to the heavenly Temple and actually moved closest to God. In our performance of this text we are the angels, praising God and getting close. And we are like Isaiah, getting purified and called.

EZEKIEL'S STORY

Ezekiel was a prophet. He told the following story.

> I was in exile in Babylon when the heavens opened and I saw God. There was a storm; a huge cloud flashed fire, and in the center of it I saw creatures with four faces, four wings, and a single rigid leg...
>
> God said to me, "Human, take all My words into your heart and listen to them with your ears. Go to the Families of Israel, who are now in exile, and say to them, 'The Eternal, my Master, is speaking to you'—even if they do not listen."
>
> Then a great wind carried me away. I heard behind me the noise of wings beating, and a great roaring voice was singing:
>
> בָּרוּךְ כְּבוֹד יי מִמְּקוֹמוֹ.
>
> *Barukh K'vod Adonai mi-M'komo.*
>
> Praise the Honor of the Eternal from God's place.
>
> A spirit seized me, and I was carried away. This is how I became a prophet (Ezekiel 1).

Immanence is a fancy way of saying that God is close and that people can feel close to God. Isaiah had an experience of getting close to God. He heard the angels singing "מְלֹא כָל־הָאָרֶץ כְּבוֹדוֹ *M'lo Kol ha-Aretz K'vodo,*" which teaches that God can be found everywhere. When you feel God in your heart, that is immanence.

Transcendence is a fancy way of saying that God is far away and beyond what a person can understand. Ezekiel's experience of God was one of terror and not quite understanding. He knew that he did not get the whole picture. He heard the angels sing "בָּרוּךְ כְּבוֹד יי מִמְּקוֹמוֹ. *Barukh*

K'vod Adonai mi-M'komo." That suggests that God has a hiding place and only sends out messages. When you feel that God is a big mystery—beyond what you can fully understand—this is transcendence.

Judaism believes that sometimes God feels immanent and sometimes God feels transcendent. When have you had an Isaiah experience of God—knowing that God is close, everywhere, and loving? When have you had an Ezekiel experience of God—knowing that God is hidden, far away, and awesome?

> Philo, a famous Jewish philosopher who lived in Egypt around 50 B.C.E., taught: "When God finished creating the world, God asked the angels if anything was lacking. The angels answered, "Everything is perfect except for one missing thing—words that praise God." God agreed with the angels, so God created people."

> Rabbi Ze'ev Einhorn taught in his commentary on the Siddur, "When Israel says that God is *Kadosh*, it helps to make them *kadosh*. One purpose of the *K'dushah* is to make us holy."

וְשָׁמְרוּ *V'SHAMRU*

THE MIDDLE *BRAKHOT*

The *Amidah* is like a sandwich. On the outside are two sets of three *brakhot*: three praise *brakhot* at the beginning and three thanksgiving *brakhot* at the end. During the week there are thirteen petition *brakhot* in the middle. Petition means "asking." During the week we ask God for the things that we need. On Shabbat we don't do "business" with God. We remove these middle *brakhot* and replace them with a Shabbat prayer.

SHABBAT

On Shabbat we say a *brakhah* called קְדוּשַּׁת הַיּוֹם *K'dushat ha-Yom*, "the Holiness of the Day." This is very much like the *Kiddush*. It celebrates Shabbat as an opportunity to experience God's holiness and create a sense of holiness of our own.

וְשָׁמְרוּ *V'SHAMRU*

Once the Shabbat commandment was read in the middle of this prayer. But in a period of time when some people began to believe that the Ten Commandments were the only important part of the Torah, the Rabbis made a switch. In the evening service they used the וַיְכֻלּוּ *Va-Y'khulu*, a piece of Torah that comes from the Shabbat part of the story of creation (Genesis 2:1-3). On Saturday morning they used the וְשָׁמְרוּ *V'Shamru* (Exodus 31:16-17), a lesson about Shabbat that Moses taught soon after the incident of the Golden Calf.

Shabbat is rooted in two big themes. The first is creation, and the second is the Exodus from Egypt. *Va-Y'khulu*, which is also said as part of the Friday night *Kiddush*, reminds us of the creation connection. *V'Shamru*, which is part of the Exodus story, is used to introduce the Saturday lunch *Kiddush*.

SHABBAT IN EGYPT

> Moses came to Pharaoh and said, "Let my people go." Pharaoh laughed and said, "No." To make matters worse, Pharaoh then told the Families of Israel that they had to work harder. Up till then, they had to make mud bricks using straw that other people had cut and brought to river's edge. Now the Jews had to make the same number of bricks every day, but they had to cut and haul their own straw. The Families of Israel were very angry with Moses because he had not set them free. Instead he made things worse.
>
> Moses went back to Pharaoh and asked, "How would you like to get twice as much work out of your slaves?" Pharaoh nodded. Moses said, "You have a choice: kill more and more of your slaves by working them to death or give them one day a week off to recover. Then you can work them twice as hard." Pharaoh asked, "What day should it be?" Moses smiled and said, "Start on Friday night." From that day on Israel had Shabbat in Egypt. It was their first taste of freedom (*Exodus Rabbah* 1:28).

In the Torah there are two versions of the Ten Commandments. One of them uses the word שָׁמוֹר *shamor* (keep) and the other זָכוֹר *zakhor* (remember). One roots Shabbat in creation and the other in the Exodus. It is easy to understand the connection between Shabbat and creation because "God rested on the seventh day" (Genesis 2:2). The connection between Shabbat and the Exodus is more tenuous. This story makes the connection. Moses brought Shabbat back to the Jews in Egypt, and it was their first experience of liberation—even if just one day a week. We ask, "How does Shabbat set us free?"

> Rabbi Shimon ben Lakish looked at the word וַיִּנָּפַשׁ *va-Yinafash*. While it sometimes is translated as "refreshed" it comes from the word נֶפֶשׁ *Nefesh*, which means "soul." In the Talmud he taught, "On Friday night God gives us a *neshamah yetera*—an extra portion of soul. On Saturday night, after Shabbat, God takes it back."

THE FIRST SHABBAT

This story is a weaving of *midrashim* and other Rabbinic pieces and is not directly about the origins of a part of *K'dushat ha-Yom*, but of the psalm for the Shabbat day. It helps us establish the spiritual connection between Shabbat and creation.

> In the beginning God was alone. So God created the angels, the other heavenly creatures, and people, too. The first thing God created was light. It was a special kind of light—one that came directly from God. On the fourth day of creation God created the sun, the moon, and the stars. The original light was hidden away.
>
> On the eve of the first Shabbat God stopped working and gathered all of creation. The angel of Shabbat got to sit on the throne of glory, and all of the angels got to rest. They gathered round and folded their six wings. On Shabbat day they could not sing. God brought Adam and Eve up to heaven to join in the Shabbat celebration. They were the ones who began to sing "IT IS GOOD TO GIVE THANKS TO GOD," the words that later started the Shabbat psalm (Psalms 92:2). The angels joined in.
>
> God told Adam and Eve that a piece of the Garden of Eden is in every Shabbat. God said, "During Shabbat you will be able to taste the world to come." God then decided that a little bit of the original hidden light would be released into the world every Shabbat. (Assembled through the notes in Louis Ginzberg's *Legends of the Jews*)

The Shabbat psalm is said at *Kabbalat Shabbat*, at *P'sukei d'Zimra* on Shabbat morning, and after the reading of the Torah on Shabbat afternoon. It is not part of the *K'dushat ha-Yom* for Shabbat, but this story connects Adam and Eve to the first Shabbat. Here we get the idea that Shabbat is redemptive, that it is our way "back to the garden" (Joni Mitchell). We realize that Shabbat takes us back into the purity of the Garden of Eden and forward to the World-to-Come. Answer this: "How can Shabbat be your experience of Utopia?"

רְצֵה *R'TZEIH*

THE FINAL THREE

The *Amidah* ends with three final *brakhot* that are blessings of thanksgiving. These final three are said both Shabbat and weekdays. They are:

- בִּרְכַּת עֲבוֹדָה *Birkat Avodah* (or רְצֵה *R'tzeih*), which thanks God for hearing our prayers and hopes that our worship is acceptable.
- בִּרְכַּת הוֹדָאָה *Birkat Hoda'ah* (or מוֹדִים *Modim*), which thanks God for the opportunity to say "thank you."
- בִּרְכַּת שָׁלוֹם *Birkat Shalom*, which thanks God for the possibility of peace (and asks God to help us finally achieve peace).

רְצֵה *R'TZEIH*

רְצֵה *R'tzeih* was originally part of what the High Priest said in the service in the Temple. Originally it asked God to accept Israel's sacrifices. Later, after the destruction of the Temple, prayer became the replacement for sacrifice, and the *R'tzeih* got expanded to include two different ideas.

While this is supposed to be the first of three thanksgiving *brakhot*, the *R'tzeih* asks God to (1) accept our prayers and (2) return the *Shekhinah* (the neighborly part of God) to Jerusalem so that sacrifices can be reinstituted.

This *brakhah* is known as the *R'tzeih* (want/favorably receive) because that is its opening word. Likewise, it is known as the עֲבוֹדָה *Avodah,* because it refers to worship. *Avodah* means "work." The original sacrifices were called *Avodah*, the "work" or "service" we do for God. Later, when prayers came to replace sacrifices, we continued the use of the term *Avodah*, making it עֲבוֹדַת הַלֵּב *Avodat ha-Lev*, "the work of the heart."

ZION IN THE WILDERNESS

God's original plan was to remain the Invisible God Who was everywhere. God's original thinking didn't involve a Temple or any place that was physical. The Golden Calf changed God's mind. God saw that Israel needed a concrete way of connecting to God. The first step was building a portable sanctuary in the wilderness. It was called the *Mishkan*, the "Tabernacle" or "Dwelling Place." It became the place where God would send the *Shekhinah*, the part of God that could come close to people, down to be Israel's neighbor.

God gave very detailed plans for the *Mishkan* to Moses. God chose Betzalel, a man with a "wise heart," to be the actual lead artist on the project. At the end of the book of Exodus all the work came together. Moses set up the *Mishkan* for the first time, and Aaron led the worship. A cloud descended, and in it was the *Shekhinah*.

At that moment, up in heaven, the angels sang what may seem like a strange prayer. They sang, "Praise are You Who returns the *Shekhinah* to Jerusalem." We are in the wilderness. Jerusalem is still hundreds of years away. It won't be Jewish until the time of King David. Why, a few months into the wilderness, do the angels sing about Jerusalem? It is because they know something. They know that God pulled back a bit from Israel when the Golden Calf happened. They know that God is now coming completely back to Israel. Just as Israel returned, God returned. The angels know that in the future the *Mishkan* will be rebuilt as the Temple in Jerusalem. And the angels know that the Temple will be destroyed twice when God again pulls back. So in this first moment of God's return, the angels pray that no matter when Israel leaves God and then returns, God will return. It isn't a Jerusalem moment yet, but the angels are already praying for the Jerusalem moment.

The *Avodah* is a difficult prayer. It has its origins in the sacrifices. Maimonides goes both ways on the future of sacrifices; Na<u>h</u>manides is a little clearer that sacrifice was a stop on the way to prayer. The Reform Movement edited this prayer heavily because sacrifice and Temple were not things to which they wanted to return. The Conservative

Movement kept the words but made them a metaphor for again being close to God. Traditional Jews keep both the meaning and the words. Regardless, *R'tzeih* is a call for our worship to reconnect us to God. It is a call for the *Shekhinah,* the part of God to which we can get close, to return to us. We ask, "When do our prayers make us close to God?" "What do we have to do to return to God?" (Maimonides, *Guide to the Perplexed* 3:46, *Shibbolei ha-Leket, T'fillah,* chapter 18. Also *Otzar ha-Tefillot,* I, 307)

בִּרְכַּת הוֹדָאָה *BIRKAT HODA'AH*

מוֹדִים *MODIM*

בִּרְכַּת הוֹדָאָה *Birkat Hoda'ah* starts with the words מוֹדִים אֲנַחְנוּ לָךְ *Modim Anahnu Lakh*. It means "We are thankful to You." These words lead us to the heart of this prayer—that God is the source of our life and of all that is good in our life.

Birkat Hoda'ah was part of the original service in the Temple. At the end of a day of sacrifice the priests would say a few prayers that included the Ten Commandments, the *Shema*, the *Modim*, and the priestly blessing for peace. When the Rabbis replaced sacrifices with the prayer service, *Modim* was still used as part of the ending.

Birkat Hoda'ah is:

- the eighteenth *brakhah* in the *Amidah* (the sixth *brakhah* on Shabbat).
- a *brakhah* during which we customarily bow at the beginning and the end.
- a *brakhah* that has a second version that is said by the congregation if the *Amidah* is repeated out loud.
- where a special Hanukkah prayer is added.
- an acting out of the story of King Solomon celebrating the grand opening of the Temple in Jerusalem.

It thanks God for four things:

- our lives
- our souls
- the miracles in our lives
- the gifts that happen evening, morning and afternoon

THE CHOREOGRAPHY

The Talmud teaches that we are required to bow at the beginning and the end of *Birkat Hoda'ah* as a way of acknowledging God's presence in our life. We are told that if one does not bend when saying *Modim*, his spine will turn into a snake (*Bava Kamma*, 16a).

Rashi explains that this does not mean that a person's spine will grow soft and bend. Rather, it means that they will become like the snake in the Adam and Eve story. The snake tried to convince Eve that what God wanted did not make a difference. He told her to do what she wanted to do rather than be grateful for everything that God did. When we don't bow before God and say "Thank You," we become the snake.

DAVID'S MEMORY MAKES A DIFFERENCE

David took the city of Jerusalem and wanted to build God's House there, but God said, "No." God was upset about all the blood that David had spilled. God was also upset that he had done a bad thing in stealing Batsheva from her husband. David asked, "Will You ever forgive me?" God answered, "Eventually, but your son, Solomon, will be the one to build the Temple."

When the Temple was finished and ready for its dedication, Solomon tried to bring the Ark of the Covenant into the Holy of Holies. The gates refused to open. Solomon said, "LIFT UP YOUR HEADS. OPEN UP THE GATES. LET IN THE RULER WITH HONOR (Psalm 24:7). The gates stayed shut and asked him, "WHO IS THE RULER WITH HONOR?" Solomon said, "The Ten Commandments that are in the Ark." The gates said, "Try again." Solomon said, "The Holy One who often comes close to us when we are near the Ark." The gates didn't move and said, "What is your third guess?" Solomon said, "David, my father, who was God's servant." The gates opened. The Ark went into the Holy of Holies. David was forgiven, and the angels sang, "בָּרוּךְ אַתָּה יי הַטּוֹב שִׁמְךָ וּלְךָ נָאֶה לְהוֹדוֹת *Barukh Attah Adonai, ha-Tov Shimkha, u'L'kha Na'eh l'Hodot* (Praised are You, Adonai, The Good-One is Your name and it feels good to praise You)" (*Shabbat* 30a, *Shibbolei ha-Leket*, 18).

בִּרְכַּת שָׁלוֹם *BIRKAT SHALOM*

בִּרְכַּת שָׁלוֹם *Birkat Shalom* is:

- the last of three thanksgiving *brakhot* that end the *Amidah* and the very last *brakhah* in the *Amidah*.
- a *brakhah* that asks for both world peace and personal inner peace.
- a prayer that has two versions. In Ashkenazic traditions שִׂים שָׁלוֹם *Sim Shalom* is said at morning services. שָׁלוֹם רָב *Shalom Rav* is said at afternoon, *Mussaf* and evening services. Sephardic[2] Jews only say *Shalom Rav.*

At the end of the service in the Temple the *Kohanim* (priests) would bless the people. This was their way of performing a biblical *mitzvah*, "THE *KOHANIM* SHOULD PUT MY NAME ON THE PEOPLE OF ISRAEL—AND I WILL BLESS THEM" (Numbers 6:27). *Shalom* is one of God's names.

This was done as part of a ceremony called *Duchinin*. The *Kohanim* would come up on the *bimah*, cover their heads with their *tallitot*, spread their fingers into two, two, and a thumb, making a *shin,* and say the words of the priestly benediction. This ceremony is still done weekly in Orthodox synagogues in Israel and in Sephardic synagogues. In some Conservative and Orthodox synagogues elsewhere this is done only on festivals. Reform synagogues have dropped the ceremony but Reform rabbis often bless the congregation with these words at the end of services. Jewish parents still use this biblical *brakhah* to bless their children on Shabbat.

Starting while there still was a Temple, a prayer called *Birkat Shalom* was said in synagogues. When the Temple was destroyed and the *Amidah* replaced the sacrifices, *Birkat Shalom* became its final *brakhah. Birkat Shalom* became the day-to-day replacement for *Birkat Kohanim* in the Temple. This pattern followed a lesson taught by Rabbi Eliezar ha-Kappar, "Great is peace. It is the end of all *brakhot*" (*Sifrei*, Numbers, 42).

[2]Ashkenazic Jews are those who came from Christian countries in North and Eastern Europe. Sephardic Jews are those who come from Muslim countries in Spain, Northern Africa, and the Middle East. Some Sephardic Jews moved to Holland, Rome, and Rhodes.

THE END OF THE TALMUD

Here is the very end of the Talmud.

> Rabbi Shimon ben Halafta said, "The Holy One found nothing that could hold all the blessings that God wanted to give Israel—except *shalom*. That is why the Torah teaches "GOD WILL BLESS GOD'S PEOPLE WITH *SHALOM*" (*Psalms* 29:11) (*Uktzin* 3:12).
>
> The *Tosefot Yom Tov* explained this *Mishnah* by saying, "When God wanted to give strength and power to Israel, God gave them *shalom*. That is why the Torah teaches יי עֹז לְעַמּוֹ יִתֵּן יי יְבָרֵךְ אֶת עַמּוֹ בַשָּׁלוֹם *Adonai Oz l'amo Yiten Adonai Y'varekh et Amo va-Shalom* (GOD GIVES STRENGTH TO GOD'S PEOPLE—GOD WILL BLESS GOD'S PEOPLE WITH *SHALOM*) (Psalms 29:11). For all the *brakhot* in the world exist only if there is *shalom*. *Shalom* is the only possible ending to the Oral Torah."

The final blessing is *Shalom*. "Where do you find *Shalom*?"

שִׂים שָׁלוֹם SIM SHALOM

ENTERING THE LAND OF ISRAEL

It is not a long walk from Egypt to Israel, yet it took the Families of Israel forty years. It took a long time because it took the Families of Israel a long time to become a holy nation.

God could have led them along the Mediterranean. That is the quick way. But God chose a longer road. God said, "If I lead them directly into the Land of Israel, they will become selfish. These former slaves will only think about what they have and what they can have. They will worry about their own fields and their own vineyards, and they will forget to take care of each other. They will forget about the Torah. If they camp together in the wilderness—if they have to ration water and gather their own food every day—they will gain discipline and become a community."

Just about as soon as they crossed the Reed Sea the people complained about the lack of water. They were afraid that they would not have enough. God talked to them directly at Mount Sinai, and within two months they were making a Golden Calf. They were worried that no one was leading them. The rebellions kept coming. Even though there was more than enough miracle food, manna, the people complained about the lack of meat. Another time they complained about the lack of "the garlic, and the onions, and the fish they used to eat for free in Egypt."

When God asked the Families to spy out the Land of Israel, the people panicked. They chickened out. They stopped trusting God. They had no faith. They said, "We can't do it." God extended the training program. The Families of Israel spent forty years in Sinai. They gathered manna every day except Shabbat. They stood in line to get water. They studied Torah with Moses and used it to solve the problems that came with living together.

Finally, after all that waiting, God told them it was time to enter the Land. For forty years they had owned nothing. They had been homeless wanderers. They had rebelled and rebelled. When Joshua led Israel into the Land they spent seven years fighting. At the end of seven years they were sick of war. They had had enough. The angels looked into Israel's hearts. The angels saw that Israel had grown. They had learned to live together and trust God. They had come to understand that *shalom* was the most important thing. At that moment the angels sang for the first time, "בָּרוּךְ אַתָּה יי עֹשֶׂה הַשָּׁלוֹם *Barukh Attah Adonai, Oseh ha-Shalom* (Praised are You, Eternal, the Maker of Peace)" (*Shibbolei ha-Leket*, chapter 18 and other midrashim).

שָׁלוֹם רָב *SHALOM RAV*

JACOB MAKES PEACE

From before their birth, brothers Jacob and Esau struggled with each other. As unborn babies they wrestled in the womb. Jacob then tricked Esau out of his birthright and later stole his blessing. Jacob ran away from home and went back to Padan Aram in "the old country" to keep his brother from killing him. He spent twenty years away from home, married two women, and had thirteen children. Before he headed back home he prayed to God, "LET ME RETURN TO MY FATHER'S HOME IN PEACE" (Genesis 28:21).

When Jacob and his holy family were about to meet Esau and his army of four hundred moving towards him, Jacob prepared three things: peace offerings, a prayer, and to fight back. He spent the night alone and wound up wrestling with a stranger who for him was the spirit of his brother. He walked away crippled and with a new name, *Yisrael*. When Esau came ready for war he saw a crippled man surrounded by women and children. He felt safe. He was transformed. Both brothers were now ready to make peace. At that moment the angels sang, "שָׁלוֹם רָב עַל יִשְׂרָאֵל תָּשִׂים לְעוֹלָם *Shalom Rav Al Yisrael Tasim l'Olam* (Much peace place on Israel)" (Torah, *Tanhuma, Yashan* 6, *Kallah Rabbati*, 3, Rashbam Ad Loc).

עֹשֶׂה שָׁלוֹם *OSEH SHALOM*

עֹשֶׂה שָׁלוֹם *Oseh Shalom* is an add-on that comes at the end of *Birkat Shalom*. Here is a story of God creating peace in the heavens above.

GOD BURIES THE TRUTH

When the Holy One was ready to create people, the ministering angels divided into groups and political parties. One side said "Let people be created," while the other said, "Let them not be created."

Love said, "Create people, because they will perform acts of love."

Truth said, "Don't create people, because they will all lie a lot."

Righteousness said, "Create people, because they do righteous deeds."

Peace said, "Don't create people, because they will get into conflict after conflict."

What did the Holy One do? God took truth and buried it in the ground. Then God created people. With truth buried, peace was possible (*Genesis Rabbah* 8:5).

עֹשֶׂה שָׁלוֹם *Oseh Shalom* is an ending chorus line. It is used in closing both the *Amidah* and the *Kaddish*. It is seen as the supreme compliment to God—being a Maker-of-Peace. The story above shows just how hard peace is to make. It sometimes means burying truth. Memory without forgiveness is the enemy of peace. In making peace we agree to become God's coconspirators. We echo Yitzhak Rabin, who taught, "One has to make peace with one's enemies, not one's friends." We ask, "Where do we need to make peace? What are the compromises we need to make?"

OSEH SHALOM CHOREOGRAPHY

At the end of the *Amidah*, during the saying of *Oseh Shalom*, one:

- takes three steps backwards.
- bows to the left (saying *"Oseh Shalom Bi-m'romav"*).
- bows to the Right (saying *"Hu Ya'aseh Shalom Aleinu"*).
- bow forward (saying, *"V'Al Kol Yisrael v-imaru Amen"*).
- pauses for a moment before moving away.

When we take three steps backwards we are like:

- A servant leaving a master. A citizen backing away from a monarch. (*Orekh Hayyim* 123:1)
- Moses leaving Mt. Sinai and going back through the cloud, the fog, and the darkness (Deuteronomy 4:11). Moses leaving the burning bush and stepping back from the holy space (*Shibbolei ha-Leket*).
- The *Kohanim* leaving the altar where they brought the people's message to God. There were three rows of stones that they stepped over (*Rav Hai Gaon*).
- The wicked King Nebuchadnezzar, who took three steps toward God and was rewarded with the victory that destroyed the Temple. If three steps could work for him, they could well work for us (*Mishnah Brurah* 123:2).

When we bow to the left, right, and forward we are acting out a scene.

- The angel *Mikhael* stands to the right of God. He represents God, the strict judge Who follows all the rules.
- The angel *Gavriel* stands to the left of God. He speaks for God's commitment to mercy—forgiving people and meeting their needs.
- The Holy One, God, is in the middle. God balances justice and mercy to fit every situation. The *Amidah* is a moment of judgment—we are asking God to balance justice and mercy and fulfill our needs (*Bet Yosef* 123, Rabbi Eli Munk).

THE WEEKDAY MIDDLE *BRAKHOT*

אַתָּה חוֹנֵן *ATTAH HONEN*

The fourth *brakhah* in the *Amidah* goes by two different names. It is sometimes called בִּרְכַּת בִּינָה *Birkat Binah* (the blessing for understanding), after its basic theme; and it is often called אַתָּה חוֹנֵן *Attah Honen,* because those are the opening words.

The first three *brakhot* and the last three *brakhot* of the *Amidah* are said every time the *Amidah* is said. The middle thirteen *brakhot* are replaced with a single *brakhah* on Shabbat and holidays. *Attah Honen* is the first of these "swing *brakhot*." On Saturday night (and after festivals) the words that transform us back into weekday time, the *brakhah* for *Havdalah,* is added to *Attah Honen*.

Birkat Binah first praises God for being the source of wisdom and then petitions God to grant us understanding. In this way *Attah Honen* makes a transition from the first three *brakhot* of the *Amidah* which primarily praise God, to the next thirteen *brakhot,* which are mainly petitions. The Rabbis believed that it was important to have דֵּעָה *de'ah* (knowledge), בִּינָה *binah* (understanding), and שֵׂכֶל *sekhel* (intelligence) at the top of our wish list.

SOLOMON ASKS FOR WISDOM

Here is a story from the Bible. It is from the second book of I Chronicles (9:28, 10:7–12), which is one of two historic summaries of the history of Israel found at the very back of the Bible. This is a story about King Solomon. As you read it, think about how it answers our question.

AND HE (DAVID) DIED AT A GOOD OLD AGE—FULL WITH DAYS, WITH WEALTH AND WITH HONOR. AND SOLOMON, HIS SON, REIGNED AFTER HIM...

THAT NIGHT GOD APPEARED TO SOLOMON AND SAID TO HIM: "WHAT IS IT THAT I SHOULD GIVE YOU?" AND SOLOMON SAID TO GOD: "YOU ACTED WITH GREAT *HESED* TOWARDS MY FATHER DAVID. NOW I AM RULING IN HIS PLACE. NOW ETERNAL, THE GOD, KEEP TRUE TO YOUR WORDS WITH MY FATHER DAVID,

> BECAUSE YOU HAVE MADE ME THE RULER OVER A GREAT PEOPLE WHO COVER THE LAND LIKE DUST. NOW PLEASE GIVE ME *HOKHMAH* (WISDOM) AND *DA'AT* (KNOWLEDGE) THAT I MAY GO OUT BEFORE THIS PEOPLE AND COME TO THEM. BECAUSE HOW ELSE WILL I BE ABLE TO JUDGE THIS GREAT NATION?"
>
> AND GOD SAID TO SOLOMON: "BECAUSE THIS WAS IN YOUR HEART, AND YOU DIDN'T ASK FOR RICHES, WEALTH, OR HONOR—NOT FOR THE LIVES OF YOUR ENEMIES AND NOT EVEN FOR LONG LIFE—RATHER, YOU ONLY ASKED FOR *HOKHMAH* AND *DA'AT* WITH WHICH TO JUDGE THIS PEOPLE OVER WHOM YOU RULE—THEREFORE *HOKHMAH* AND *DA'AT* WILL BE GIVEN TO YOU, AND I WILL GIVE YOU RICHES AND WEALTH AND HONOR. THERE WILL NEVER BE ANOTHER KING LIKE YOU—NOT BEFORE AND NOT AFTER." *(CHRONICLES* 9:28, 10:7-12)

The lesson of this biblical text is simple. Make wisdom the first thing for which you ask. We need to be like Solomon, understanding the importance of *hokhmah* and *da'at* in our life. If God offers you a gift, you know for what to ask. When you go through life, your choice should be the same.

JOSEPH LEARNS A LOT

Joseph was sold into slavery. He rose as a slave until he became the head of his owner's house. The Torah tells us that God was with him. Things were good until they became bad. The owner's wife accused him of fooling around, and Joseph wound up in jail. God was with him in jail. Again things turned out well, and he became the second-in-command to the head of the jail.

We have one memory that Joseph learned the seventy languages spoken in the world while he was in jail. He wanted to be able to speak to every prisoner who was with him.

We also have a different memory that the angel Gavriel taught him the seventy languages that were spoken in the world. Pharaoh knew all seventy of these languages. He sat on a throne that had seventy steps. Each time a person showed that he knew a language that person got to ascend one step.

When Joseph reached the seventieth step the angels sang "בָּרוּךְ אַתָּה יי חוֹנֵן הַדָּעַת *Barukh Attah Adonai Honen ha-Da'at* (Praised are You, Eternal, Giver-of-Wisdom)." One had to speak all seventy languages to run Egypt. Pharaoh picked Joseph to be his number two, to run Egypt.

Joseph warned Pharaoh that there would be seven good years followed by seven years of famine. When the famine hit, people came to Egypt from all over the world looking for food. Joseph used his mastery of the seventy languages to speak each of these needy people in his own language (*Numbers Rabbah* 19:3, *Sotah* 36b, *Zohar Pinhas* 5).

You already know that we need to be Joseph learning what we need to make a difference—and using what we know. The question is "What do you need to know to change the world, to make it better?" The lesson of this prayer is "What we learn can be used to make a difference."

MOSES LEARNS GOD'S NAME

According to the Midrash, God came down to earth ten times. The fifth visit was to meet Moses at the burning bush. There, standing next to a bush that burned and was not consumed, Moses asks God a hard question: "What's Your name?" This may not seem like a big deal, but God's name gives people direct access to God. Moses learned it. Aaron knew it. And from then on, only one person in the world, the High Priest, knew it. After the Temple was destroyed, the people who knew it were secret. They were able to do amazing things. Each of them was called a *Baal Shem* (Master of the Name). The Baal Shem Tov, the founder of Hasidism, was supposed to be one of these. God's real name is the biggest secret in the world. When God taught this most import piece of information to Moses, the angels sang: "בָּרוּךְ אַתָּה יי חוֹנֵן הַדָּעַת *Barukh Attah Adonai Honen ha-Da'at* (Praised are You, Eternal, Giver-of-Wisdom)" (*Pirkei d'Rabbi Eliezer* 40).

Think of your burning bush moment. "When have you felt closest to God?" "What name got you there?" "What is the knowledge you need to call upon God?" "What is your name for God?"

בִּרְכַּת תְּשׁוּבָה
BIRKAT T'SHUVAH

The fifth *brakhah* is called both בִּרְכַּת תְּשׁוּבָה *Birkat T'shuvah* (because of its theme) and הֲשִׁיבֵנוּ *Hashiveinu* (because of its first word).

In Hebrew תְּשׁוּבָה *t'shuvah* actually means "return," but in English we often call it "repentance." Repentance is when you feel sorry about something you've done wrong and you promise to change. The idea of *t'shuvah* is that making repentance is "returning" to the good relationship, because once you "understand," you know that you have done something wrong, and you want to return to better relationships.

JUDAH RETURNS

We are taught that true repentance is when a person has an opportunity to repeat a sin and acts differently the second time. This is Judah's story.

Judah was one of Jacob's sons. When Joseph came out to see his brothers, they wanted to kill him. Judah was the one who talked them into selling him into slavery. Selling him into slavery is better than killing him, but it still is a sin.

Years go by. There is a famine in the land of Canaan. Jacob sends most of his sons to buy food in the land of Egypt. Joseph is in charge of the food, but his brothers don't recognize him. Joseph sends them back to get their youngest brother, Benjamin. Some people think that Joseph is playing games with his brothers when he sends them back to Egypt with gold in their bags of grain and says, "I am going to keep your youngest brother as a slave." Judah speaks up and offers to take Benjamin's place. You could say that Joseph is playing games, getting even, but the Rabbis teach us that Joseph was actually giving his brothers a chance to repent.

When Judah speaks up to protect Benjamin, he is responding differently. When Joseph was sold into slavery, he helped it to happen. When Benjamin is going to be held, Judah says, "Take me instead." He argues for his brother's freedom. This was repentance. It was being in the same situation and acting differently. When he repented, the angels sang, "בָּרוּךְ אַתָּה יי הָרוֹצֶה בִּתְשׁוּבָה *Barukh Attah Adonai, ha-Rotzeh bi-Tshuvah* (Praised are You, Eternal, The One Who wants repentence)." Joseph then forgave his family and brought them to safety in Egypt. (Nissan Mindel [*As for Me—My Prayer.* Brooklyn: Merkos L'Inyonei Chunich, Inc. 1972] connects this prayer to Reuben's repentance after his sin against his father.)

Malakhi 3:7 teaches that God says, "IF YOU WILL RETURN TO ME, I WILL RETURN TO YOU." The lesson here is that sin causes distance, not only between us and God, but between us and other people. When we do *t'shuvah* and return, that distance closes. Joseph's story teaches us that lesson. When he gives his brothers a second chance, a chance to respond differently, he closes the distance. We should always be looking to close distances and end exiles. We want to "get back to where [we] once belonged" (Lennon/McCartney, 1969). We ask, "Where do I need to react differently and change?" "Where can I help others to return?" "How do I close the gap between me and God?"

ELIJAH TEACHES ABOUT RETURN

Rabbi Judah said: "If Israel will not repent, they will not be redeemed." Israel only repents when they are in trouble. Israel only repents because of powerful enemies, exile, or poverty. Israel will only do complete repentance when Elijah returns. Elijah is the prophet who did not die, who went up to heaven, alive, in a fiery chariot. And it is Elijah who will come back to announce the coming of the Messiah.

The Prophet Malakhi taught, "BEHOLD, I WILL SEND YOU ELIJAH THE PROPHET BEFORE THE GREAT AND TERRIBLE DAY OF THE ETERNAL COMES. AND HE SHALL TURN (הֵשִׁיב) THE HEART OF THE FATHERS TO THE CHILDREN, AND THE HEART OF THE CHILDREN TO THEIR FATHERS, LEST I COME AND SMITE THE LAND WITH UTTER DESTRUCTION."

When Malakhi announced Elijah's return, the angels sang, "בָּרוּךְ אַתָּה יי הָרוֹצֶה בִּתְשׁוּבָה *Barukh Attah Adonai, ha-Rotzeh*

> *bi-Tshuvah* (Praised are You, Eternal, The One Who wants repentance)" (*Malakhi* 3:23-4 *Pirkei d'Rabbi Eliezer*, 43).

This story is both cynical and hopeful. It suggests both that *t'shuvah* is difficult and that *t'shuvah* will happen. When Maimonides teaches about *t'shuvah* (*Mishneh Torah, Laws of Repentance* 7:2) he compares sin to addiction. Addictions can be hard to break. They may take several tries, but they can be broken, a new response can be built, and lives can change.

BEIT T'SHUVAH STORY

> The rabbi was a contradiction. On one hand he always had his nose in a book. He rarely left his study. He almost never went into the real world. The rabbi lived a sheltered life. On the other hand, he did a lot of counseling. All of the lowlifes came to him for advice. He attracted drug dealers and prostitutes, pimps and criminals. No one could figure out how this scholarly rabbi knew what to tell the street folk.
>
> Finally one of the students had the courage to ask, "How can a person who almost never leaves the house know what to tell the shady characters who come to you?"
>
> The rabbi answered, "Easy. There is no feeling, no urge, no desire that they have that I can't find in myself. And if there is something I can't find inside, then I have to look harder."
> (Taught by Becca Kesuvie on Yom Kippur at *Beit T'shuvah*, Los Angeles, California. Rabbi Jay Siegel believes it is based on a story told by Rabbi Harold Schulweis. Janie Grackin learned that it was rooted in a story told by a former Lubavicher Rebbe.)

One Jewish practice is *heshbon ha-nefesh*, the accounting of the soul. It is inventorying not only our actions but our feelings and tendencies. It is the job of understanding how we work. This story says that we have the capacity for every sin in us. It also suggests that we have the capacity for *t'shuvah* for every sin within us. We can change that which we can understand. If that doesn't make sense, look harder.

סְלַח לָנוּ *S'LAH LANU*

The sixth *brakhah* is about סְלִיחָה *s'lihah* (forgiveness). Forgiveness comes after repentance. When we do *t'shuvah*, we tell God, "We are sorry." Then God grants *s'lihah* and says, "I forgive you." Like other *brakhot* in the *Amidah*, this *brakhah* is sometimes called by its theme, בִּרְכַּת סְלִיחָה *Birkat S'lihah*, and sometimes called by its opening words, סְלַח לָנוּ *S'lah Lanu*.

On the High Holidays we say a prayer called עַל חֵטְא *Al Het* (*For the Sin*) that is a long list of things we may have done wrong during the past year. We hit our breasts once for each item on the list. It is a way of reminding ourselves that we want these words to reach our heart. When we say the words כִּי חָטָאנוּ *Ki Hatanu* in *S'lah Lanu* we also hit our breasts once. This prayer is like a mini-High Holiday season.

JUDAH AND TAMAR

This is a biblical story, but it is not PG. Tamar is married to Judah's oldest son, Er. Er dies before they have any children. Following an ancient tradition, wanting Er to have an heir, Judah then gives Tamar to his middle son, Onan. If Tamar had given birth to a child, it would have been considered Er's heir. Onan doesn't do the right thing, completely, and he dies. Judah is then afraid to connect Tamar and son number three, Shelah.

Judah's wife dies, and he makes a visit to a professional woman. It turns out that this professional was really Tamar in costume. Judah doesn't have any money with him, so Tamar takes his staff and seal as a security deposit. When Judah finds out that Tamar is pregnant, he is ready to burn her, literally. Tamar discreetly returns the seal and the staff. When Judah realizes that Tamar could have told everyone what he had done, Judah forgives her and admits that he was wrong.

When he does this, the angels sing,

"בָּרוּךְ אַתָּה יי חַנּוּן הַמַּרְבֶּה לִסְלֹחַ" *Barukh Attah Adonai Hanun ha-Marbeh li-S'lo'ah* (Praised are You, Eternal, The One Who Greatly-Forgives)" (Genesis 38, Nisssan Mindel, *As for Me—My Prayer* [Brooklyn: Merkos L'Inyonei Chinuch, Inc., 1972]).

We are created in God's image. When we say that God greatly forgives, we are saying that we, too, have the capacity to forgive. Thinking of forgiveness should teach us "I am worthy of being forgiven." It should also get us to ask "What do I need to do to be forgiven?" "What gets me to forgive?" We are like Judah, we can grow in our understanding.

MOSES ASKS FOR FORGIVENESS

Moses had the two tablets of the Ten Commandments in his arms. They were heavy, but the letters were special. They went all the way through the tablets and could be read correctly from both sides. Even the center of the ס *samekh* stayed in place.

Moses heard noise from the camp. He though it was the sound of fighting. He then saw it was the celebration at the Golden Calf. His anger burned. The letters flew off of the tablets. They became too heavy to hold. Moses couldn't hold them up. They fell and broke. God's anger burned, too.

Moses acted to protect the people. He said the words we now use when we ask for forgiveness on the high holidays: "THE ETERNAL, THE ETERNAL GOD, MERCIFUL AND GRACIOUS, LONG-SUFFERING, AND ABUNDANT IN GOODNESS AND TRUTH; KEEPING MERCY TO THE THOUSANDTH GENERATION, FORGIVING INIQUITY AND TRANSGRESSION AND SIN" (Exodus 34:6-7).

The Torah tells us, "THE ETERNAL REPENTED OF THE EVIL THAT GOD SAID GOD WOULD DO TO GOD'S PEOPLE."

At that moment the angels sang,
"בָּרוּךְ אַתָּה יי חַנּוּן הַמַּרְבֶּה לִסְלֹחַ" *Barukh Attah Adonai Hanun ha-Marbeh li-S'lo'ah* (Praised are You, Eternal, The One Who Greatly-Forgives)" (*Pirkei d'Rabbi Eliezer* 46, and other midrashic sources).

With this prayer we have a Moses moment. We pray for others' forgiveness—and in doing so we pray for our own. In knowing that God accepts and wants *t'shuvah* we know that we can ask for forgiveness. We ask, "Who do I need to forgive?" and "Who needs my help in earning forgiveness?"

רְאֵה נָא בְעָנְיֵנוּ *R'EIH NA V'ONYEINU*

The seventh *brakhah* is called בִּרְכַּת גְּאֻלָּה *Birkat G'ulah*, the blessing of redemption. Redemption is clearly the central theme of this *brakhah*. In two sentences the root גאל is used three times. However, the seventh *brakhah* begins רְאֵה נָא בְעָנְיֵנוּ *R'eih Na v'Onyeinu* ("See our suffering"). The Rabbis point out that the redemption asked for in this *brakhah* is short-term redemption from our immediate problems. The long-term final redemption is asked for in later *brakhot* in the *Amidah*.

ISRAEL IS REDEEMED FROM EGYPT

Israel was enslaved in Egypt for four hundred years. It took ten miracles and a lot of work for them to be freed. When they were finally redeemed, the angels sang, "בָּרוּךְ אַתָּה יי גּוֹאֵל יִשְׂרָאֵל. *Barukh Attah Adonai, Go'el Yisrael* (Praised are You, Eternal, The One Who redeems Israel)" (Nissan Mindel [*As for Me—My Prayer*. Brooklyn: Merkos L'Inyonei Chunich, Inc. 1972].

It is a regular Hasidic teaching (many different *rebbes* have said it) that "each of us has our own Egypt." On Passover we focus on this present-tense, personal Egypt and our redemption from it. We are to bring that to this blessing each time we are redeemed from an "Egypt" that has enslaved us, that has burdened us with slavery. This blessing does not say that God "has redeemed" us, but that God "is redeeming" us. Ask "What are my slaveries?" "When were my redemptions?" 'What do I need to be released from this time?"

ISRAEL IS REDEEMED FROM HAMAN

"Oh once there was a wicked, wicked man and Haman was his name–O" (Traditional Purim song, composer unknown). You know the story. Mordechai saves the king's life. Esther hides her Jewishness and becomes queen. Haman plots, and Esther and Mordechai outsmart him. The king comes to the rescue and gives the Jews permission to defend themselves. The story ends with a redemption of the Jewish people from the evil that was planned. God doesn't appear in the book. But we can see God's wake in the results: "Oh, today we'll merry, merry be..."

When the Jews were saved from Haman's evil the angels sang, "בָּרוּךְ אַתָּה יי גּוֹאֵל יִשְׂרָאֵל *Barukh Attah Adonai, Go'el Yisrael* (Praised are You, Eternal, The One Who Redeems Israel)" (Implied by *Pirkei d'Rabbi Eliezer* 50).

Redemption in this blessing does not refer to redemption from exile, but rather asks God to deliver us from the troubles that constantly bother us (Rashi on *Megillah* 17b).

We experience many redemptions, and we are saved many times. Not always do the tracings of God become clear. I was once doing a program with high school students near the Claremont Colleges. One sixteen- or seventeen-year-old explained the Holocaust this way: "God did stop the Holocaust. God did it through us. It just took longer than we would have liked." When we live in the Mordechai/Esther place we remember that God acts through people—and we give God credit for the people who have redeemed us. That is the secret of redemption that happens in a book that doesn't mention God's name.

רְפָאֵנוּ *R'FA'EINU*

בִּרְכַּת רְפוּאָה *Birkat R'fu'ah* (a.k.a. רְפָאֵנוּ *Refa'einu*) is the eighth *brakhah*. It describes God as the ultimate healer, the source of all healing, and in the process asks that all our illnesses be healed.

This blessing is based on a passage in the book of Jeremiah, "HEAL ME, ETERNAL, AND I SHALL BE HEALED; SAVE ME, AND I SHALL BE SAVED; FOR YOU ARE MY PRAYER (Jeremiah 17:14)."

When they made it part of the daily service the Rabbis changed *R'fa'eini* (heal me) into *R'fa'einu* (heal us), turning singular into plural and expressing the idea that "any prayer not asked in the name of all Israel is not a valid prayer."

However, *Birkat R'fu'ah* is a *brakhah* with which it is traditional to insert personal prayers for the healing of a friend or relative who is sick.

ABRAHAM HEALS

When Abraham was ninety-nine years old God commanded him to circumcise himself and his family. It was the big moment when Abraham and God cut a covenant. After the operation Abraham sat in the door of his tent, recovering. God sent three angels to do בִּקּוּר חוֹלִים *Bikkur Holim* (the mitzvah of visiting the sick). When Abraham was healed the angels sang בָּרוּךְ אַתָּה יי רוֹפֵא חוֹלֵי עַמּוֹ יִשְׂרָאֵל *Barukh Attah Adonai Rofei Holei Amo Yisrael* (Praised are You, Eternal, The One Who heals the sick of the people, Israel).

We heal in many ways. Our bodies do much of the job. So does our mind. Doctors help. And even visitors make a difference. All of these are God's gifts. Simple questions: "Am I in need of healing?" "Who do I know who is ill?" We have no reason to be afraid to believe: "Even if we don't affect God, we may affect ourselves."

Only after a person prays for the needs of all Israel is it permissible to insert personal requests, and then only in the places reserved for them. A prayer, in order to be heard, must be recited for the community, in the midst of the community, or for an individual who is part of the community (Judah Ha-Levi, the *Kuzari*).

בָּרֵךְ עָלֵינוּ BARE KH ALEINU

בִּרְכַּת הַשָּׁנִים *Birkat ha-Shanim*, the blessing for the years, begins with the words בָּרֵךְ עָלֵינוּ *Barekh Aleinu* and is really the *brakhah* that asks God to provide us with sustenance. Sustenance is a fancy word that means "stuff" (stuff like food, money—the things we need to live).

This is the last of six *brakhot* that ask God to meet our individual needs: knowledge, repentance, forgiveness, protection (redemption), health, and now "a living."

In the first part of the *Amidah*, while we were praising God, we reminded God that rain and dew were important *brakhot* we receive. Now that we are in the petition part of the *Amidah* we add dew and rain as requests, changing this *brakhah* depending on the season. (Remember, in Israel where this *brakhah* was written, rain can only fall in the winter.)

REDIGGING OUR FATHERS' WELLS

There was a famine in the Land of Canaan. God told Isaac not to go down to Egypt the way that Abraham did and that Jacob will do. So Isaac moved to Gerar. Gerar was a place in the Negev near the border with the Philistines. Isaac had some trouble there but got past it. The Torah tells us: ISAAC SOWED IN THAT LAND (Gerar) AND REAPED IN THE SAME YEAR (of famine) A HUNDREDFOLD. THE ETERNAL BLESSED HIM (Genesis 26:12). His flocks grew, too. The people would say about him, "The manure of Isaac was better than the gold of Avimelekh, the local king" (Rashi ad loc). He went and redug all the wells that had originally been dug by his father, Abraham.

When the angels saw that God had blessed Isaac they sang בָּרוּךְ אַתָּה יי מְבָרֵךְ הַשָּׁנִים *Barukh Attah Adonai M'varekh ha-Shanim* (Praised are You, Eternal, The One Who blesses the Years) (*Shibbolei ha-Leket*, 18. *Otzar ha-T'fillah* I. 307).

"A living." We all want to earn "a living." There is no embarrassment in asking God's help, even if we are just looking to actualize our own inner-resources. Isaac worked hard for his success. He didn't use magic beans. Asking God's help with *parnasah* is something we should do, but we should do it by remembering that we also have work to do. We may have to redig our father's wells.

תְּקַע בְּשׁוֹפָר גָּדוֹל
T'KA B'SHOFAR GADOL

The tenth *brakhah* in the *Amidah*, begins with the words תְּקַע בְּשׁוֹפָר גָּדוֹל *T'ka b'Shofar Gadol* (sound a great shofar). The *Shofar Gadol* is a symbol of קִבּוּץ גָּלֻיּוֹת *Kibbutz Galuyot* (the ingathering of the exiles) that is the first step in the final redemption. It is not surprising that this *brakhah* is known both as *T'ka ba-Shofar Gadol* and as the בִּרְכַּת קִבּוּץ גָּלֻיּוֹת *Birkat Kibbutz Galuyot.*

It is rooted in this verse from the Prophet Isaiah: "In that day, a great shofar will be blown, and the lost from the land of Assyria and the dispersed from the land of Egypt will come and bow down to God in the holy mountain in Jerusalem" (Isaiah 27:13).

This *brakhah* is found in the middle of the second part of the *Amidah* (the petition part) and starts the second part of the petitions. Up to now, we have been asking (in a collective way) for things that each of us needs as individuals. Now (still in a collective way) we are asking for the things we need as a Jewish community.

Each of the six *brakhot* in this second half of the *Amidah* represents a request for one of the necessary steps toward bringing about the Messianic Era. Just as the sounding of the great shofar will serve as the announcement that the redemption has begun, the prayer *T'ka b'Shofar Gadol* serves as the way we begin our specific requests for the final redemption in the *Amidah*.

JACOB GATHERS HIS EXILES

Remember, Jacob is Israel. From his perspective, his son Joseph is dead. Eleven of his sons, including the youngest, the one whose birth caused the death of Rachel, have gone down to Egypt. There has been no choice. He feels abandoned, scared.

Then his sons return with the news that Joseph is alive. Jacob doubts their words. They work hard to convince him. Eventually he says, "My son Joseph still lives. I will go and see him before I die" (Genesis 45:28). He goes as far as Beersheva and asks God's permission. God tells him, "I am God, the God of your father; do not be afraid to go down to Egypt; for there I will make of you a great nation" (Genesis 46:3). Jacob goes to Egypt. "Joseph went to meet him in his chariot of gold" (Tim Rice).

The family that had been divided is reunited. The angels sing בָּרוּךְ אַתָּה יי מְקַבֵּץ נִדְחֵי עַמּוֹ יִשְׂרָאֵל *Barukh Attah Adonai M'kabetz Nidhei Amo Yisrael* (Praised are You, Eternal, The One Who gathers God's scattered people, Israel)." At that moment the family was gathered. In the future the nation will return from their exiles (*Shibbolei ha-Leket* 18. *Otzar ha-T'fillah* I. 307).

Exile is a national reality. It is also a psychological truth. For the tradition the ingathering of the exiles is a Messianic beginning. It is part of the redemption. For a community the ingathering often involves bands and fireworks. For a family the ingathering is often a holiday celebration and involves brisket and turkey. For an individual, ingathering is a sense of wholeness and connection. We pray for many different gatherings of the exiled. Our exile involves friends and family, communities, nations, peoples, and the world. We look for the Joseph moment. "What are the once and future ingatherings?"

We pray we will be redeemed by a "great shofar." We do not wish to be awakened by the calamitous call of the shofar of persecution, nor by the middle shofar of ordinary aspirations. We yearn for the shofar that is suitable for a holy nation, the shofar of spiritual greatness and true freedom. We await the call to complete redemption, inspiring the people of Israel to the sacred ideals of Jerusalem and Mount Moriah (Rav Kook).

הָשִׁיבָה שׁוֹפְטֵינוּ *HASHIVAH SHOFTEINU*

In the previous *brakhah* (*T'ka b'Shofar Gadol*) we made a transition from petitioning for the things we need now to petitioning for the beginning of the steps in the final redemption. This, the eleventh *brakhah*, which begins הָשִׁיבָה שׁוֹפְטֵינוּ *Hashivah Shofteinu* (Return Our Judges), continues with the same concerns. It is known as the *brakhah* that focuses on דִּין *Din* (judgement) because reestablishment of fair and just courts headed by outstanding judges was seen as an important step in bringing the Messianic Era. In *Pirkei Avot* (a part of the Talmud) we are told "Destruction comes into the world only because of corruption of the law" (*Pirkei Avot* 5:8).

This prayer begins with a petition for the return of "quality leadership," but it ends with a series of statements of praise. God is described as the ideal ruler, a מֶלֶךְ *Melekh*, who rules with צְדָקָה וּמִשְׁפָּט *Tzedakah u'Mishpat* (righteousness and justice).

MOSES AND THE JUDGES

Jethro, Moses' father-in-law, shows up at Mount Sinai. He brings Moses' wife and sons. He also gives Moses some advice: "Choose able men from all the people, those who fear God, men who are trustworthy and who hate bribes; and place such men over the people as leaders of thousands, of hundreds, of fifties, and of tens" (Exodus 18:21). This was the creation of the first judges in Israel.

Moses received the law on Mount Sinai. He received more laws as the Families of Israel moved through the wilderness. Each time Israel was given more laws, the angels would sing בָּרוּךְ אַתָּה יי מֶלֶךְ אֹהֵב צְדָקָה וּמִשְׁפָּט *Barukh Attah Adonai Melekh Ohev Tz'dakah u'Mishpat* (Praised are You, Eternal, the One Who loves righteousness and justice) (*Shibbolei ha-Leket* 18. *Otzar ha-T'fillah* I. 307).

Judaism is a religion of law. It is laws, Torah, that teach us how to celebrate Jewish events. It is laws that transmit Jewish values. Even if we come from liberal strands of Judaism, laws serve a role. Even the laws we reject or compromise define our relationship with the tradition. When you look at the final line in this *brakhah*, ending in "righteousness and justice," it becomes clear that the "restoration of judges" represents the return to justice. We all need more justice, more righteousness. The questions: "Where can I contribute to the justice in the world?" "Where do I need justice?"

בִּרְכַּת הַמִּינִים *BIRKAT HA-MINIM*

The twelfth *brakhah* begins וְלַמַּלְשִׁינִים אַל תְּהִי תִקְוָה *V'laMal'shinim Al T'hi Tikvah* (Let there be no hope for the slanderers/informers). It is known both by its first word, וְלַמַּלְשִׁינִים and as בִּרְכַּת הַמִּינִים *Birkat ha-Minim*, the blessing about the *Minim* (also known as the Samaritans, a religious group that threatened Israel and often informed the Romans about Jewish groups).

While this is the twelfth *brakhah* in the *Amidah*, it is actually the "nineteenth blessing," the one that was later added to the already organized *Shmoneh Esrei,* the eighteen benedictions. Here is the way that the Talmud tells the story.

> Rabban Gamliel says, "Every day one prays eighteen (blessings)..."
>
> Rabbi Levi said, "These eighteen *brakhot* are actually nineteen. The 'blessing of the heretics' was drafted in Yavneh at a later date…"
>
> The Rabbis taught: Shimon ha-Pakuli ordered the eighteen blessings before Rabban Gamliel in Yavne.
>
> Rabban Gamliel said to the Sages: "Is there no one who knows how to draft the *Birkat ha-Minim* (the blessing of the heretics)?"
>
> Shmuel ha-Katan stood up and drafted it. The next year he forgot it and paused for two or three hours (trying to remember it), but they did not replace him (*Brakhot* 28b).

The Talmud understands that this *brakhah* is a problem. It represents a major Jewish values conflict. On the one hand, Jews believe that there is the potential for goodness in every person and that people have the potential for *t'shuvah* (growth and change). On the other hand, Jews believe that evil must be destroyed. This *brakhah* asks God to destroy evil; that will take away people's potential to change.

Shmuel ha-Katan quoted Torah (*Pirkei Avot* 4:24): "At your enemy's fall do not rejoice, and when your enemy stumbles don't let your heart be joyous, lest the Eternal see and be unhappy and turn back God's anger to you" (*Proverbs* 24:17–18). Clearly he was chosen to compose this prayer, for he can be counted upon not to allow the war with evil to become a personal vendetta. One year later he cannot remember the text. The words remain foreign even when they are necessary.

Reform Judaism chose to eliminate this *brakhah* from their Siddur. It has been retained in both the Conservative (with careful translation) and the Traditional siddurim.

THE EGYPTIANS DROWN

The Midrash teaches that while the Egyptians were drowning in the Reed Sea the angels sang: "בָּרוּךְ אַתָּה יי שֹׁבֵר אֹיְבִים וּמַכְנִיעַ זֵדִים *Barukh Attah Adonai Shover O'y'vim u'Makhni'a Zedim* (Praised are You, Eternal, the One Who shatters enemies and humbles the sinners) (*Shibbolei ha-Leket*, 18. *Otzar ha-T'fillah* I. 307).

We have already learned in another midrash that when the angels wanted to sing praises while the Egyptians were drowning, God stopped then by saying "How can you celebrate while My troops are drowning?" (*Megillah* 10b).

What we learn from this *brakhah* is the post-modern dilemma of how we "support the troops" without reducing the enemy to becoming "The Other." Having seen the original *Invasion of the Body Snatchers* (Daniel Mainwaring along with an uncredited Richard Collins) this prayer is difficult for me.

> The film has been read as both an allegory for the loss of personal autonomy in the Soviet Union and as an allegory of Cold War paranoia...It has also been read as a metaphor of alienation in modern mass civilization or a covert indictment of McCarthyism. *(Wikipedia)*

Consider the prayer a challenge: "How do we wish to defeat evil without being reduced to hatred?" Consider the following story a partial solution.

BRURIA'S PRAYER FOR EVIL

There once were some highwaymen in Rabbi Meir's neighborhood who caused him a great deal of trouble. Rabbi

> Meir prayed that they should die. His wife, Bruria, said to him: "How can you believe that such a prayer should be permitted? Isn't is written 'LET SINS CEASE'? Does that verse say 'sinners'? No. It says 'sins'! Now look at the end of the verse: 'LET THE WICKED BE NO MORE' (Psalms 105:35). Since the sins will cease, there will be no more wicked people! Rather pray for them that they should repent, and there will be no more wicked people." He did pray for them, and they repented (*Brakhot* 10a).

This story is very Hannah Arendt. Arendt was a German Jew who escaped Hitler and reported on the Eichmann trial. She coined the phrase "the banality of evil" to express the notion that much evil is done by ordinary people who allow it, rather than by truly evil people. Her book on Eichmann was titled *Eichmann in Jerusalem: A Report on the Banality of Evil* (1963). Leonard Cohen, poet and songwriter, in his poem "All There Is to Know about Adolph Eichmann," writes about how ordinary Eichmann was and then ends, "What did you expect? Talons? Oversize incisors? Green saliva? Madness?" (*Flowers for Hitler*, 1964). There may be Hitlers in the world, there may be Amalek (the midrashic tribe of Hitlers), but most evil is done by people who just go along, who have not reached the point of saying "No." Like Rabbi Akiva, we can ask, "How can I stop people from allowing evil to flourish?"

עַל הַצַּדִּיקִים *AL HA-TZADDIKIM*

The thirteenth *brakhah* in the *Amidah* begins with the words עַל הַצַּדִּיקִים *Al ha-Tzaddikim* (For the Righteous) and asks God to take special care of four categories of people: the righteous, elders, the surviving scribes (a scholar class), true converts, and finally us. We hope that we can be worthy to be included in the list of *tzaddikim*, and we hope that their *z'khut* (merit) will rub off on us.

The eleventh *brakhah* of the *Amidah* was the *brakhah* that asked for the restoration of judges and justice. The *twelfth brakhah* (as we learned) was an insertion that asked for the punishment of those who endangered the Jewish people (and did an injustice). Now *brakhah* thirteen is a *brakhah* for *tzaddikim*. We ask a blessing for *tzaddikim*, who are the opposite of the *malshinim* we asked God to punish in *brakhah* twelve, and who are those most likely to enact the justice requested in *brakhah* eleven. *Tzaddikim* are those people most likely to enable the coming of the Messianic Era.

JOSEPH BURIES JACOB

Joseph had brought his family to Egypt. He had allowed his brothers to repent. He spent much of his time making sure that the people who came to Egypt for food were cared for. The tradition remembers him as Joseph *ha-Tzaddik*.

When Jacob was dying all the brothers gathered around his bed. There is a midrash we have told that they said the *Shema* together (*Pesahim* 56a). When Joseph closed his father's eyes, the angels sang בָּרוּךְ אַתָּה יי מִשְׁעָן וּמִבְטָח לַצַּדִּיקִים *Barukh Attah Adonai Mish'an uMivtah la-Tzaddikim* (Praised are You, Eternal, the One Who supports and is the trust of the *tzaddikim*).

Joseph and his brothers brought their father's body back to Canaan. They buried him in the Cave of *Makhpelah*. On the way back Joseph led the brothers a different way. They stopped at the pit that had begun the adventure. Joseph said a silent prayer: "Praised be The One Who did a miracle for me in this place." He wanted to thank God. His brothers didn't understand. Their father was dead. They thought Joseph wanted revenge. They went back to Egypt with very little talking.

The family used to eat at Joseph's house every week for Shabbat. Jacob would always sit at the head of his son's table. Jacob was now dead. Joseph didn't want to sit at the head of the table ruling over his brothers. He stopped having them over. He was trying to be an equal. They thought he was going to take revenge. The family stopped talking.

The brothers went to Bilhah with their fears. Bilhah was the servant who was like Joseph's second mother. She went to Joseph. After some talking and some crying the brothers were a family again. Once again they made Shabbat together (*Shibbolei ha-Leket* 18. *Otzar ha-T'fillah* I. 307, *Midrash Lekakh Tov*).

The idea of the *tzaddik* is both a practical and a redemptive idea. On the one hand, the result of all our good work as Jews is *tzedakah* (righteousness). On the other hand, the ideal of the *tzaddik* approaches perfection. We exhibit *tzedakah* whenever we do good, but we approach being a *Tzaddik* when we compile enough acts of *tzedakah*.

There is a legend that thirty-six righteous people exist in the world at any given time. The *Shekhinah* (the neighborly part of God) rests on them. It is for their sake that God sustains the world. The messiah comes when they are no longer hidden (*Sanhedrin* 97a-b; *Sukkah* 45b).

Imagine a court system run by a set of really *mensch-y*, Torah-learned, caring, God-fearing justices. That is the fantasy of this prayer. Connecting *tzedek* (Justice) to *tzedakah* (righteousness) leads us to ask, "Where am I on my path to being a *tzaddik*?" "Where is the world on its journey towards redemption?" "How can I help?"

וְלִירוּשָׁלַיִם *V'LI'Y'RUSHALAYIM*

We are now nearing the end of the *Amidah*. This is the fourteenth *brakhah*; there are five more *brakhot* to go. This *brakhah* is the next-to-last specific petition. This one asks for the establishment of David's throne and the rebuilding of Jerusalem. That leads to our final specific request, the redemption. Finally there is an overall request that all of our petitions be answered. That leads in turn to the three concluding *brakhot*.

Jerusalem isn't just a city, it isn't just the capital of Israel, and it isn't just a place where a lot of historic events take place. Jerusalem is all of that and more. For the Jewish tradition, Jerusalem is the place where Jews have their most direct and extended relationship with God.

This *brakhah* asks God to quickly allow Jerusalem to be rebuilt. This rebuilding isn't just a question of sewers and walls—it is the rebuilding of a spiritual connection. The Midrash explains that יְרוּשָׁלַיִם *Yerushalayim* is the עִיר *ir* (city) that is יְרֵא *yirei* (in awe of) שָׁלוֹם *shalom* (peace). Rebuilding Jerusalem is reestablishing that sense of awe and holiness. When that Jerusalem again exists, the End of Days is near.

SOLOMON FINISHES THE TEMPLE

Jerusalem was a Jebusite city. By sneaking up a water shaft, King David conquered the city and made it the capital of Israel. David built up the city, but God would not let him build The Temple. God said that there was too much blood on David's hands. God told him, "BEHOLD, A SON SHALL BE BORN TO YOU; HE WILL BE A MAN OF PEACE. I WILL GIVE HIM PEACE FROM ALL HIS ENEMIES ROUND ABOUT. HIS NAME SHALL BE SOLOMON, AND I WILL GIVE PEACE AND QUIET TO ISRAEL IN HIS DAYS" (1 Chronicles 22:9).

Solomon built the Temple. This is the story of his finding the right place.

Elijah helped Solomon find the right place to build the Temple. It was built on a field owned by two brothers. One of them had a wife and children, while the other had no wife or children.

Elijah led Solomon to see the field one night. The two brothers had made two equal piles of the grain, one pile for each of them. The brother who had neither wife nor children lay in his bed and thought to himself: "I am all by myself and have nobody who is dependent on me for his daily bread. But my brother has a wife and children, so why should my portion be as big as his?" He rose in the middle of the night, sneaked like a thief, took sheaves from his own pile, and placed them on his brother's pile. And his brother said to his wife, "It is not fair to divide the corn in the field into two portions, half to me and half to my brother. My fate is so much better than his, since God has given me a wife and children, while he goes alone. Come with me, wife, and we shall secretly add to his portion from our own." And they did so. The next morning both brothers saw that their piles were still the same size.

Solomon saw the brothers figure this out and embrace and kiss. He realized that this was the place that God desired, the spot where the two brothers had thought the good thought and done the good deed.[3]

When the Temple was completed the angels sang בָּרוּךְ אַתָּה יי בּוֹנֵה יְרוּשָׁלָיִם *Barukh Attah Adonai Boneh Y'rushalayim* (Praised are You, Eternal, The One Who builds Jerusalem) (*Shibbolei ha-Leket*, 18. *Otzar ha-T'fillah* I. 307).

The story of the redemption includes the coming of the Messiah, who is to be a descendant of King David; the rebuilding of Jerusalem as a spiritual center that includes a new Temple;, and the coming of a Messianic Era. The rebuilding of Jerusalem is metaphoric, not literal. It goes back to the *aggadah* about the love and support of the two brothers. Jerusalem is to be built and rebuilt out of those kinds of relationships. Think Jacques Brel: "If we only have love, then Jerusalem stands." Ask:

[3]One can find this story in L. Ginzberg's *The Legends of the Jews* and in his footnotes. Ginzberg refers one to Israel Costa's *Mikveh Yisrael* (Livorno, 1851). A number of years after the publication of *The Legends of the Jews* Alexander Scheiber published a number of articles examining the origins and different versions of this story. First, the story is not found in the Talmud or Midrash; rather, the first evidence that we have of it is from Palestinian Arabs. Alphonse de Lamartine recorded it from Palestinian Arabs in 1832, and it was later reworked and recorded in a number of other 19th- and 20th-century sources. In Jewish literature we find it first in Israel Costa's *Mikveh Yisrael* and Shlomo Bakhor Hutzin's *Maasei Nissim* (Baghdad, 1890). This version was built using *Mimekor Yisrael, Bin Gurion* I, 491-2; *Bin Gurion* II, 272-3. Sourcing from MenahemMendel.Net

"Where is my Jerusalem? How am I helping to build it? How do I live the story of the two brothers?"

אֶת-צֶמַח דָּוִד *ET TZEMAH DAVID*

In many ways אֶת-צֶמַח דָּוִד *Et Tzemah David* (The Offspring of David), *brakhah* fifteen, is *V'li'Y'rushalim*, part two. In fact, in some ancient versions of that prayer they were combined. (It is suggested that when *Birkat ha-Minim* was originally part of the *Amidah*, they were one *brakhah*. Then, when *Birkat ha-Minim* was later removed, the Rebuilding Jerusalem part and the Coming of the Messiah part were split in two, keeping the number at 18. Later, when *Birkat ha-Minim* was added again, these ideas were left as separate *brakhot*, and the *Shmonah Esrei* became nineteen *brakhot*.)

Perhaps the most important idea in this prayer comes from the words כִּי לִישׁוּעָתְךָ קִוִּינוּ כָּל הַיּוֹם *Ki liY'shua't'kha Kivinu Kol ha-Yom* (for redemption we hope every day). From it comes the idea of waiting. It expresses an important truth—that while we have faith that God will help us to create a perfect world, a perfect way for people to live together, we really hope that it would and could happen today. Waiting is hard.

> Why does this prayer use the image of a *tzemah* (a sprouting plant) for the coming of the Messiah? Like a plant that has a small and insignificant beginning, then grows imperceptibly toward maturity, redemption, too, will come gradually, not abruptly and suddenly, but slowly, bringing Israel out of despair and distress toward freedom (Eli Munk).

> ...the redemption process, like creation, must of necessity sprout forth and grow by means of the cultivation of the human heart.. (B.S. Jacobson).

WAITING FOR THE MESSIAH

Rabbi Joshua ben Levi met Elijah standing by the entrance of Rabbi Shimon Bar Yokhai's tomb. Rabbi Joshua said, "Have I a portion in the World to Come?" Elijah answered, "If God wills it." Rabbi Joshua continued: "When will the Messiah come?" Elijah answered: "Go and ask him."

Rabbi Joshua then asked, "Where?" Elijah answered, "He is sitting among the poor lepers. All of the lepers tie and untie all of their bandages at once. The Messiah is doing it one bandage at a time."

Rabbi Joshua went to the Messiah and said, "*Shalom Aleikhem,* Rabbi and teacher." He answered, "*Aleikhem Shalom,* Son of Levi." Rabbi Joshua asked: "When will you come?" The Messiah answered, "Today."

On his way back he met Elijah again. Elijah asked, "What did he say?" Rabbi Joshua said,"*Alekhem Shalom,* Son of Levi." Elijah said: "That means you've got a portion in the World to Come." Rabbi Joshua then said, "But he lied to me. He said that he would come today. He hasn't come." Elijah said: "What he meant was for you to read Psalm 95, verse 7, where it says, 'TODAY, IF YOU HEAR GOD'S VOICE'" (*Sanhedrin* 98a).

In his commentary on the Mishnah Maimonides presents his Thirteen Articles of Faith, which includes "I believe with perfect faith in the coming of the Messiah; and though he tarry, I will wait daily for his coming." Jewish belief is a lot about waiting. Whether you think of it as a human Messiah or a temporal Messianic Era, we are still circling and waiting. In chapter two of *Pirkei Avot* Rabbi Tarfon tells us: "We are not required to finish the work; neither are we free to desist from it"(*Pirkei Avot* 2:6). Continuing to work toward a best possible future is the Jewish way of waiting. That future can "come today" if people finally listen to God's voice. We ask ourselves, "Do I still have hope in the future?" "Am I working to bring that future?"

שְׁמַע קוֹלֵנוּ *SHEMA KOLEINU*

שְׁמַע קוֹלֵנוּ *Shema Koleinu* (Hear Our Voice), also known as שׁוֹמֵעַ תְּפִלָּה *Shomei'a T'fillah*, is the sixteenth *brakhah*, the end of the thirteen "middle" *brakhot*, the petition part of the service. This is a prayer that literally asks God to listen to (and answer) all of our other prayers. It is a petition to grant all of our other petitions—that is why it comes last.

Shema Koleinu started out as one of the prayers the High Priest said during the daily sacrifices. We learn in the Talmud (*Yoma* 7:1) that a different version of *Shema Koleinu* was used in those days and was then changed to emphasize "prayer" rather than "sacrifice" after the destruction of the Temple.

Because *Shema Koleinu* is the end of the *brakhot* of petition, it is a place where we are encouraged to expand and extend our own prayers, adding our own special requests.

GOD HEARD

The Jews spent four hundred years in slavery in Egypt. The Egyptians made their lives bitter with hard work and slavery. The Torah tells this story:

AND IT CAME TO PASS IN THE COURSE OF THOSE MANY DAYS THAT THE KING OF EGYPT DIED; AND THE CHILDREN OF ISRAEL SIGHED BECAUSE OF THE BONDAGE, AND THEY CRIED, AND THEIR CRY CAME UP TO GOD...AND GOD HEARD THEIR GROANING, AND GOD REMEMBERED THE COVENANT WITH ABRAHAM, WITH ISAAC, AND WITH JACOB. AND GOD SAW THE PEOPLE OF ISRAEL, AND GOD KNEW THEIR CONDITION (Exodus 2:23-5).

This is when the Exodus really began. It began with God hearing Israel's prayer at the moment that God heard the angels sing בָּרוּךְ אַתָּה יי שׁוֹמֵעַ תְּפִלָּה *Barukh Attah Adonai Shomei'a T'fillah* (Praised are You, Eternal, The One Who hears prayer) (*Shibbolei ha-Leket*, 18. *Otzar ha-T'fillah* I. 307).

Prayer is supposed to be an answer. It is often a question. We wonder, "Is God listening?" "Does prayer make a difference?" In saying this prayer we willingly suspend those doubts. We have an Israelite moment. We are enslaved (we have talked about this already). We are desperate. We know that we need both strength and help to solve our enslavement. It is a Twelve Step moment:

> We admitted we were powerless over our addiction—that our lives had become unmanageable. We came to believe that a Power greater than ourselves could restore us to sanity. We made a decision to turn our will and our lives over to the care of God… (*Alcoholics Anonymous: The Story of How More Than One Hundred Men Have Recovered From Alcoholism, 1939*).

This is the moment the Families in Egypt knew that their slavery was not tolerable, that they did not have the strength to end it on their own, and that turning to God was the only way to find the resources. "What are the things I really need solved?" "Where can I turn for strength to solve these?" "What role do I let God play in my life?"

The last three *brakhot* of the *Amidah* are found in the Shabbat *Amidah* section.

הַלֵּל *HALLEL*

The הַלֵּל *Hallel* is:

- a collection of six psalms (113–118). The Jewish tradition remembers that King David wrote the psalms.
- said on the three festivals, *Pesah*, *Shavuot*, and *Sukkot*. It is also said on *Hanukkah* (but not Purim) and most Jews also say it on *Yom ha-Atzma'ut* (Israeli Independence Day) and *Yom Yerushalayim* (Jerusalem Day).
- also said as part of the Passover seder.
- the oldest part of the Siddur, a cycle of prayers that goes all the way back to the service in the Temple.
- prayers with really good melodies that are a lot of fun to sing.

הַלֵּל *HALLEL*

הַלֵּל *HALLEL*

The Talmud (*Pesaḥim* 117a-118a) helps us understand the *Hallel*. It teaches that:

- *Hallel* is said when Israel is in danger and when Israel has been rescued. This teaches us that we can call on God when we need help, because God has been there for us in the past when we have needed help.
- *Hallel* traces the history of the Jewish people. It has five themes: (1) the Exodus from Egypt, (2) the crossing of the Reed Sea, (3) the giving of the Torah, (4) the giving of Eternal Life, (5) the coming of the Messiah.
- We cannot change the order of the *Hallel* because it tells a story that starts in the past, leads to the present, and has faith in the future. We believe that God will take care of us because God has taken of us in the past (*Megillah* 17a *Otzar ha-T'fillah* 487:4).

In the Talmud there are two different stories of the first time the *Hallel* was said. One story is that Israel first sang these words (echoed by the angels) when they were escaping from Egypt. The other is that King David wrote these words out of the experience of first being a criminal chased by King Saul, then being rescued and becoming the King of Israel.

DAVID AND THE SPIDER

When David was a boy he once got mad at a spider for making a web David ran into. He asked God, "Why did You ever create something as useless as spiders?"

David wound up working for King Saul. When he was a boy he ran an errand for his father. His older brothers were soldiers. He showed up in the camp at the right moment. When everyone else chickened out, David faced the giant Goliath with his slingshot. After his victory he became an important member of Saul's court. He grew and scored a lot more victories. The king became jealous of David and tried to kill him. David fled, and Saul declared him a criminal and started to chase him with his army. David hid in a cave and fell asleep. While he slept a spider wove a thick web at the cave's entrance. David woke up just before Saul and his soldiers showed up there. Saul saw the spiderweb and said, "He couldn't be in here." This web saved David, who then sang a piece of *Hallel:* "You who believe in the Eternal—trust in the Eternal. God is their help and shield" (*Alphabet of Ben Sira* 24b).

In many ways, the story of the Exodus and the story of David's rescue are one story. People are in trouble. They pray to God and ask for help. Then they find the strength and help they need to get through the crises. When has that story been your story?

HALLELUYAH

Psalm 113 speaks of שֵׁם יי *Shem Adonai* (God's Name) and not "God." The Dubner Maggid told this story to explain why.

Once there was a queen with a huge empire—it was too big for her to visit every place. One day an impersonator dressed up like a queen and visited a part of the empire where the real queen had never been. The people all treated her warmly, with great respect and honor.

When the real queen heard about this everyone expected her to be angry, but she wasn't. They thought that she would punish the people for worshipping the wrong queen, but she said, "They thought that they were honoring me, not the imposter. They just need to be introduced to the real me."

The Dubner Maggid explained, "Many different people see the things that God does in the world, but not all of them figure out which Power was responsible. God says the same thing as the queen. "They need to learn My name. They need to be introduced to the real Me" (Reworked from Rabbi Abraham J. Twerski, *Prayerfully Yours: Creating the Bond Between Man and His Maker* [Shaar Press/Artscroll Mesorah Publications, 2001]).

Once again we are talking about God. In the *Book of the Kuzari,* Yehudah ha-Levi teaches that אֱלֹהִים *Elohim* stands for the God of Aristotle and יי *Adonai* is the God of Moses. Aristotle, who was a philosopher, could look at the world and know that a greater power had been at work. Moses, who spoke to God face to face, was told God's name and knew the context of the Jewish experience. For Jews, it is one thing to be aware of God; it is another thing to know God's name and our history with God. This phrase from Psalm 113 forces us to ask, "Do I have a history with God?"

LEAVING EGYPT

In Hebrew the Exodus from Egypt is called יְצִיאַת מִצְרַיִם *Y'tzi'at Mitzrayim. Mitzrayim* is the Hebrew word for Egypt. It is built around the three-letter root [מצר]. A מֵצַר *metzar* is a "pit." *Mitzrayim* is plural. That makes Egypt "the pits." The word *metzar* is built out of the two-letter root צר. צַר *Tzar* means "narrowness."

A rabbi named the S'fat Emet taught, "We each have our own Egypt, our own narrowness that we have to escape."

Another rabbi, Isaac of Gur, taught the same lesson in a different way. He said, "In every generation there is a new understanding of leaving Egypt. Egypt is inside of us. We all have our own Pharaohs. Not only in every generation but in every person there is a point of freedom. To touch that point is to exit the inner Egypt. That point can only be found individually by each person."

The second psalm in *Hallel*, Psalm 114, begins בְּצֵאת יִשְׂרָאֵל *B'Tzet Yisrael* (When Israel left Egypt).

בְּצֵאת יִשְׂרָאֵל *B'TZET YISRAEL*

There are two stories about the first time that *B'tzet Yisrael* was sung. One version says that Israel sang it once they successfully crossed the Reed Sea (and while the Egyptians were drowning).

The other says that King David was studying about *Y'tzi'at Mitzrayim.* David learned that there were many reasons that God found the Families of Israel to be worth saving. There

> were four: (1) They kept their Hebrew names, (2) they did not give up Hebrew as their language, (3) they did not tell each other's secrets, and (4) husbands and wives were good to their partners. And there were more reasons: because they celebrated a Passover on their last night in Egypt, because they passed the Covenant with God on to their children, and because in the future they would accept the Torah and would build the Tabernacle. When David learned about all of these good things that Israel did because of their faith in God, he just had to sing. Out came *B'tzet Yisrael* (*Midrash Tehillim* 114:4).

The Exodus from Egypt is central to Jewish identity. It is the primal Jewish experience. We experience it firsthand every Passover. We experience it again through the teachings of many Jewish scholars. The core questions remain: "What is my Egypt?" "What do I need to do to be liberated from my Egypt?" "How can God help to set me free?"

PSALM 118.19: פִּתְחוּ לִי שַׁעֲרֵי צֶדֶק *PITHU LI SHA'AREI TZEDEK*

פִּתְחוּ לִי שַׁעֲרֵי צֶדֶק *Pithu li Sha'arei Tzedek* (Open for me the Gates of Righteousness) is found near the end of this psalm. One big question about this psalm is "What gates are we talking about?" Rashi, a famous medieval biblical commentator, said, "This is a dream of the future. In the future, after the Messiah comes, the Temple will be rebuilt in Jerusalem. In that Messianic future, all good people will gather and enter and come close to each other and to God."

Rashi lived around the year 1000. Today not all Jews believe that it would be wonderful to rebuild the Temple. So Rashi's comment could be understood to mean "The gates lead to a time when all people live in peace, safety, and prosperity."

KING DAVID LEARNS ABOUT THE MEANING OF LIFE

> King David learned that when a person is ready to enter the life after this life he will be asked, "What was your work?" If he answers "I fed the hungry," they will say to him, "This is God's gate" and let him in. If he answers "I gave drink to those who are thirsty," they will say to him, "This is God's gate" and let him in. If he answers "I gave clothes to those who

> need them," they will say to him, "This is God's gate" and let him in. If he answers, "I took care of orphans, gave *tzedakah,* or performed other deeds of lovingkindness," the same will happen. David said, "I do all of these things, so let all the gates be opened for me." He then wrote *"Pitḇu Li Sha'arei Tzedek,* OPEN FOR ME THE GATES OF RIGHTEOUSNESS" (Midrash on Psalms 118).

Max Kadushin wrote a book called *Worship and Ethics* (Global Publications, 2001) that is kind of a lost classic. In it he argues that in addition to the spiritual connections made by prayers, the Jewish liturgy has an ethical component. Essentially, in praising what God does, we are obligated to do the same. Because we are created in God's image, we have a model up to Whom we must live. This particular story and this particular phrase, "THE GATES OF RIGHTEOUSNESS," sets a standard for our behavior. The questions: "Will I be admitted through the Gates of Righteousness?" "What else do I have to do?"

אָנָּא יי *ANNA ADONAI*

Starting a few lines before the אָנָּא יי *Anna Adonai* we begin singing Psalm 118 differently. First the *ḥazzan* or service leader sings a verse, then the whole congregation repeats it. Every time we sing a Hebrew prayer responsively (back and forth between the service leader and the congregation) we are acting out a story.

According to the Talmud, these words were first said by Samuel, the prophet, when he came looking for a king. David, his brothers, and his father Jesse all echoed Samuel's words because they were in shock. They didn't believe God would want David. He was the youngest and scrawniest of the brothers.

DAVID ASKS FOR HELP

> When David was finally appointed king, he realized that two stories were true at the same time. Just as God had saved him from Goliath, Saul, and the Philistines and brought him to this great moment of his becoming king, so God had taken Israel out of slavery, protected them in the wilderness, and brought them into the promised land. David

> knew that God could be counted on for help. That is why we ask God for help—just as David did (*Pesa<u>h</u>im* 119a).

We ask: "In what one way is your life story like the story of the Families of Israel?"

TORAH SERVICE

This material is somewhat different from the earlier parts of the service. The Torah Service, for the most part, is not found in the Torah or the Talmud; it is outlined in a volume called *Masekhet Sofrim*. This text is like the Talmud but was put together after the Talmud was finished. The Talmud was closed around 500 C.E.; *Masekhet Sofrim* was probably put together in the middle of the eighth century. What that means for us is that there are many fewer Rabbinic origin stories for this material, and we will have a greater reliance on folk literature and literature written to resemble folktales.

BEING AT MT. SINAI

God gave the Torah to Israel at Mt. Sinai. God gave it to Israel a second time as part of the teachings that were done in the Tabernacle. God then regave it to them a third time when Israel was on the steps of Moav. Israel actually received the Torah three times (The Rokeah, *Ma'aseh Rokeah*).

In the Talmud we are told that it is a *mitzvah* to read the *sidrah* (the weekly Torah portion) three times in a week: twice in the original Hebrew and once in translation. We are then told that anyone who completes this third time with a congregation, as part of the communal reading, will be rewarded (*Brakhot* 8a/b).

When we study Torah with the congregation we are returning to Mt. Sinai (The Rokeah).

In the Midrash we learn that every single Jew was at Mount Sinai and heard the Torah (*Midrash ha-Gadol*).

Rabbi Menachem Mendel of Kotzk taught: "Every Jew should try to imagine the event at Sinai" (*Emet V'Emunah*).

Rabbi Elimelekh of Lyzhansk said, "Not only do I remember being at Sinai, but I also remember who was standing next to me" (*Binat Ya'akov*).

Rabbi Kook taught, "When we pray we take that which is in us and reach up...When we study Torah we take the light from above and plant it in our deepest nature" (*Olat Re-iyah*, Vol. 1, pp 19, 20).

When we read Torah in community, when we study Torah, we have a Mount Sinai moment. We reenact and deepen our memory of being at Sinai. And we connect and associate other memories of revelation to the Sinai experience.

THE TORAH SERVICE IS LIKE...

The Torah service acts out the years that the Families of Israel spent wandering in the wilderness. In the Torah we are told Israel suffered because "THEY TRAVELED THREE DAYS IN THE WILDERNESS AND DID NOT FIND WATER" (Exodus 15:22). The Talmud uses this verse to explain why we read Torah on Mondays, Thursdays, and Shabbat. It teaches that Torah is like water and we should never go more than three days without having a "drink of Torah" (*Bava Kamma* 82a).

The Torah service is like being at Mt. Sinai when the Torah is given. Rabbi Joseph Soloveitchik taught that the Torah Service is "a new giving of the Torah, the amazing standing under the mountain that burned with fire...each time we take out the Torah" (*Halakhic Man*, pp. 227–8).

The Torah service is also a Torah class. In the Talmud, when Ezra makes it a rule that the Families of Israel will read Torah on Shabbat, he explains that this is because people who did not work in the marketplace on Mondays and Thursdays would miss their chance to learn Torah (*Bava Kamma* 82a).

THE TORAH IS GIVEN EVERY DAY

When God was teaching the Torah to Moses, God told him to put little crowns on the top of some letters. Making all those extra pen strokes was a lot of work.

Moses asked God, "Why go to all this effort to put crowns on all these letters?"

God answered him, "In the future there is going to be a man, Akiva ben Yosef, who will learn things from the details of the crowns."

Moses demanded, "Take me to this man."

Moses was immediately zapped into Akiva's school. He was placed in the last seat in the last row. This was the dunce seat. He listened to the lesson and could not understand a word that Akiva was teaching. He felt like the dunce.

When the lesson ended, one of the students asked, "Rabbi, where did you learn this lesson?" Rabbi Akiva answered, "All this we learned from Moses our teacher." Moses felt much better (*Avodah Zara* 19a).

How could Akiva learn something in the Torah that Moses did not know? The Zohar teaches, "When a person speaks words of Torah, those words come before God. God takes those words and kisses them" (*Zohar* 1:4b).

BEGINNING THE TORAH SERVICE

אֵין כָּמוֹךָ *EIN KAMOKHA*

The Torah service begins with the אֵין כָּמוֹךָ *Ein Kamokha.* These are words that are said before the ark is opened. It starts by praising God. It says:

- God is the ultimate.
- God rules everywhere/everywhen.
- God was/is/always will be The Ruler.

אָב הָרַחֲמִים *AV HA-RA<u>H</u>AMIM*

It continues with אָב הָרַחֲמִים *Av ha-Ra<u>h</u>amim,* which makes two requests:

- Be good to Zion.
- Rebuild the walls of Jerusalem.

It ends by:

- telling God, "We trust in You alone."
- praising God as "Ruler, high and exalted God, Master of Eternity."

In a moment we will rise and open the ark. The Torah will be taken out, and we will busy ourselves, first with the Torah as a symbol, and then with the Torah as words. Before there can be any confusion, before we can fool ourselves into thinking that it is the Torah we are worshiping, we start with the Source. We remember that Torah is a way of bringing God into our lives.

THE WALLS OF JERUSALEM

Here is a folktale that expands our understanding of "the walls of Jerusalem" as manifest in *Av ha-Ra<u>h</u>amim.*

> The year was either 1539 or 1540. Suliman the Magnificent, the Sultan, had a palace in Jerusalem. He was looking out one of its many windows and saw an old woman climb up on a hill and dump out a sack of garbage. He was angry to

think that some poor woman wanted to turn his neighborhood into a garbage heap. He sent his soldiers to arrest her.

When she was brought into the palace she told Suliman: "I am sorry, Your Grace, but I am carrying out the commandment of my ancestors." When the Sultan questioned her further she explained, "I am a descendent of the Romans who conquered and destroyed Jerusalem in the year 70. While they destroyed the city, they were unable to destroy the foundations of the Jewish Temple. My ancestors therefore commanded that all Romans in the city had to daily dump garbage on the site where that Temple used to be. Everyone who lived outside the city had to dump garbage there twice a week. And anyone who lived further than three days away from Jerusalem had to bring garbage to the site at least once a month. When my ancestors couldn't destroy the foundations of the Temple, they decided to make sure that it would always be buried in filth and street mud, to make it a place that no one would want to be. They ordered us to continue to dump garbage on this site so that the Jewish Temple would soon be forgotten."

After hearing this story the Sultan ordered his men to arrest anyone else who tried to dump garbage there. Over the next few weeks several people were arrested every day. Each of them told the same story. Each was bringing garbage to this site because it was a family tradition to make sure that no one remembered the place.

The Sultan then issued a royal edict that said "People who wants to find favor in my eyes should come to this location and do the things that they see me do." The Sultan then went to the site with a sack of money, a basket, and a broom. First, while he was alone, he threw silver and gold coins all over the mound. Then he began to pick up the big pieces of garbage and put them in his basket. By the time he got to sweeping one small part of the hill, lots of people had joined him. Some of them came to look for gold and silver coins. Others came because they wanted to make the Sultan happy. Soon the hill was covered with people sweeping and shoveling, picking up and cleaning. It took more than a month. Every day the Sultan came and worked with them. Every night he seeded the site with a few more coins. When the work was done the foundations of the Temple could be seen, and a wall, the one we now call the Western Wall, was uncovered.

The Sultan issued another royal edict. This one made it a crime to litter or even spit in this area.

Next the Sultan invited the Jewish community to come and rebuild their Holy Temple at his expense. They politely refused, him saying, "We are not allowed to rebuild God's House until the world is ready. We cannot do it until we have a world where everyone lives in peace." When they said, "No," the Sultan informed them that he would build his own place of prayer nearby. He explained, "I know that your God's house will be a place of prayer for all people. God will listen to people who pray there." The Sultan made sure that there was freedom and respect for all Jews who lived in the Ottoman Empire. Last Suliman, built a wall around Jerusalem to protect Her (M.M. Reischer, *Sha'arei Yerushalayim*, No. 10, pp 42–3).

This story teaches us that the existing walls of Jerusalem are a memory, an important memory. The walls that need to be rebuilt are spiritual. They are walls built of peace and freedom, walls built of redemption. Midrash speaks of an earthly Jerusalem and a heavenly Jerusalem. The process we are seeking in our hearts is to make the earthly Jerusalem heavenly. The question here, as we stand for the Torah, is "How do we make use of Torah to rebuild Jerusalem?"

204—STORIES WE PRAY

THE ARK IS OPENED

When we open the ark, we begin by remembering two moments in Jewish history.

CARRYING THE ARK

The first moment we act out comes from the time when Israel spent forty years in the wilderness. Every time they moved their camp the Families of Israel were led by the Ark of the Covenant. The Ark followed a pillar of fire at night and a pillar of clouds by day. It was a wooden box covered inside and out in gold, with winged *cherubim* on top. It was carried on long poles by the *Kohanim* (priests). Inside were (a) the two tablets of the Ten Commandments, (b) the broken fragments of the first set of the Commandments, (c) a jar with a sample of manna, and (d) a copy of the Torah scroll. Today in our synagogue we still keep the *Sefer Torah* in an ark.

In the Book of Numbers there is a two-sentence passage that is surrounded by a pair of upside-down versions of the Hebrew letter נ *Nun* like parentheses (Numbers 10:35–6). One sentence talks about picking the ark up. The other sentence talks about putting it down. The first sentence is used at the beginning of the Torah service. The second is used when we return the *Sefer Torah* to the ark. When we take the Torah out and when we carry it around the synagogue we are like the Families of Israel being led by God through the wilderness.

JERUSALEM

The second moment comes from a vision about the future shared by the prophets Isaiah and Micah. They both saw Jerusalem as a center from which the wisdom of Torah would be distributed around the world. The second part of opening the ark involves remembering their dream. Just before we take the Torah out of the ark and begin to make it our own, we share the hope that all people will join in its dream of peace and freedom, justice and kindness. When we take the Torah out of the ark we accept that hope for the future. It comes with the words כִּי מִצִּיּוֹן תֵּצֵא תוֹרָה וּדְבַר יי מִירוּשָׁלָיִם *Ki mi-Tzion Tetzei Torah u-D'var*

Adonai mi-Y'rushalayim (From Zion Torah goes out, and the Eternal's word from Jerusalem) (Isaiah 2:3, Micah 4:2).

BEING LIFTED

THE ARK

The Ark led the Families of Israel through the wilderness. First came a column of smoke or a pillar of fire, then came the Ark, and then came the Families of Israel. The Ark used to clear the way for the people; out of it would come bursts of fire that zapped the scorpions and the snakes out of the way. When God used to talk to Moses, God would speak to him from above the wings of the *cherubim*.

The Ark was very heavy to lift. The Levites would have to struggle with all their might just to lift it a tiny bit above the ground. But once they did that, the Ark took over and carried them (*Numbers Rabbah* 4:20).

THE TORAH

Rabbi David Moshe Chortkov was a Hasidic rabbi. He once had to hold a large, heavy Torah for a long time. One of his students offered to share the weight, but Rabbi David said to him, "Once you've picked up the Torah, it is no longer heavy. It carries you" (Martin Buber, *Tales of the Hasidim*).

THE GRANDSON

November 9, 1938 was Kristallnacht, "The Night of Broken Glass." Gangs of Nazi youth roamed through Jewish neighborhoods breaking windows of Jewish businesses and homes, burning synagogues, and looting. One hundred and one synagogues were destroyed, and almost 7,500 Jewish businesses were destroyed. Twenty-six thousand Jews were arrested and sent to concentration camps. Jews were physically attacked and beaten, and ninety died (Louis L. Snyder, *Encyclopedia of the Third Reich*).

It was just before sundown, and the burning and the breaking had started. A Jewish grandfather and his son were too far away from home. Around them gangs of youth, whipped into craziness by the Nazi machine, were throwing rocks and destroying. The grandfather took the young boy's hand. He began to walk more quickly. He looked behind and saw that they were being followed. They broke into a run. The boy fell, hurt his knee, and started to cry. The grandfather threw down his cane, scooped up the boy, and continued running. The gangs were closing on him. Out of a window people called to him, "Put the boy down. You need all your own strength. The boy can run faster than you." The grandfather called back, "I am not carrying him—he is lifting me up" (Morris Silverman, *Heaven on Your Head: Interpretations, Legends and Parables, Comments on the Torah and the Holidays.* Hartmore House, 1964).

These three stories are one story. Each says "It was heavy to lift, but when I had it up it carried me." In each case the "it" involves Torah: Torah as the Ark of the Covenant, Torah as the Torah scroll, and human life as Torah. The act of lifting leads to being carried. "When do you lift Torah? When does Torah carry you?"

THE LAST KOPECK

In a little village called Smunefka the impossible happened. There was not a single kopeck left in the village. In fact, there was no money of any kind. Even if you offered someone a ruble for a kopeck, they would be unable to give you one. People came running to the rabbi and asked, "What should we do?" The rabbi washed his hands and said the *She-heheyanu brakhah* over something new.

Still the panic went on, so the rabbi called a meeting. People gathered at the synagogue and waited for the rabbi to speak. He ascended the *bimah* and said, "Jews, it will do us no good to get angry at God. Everything that God does is either because of *Z'khut Avot v'Imahot,* the merit of our ancestors, or for the coming of the Messiah. While it is hard to believe that our little town is so important, the lack of money here assures the coming of the Messiah. In the Talmud we are taught, 'The seed of David will not come until no Jew has a single coin in his pocket.' That time is now, and that place is here."

Reb Hayyim said, "But what about the Zionists and all their settlements in *Eretz Yisrael?* Do they have nothing to do with the Messiah?"

The rabbi answered, "Prepare for your journey to Zion. When the Messiah comes we will all return there. The pioneers have prepared our path."

The joyful mood was interrupted by Menahem Mendel, the contractor. He said, "I have been going over the accounts for the building of the new public baths, and one kopeck is left over." He pulled out a ream of papers and found a small envelope with one kopeck in it. He put the coin down on the table and said, "This belongs to the community." Everyone looked at it as if it were the first coin in the world.

Shmuel yelled at him, "Go and check your records. Last month you told us we were 138 rubles short—now you say we are one kopeck over. Check your records."

The rabbi said, "The records do not matter. The Messiah cannot come because we have a coin here."

One person said, "Throw the coin into the river. It will be gone, and the Messiah will come."

Another person said, "Not into the river. It is a *mitzvah, bal tash'bit,* never to destroy anything useful. Besides, a fish might swallow it, and someone would catch it, and we would have the coin back. We should throw it into the public baths. There is so much mud on its floor that no one will ever find it there."

David, the principal of the Talmud Torah, said, "The roof of the Talmud Torah, the school, leaks. We should assign the kopek to repair the roof of the school. That would be using it to do a *mitzvah.*"

Barukh, the *shamas,* said, "No, not the Talmud Torah! When the Messiah comes we will not use it anymore. We should use it to repair the synagogue, which also leaks. It is more of an embarrassment to have a leaky synagogue."

Mr. Kaufman, head of the Shmunefka burial society, argued, "The synagogue is holy, but what about a cemetery? When the Messiah comes we will take the holy things out of the synagogue and take them to Jerusalem with us. When he comes the synagogue will be only the four walls—but the cemetery will be here. We need to protect the cemetery from all the animals breaking in and walking through. It needs a new fence."

The arguing went on; the rabbi tried to keep order. In heaven the Holy One sent a message to the Messiah. It told him to get ready, and explained that there was no one in Shmunefka with a single coin—and that the community was having a meeting to get rid of the single communal kopeck. "Jewish communities," the message explained, "are good at spending money."

The Messiah sent for his white donkey and his shofar. Both had been sitting and waiting for hundreds of years. The donkey was covered in dust and had to be washed twice; the shofar had to be soaked in vinegar for hours. Finally they were ready, and the Messiah mounted the donkey and flew to Shmunefka. He said the words of the psalm, "WHEN THE ETERNAL BROUGHT US BACK TO ZION WE WERE LIKE DREAMERS" (Psalm 126:1). On his face was a huge smile.

As he came into the town the meeting was ending. The Jews of the town were screaming and fighting, "For the cemetery." "No. For the school." "Throw it away." There was kicking and screaming. Everyone was angry. The Messiah said quietly, "No, I have come too soon" (Based on a story by Shimon Frug).

This story could easily have fit into the *Amidah brakhah* about the Messiah, but it also teaches us a lot about the rebuilding of Jerusalem. We rebuild (or don't rebuild) Jerusalem where we live and where we act. The story makes clear that something as small as a penny can determine the redemption of the world—the actualization of the Torah. "How do my actions rebuild Jerusalem?" "How do I use Torah to do it?"

PRAYERS BEFORE THE ARK

Between the time we open the ark and the time we take the Torah out of the ark, some communities use this moment to say a few prayers. Some of these are said only on holidays, others are said every Shabbat.

שְׁמַע SHEMA

The שְׁמַע *Shema* makes the moment when we take the Torah out of the ark feel like the moment when Israel stood at Mt. Sinai. According to a midrash, the Families of Israel were all standing at the foot of Mt. Sinai, and Moses led them in the *Shema* (just as we do when we take the Torah out of the ark) when God spoke words of Torah to them (*Deuteronomy Rabbah* 2:31). It was the moment when Israel said, "*NA'ASEH V'NISHMA*. WE WILL DO. WE WILL OBEY" (Exodus 24:7).

אֶחָד אֱלֹהֵינוּ EHAD ELOHEINU

Next comes a sentence that is not in the Bible. אֶחָד אֱלֹהֵינוּ *Ehad Eloheinu* is found in a book called *Mesekhet Sofrim* 14.8 that is not part of the Talmud but is often found with it. It gives lots of rules about the Torah. This verse is an echo of the *Shema*. It is made up of biblical phrases (Psalms 147:5, Isaiah 57:15).

גַּדְּלוּ לַיי אִתִּי GADLU L'ADONAI ITI

The third verse in the taking out of the Torah comes from Psalms 34:4. It tells a story. In Hebrew גַּדְּלוּ *Gadlu* is made up of six words. In II Samuel 6:13 we learn that when David brought the Ark up to Jerusalem he stopped and had a celebration every six steps. The *Shema* has us receiving the Torah with Moses. *Gadlu* has us bringing the Ark with the Torah up to Jerusalem.

לְךָ יי LEKHA ADONAI

With לְךָ יי *Lekha Adonai* the Torah processional begins. The *Lekha Adonai* is made up of two verses from two different places. The first comes from the story where David announces that his son Solomon will be building the Temple (1 Chronicles 29:11). We begin by following the

Ark into Solomon's Temple, its home. The second verse comes from Psalms. It was written by David and it praises the establishment of the Temple mount as a holy place of Torah (Psalms 99:5, 9). The celebration continues.

ANOTHER SHEMA STORY

Why was Israel considered holy enough to recite the *Shema*? Rabbi Pinhas ben Hama told this story: "Israel earned the right to recite the *Shema* on Mt. Sinai. God first began to speak to them at Mt. Sinai by saying, שְׁמַע יִשְׂרָאֵל *Shema Yisrael* (LISTEN ISRAEL). Then God said, "I AM THE ETERNAL YOUR GOD." Israel immediately answered יי אֱלֹהֵינוּ יי אֶחָד *Adonai Eloheinu Adonai Ehad* ("THE ETERNAL IS OUR GOD, THE ETERNAL ALONE). Then Moses said, בָּרוּךְ שֵׁם כְּבוֹד מַלְכוּתוֹ לְעוֹלָם וָעֶד *Barukh Shem K'vod Malkhuto L'Olam Va'ed* Blessed be the Name of Whose glorious empire is for ever and ever (*Deuteronomy Rabbah* 2:31).

This simple story (1) connects the *Shema* to the giving of the Torah, (2) explains how the *Barukh Shem K'vod* was added to the *Shema*, and (3) teaches that Torah is a dialogue between God and us. In between times remembering that God is One, think about being at Sinai and saying the *Shema* with God.

THE SYNAGOGUE THAT CRIED

At the edge of town there is an abandoned synagogue that people call the weeping synagogue. Birds nest there. Squirrels come and play there. But no one prays there. Many of the local Jews believe that it is haunted. They abandoned it, moved the Holy Torah scrolls, turned off the Eternal Light, and built a brand-new synagogue on the other side of town. This is the story the oldest members of the community tell about it.

Once, long ago, we had a rabbi who was a scholar. He taught brilliant classes and gave astounding sermons. Late at night he could often be found alone in the synagogue, the old synagogue, studying the holy books. He would study late into the night, early into the next morning.

One night, when the rabbi was the last person awake in the whole town, a voice spoke to him from inside the Holy Ark. It said, "Make a wish. Heaven has seen how good and how holy you are, so make a wish."

The rabbi thought and thought, then said, "I have nothing for which to wish. I have health and family. I have enough to eat and wear, enough things, enough of a place to live. I am happy with my work. I am happy with my portion in life."

At that moment the ark began to cry. A huge sobbing started. Then the voice began to speak again. "You could have done so much. You could have brought peace or ended hunger. Human suffering could have ended, but you thought of wishes as only for you." The crying continued.

In the morning they found the rabbi collapsed on the floor. They woke him, took him home, washed his forehead, and fed him soup. By evening he was gone. He said nothing to anyone. But the crying started that day. From then on the synagogue felt like a sad place. At night, when the wind blew, it became a sobbing voice that seemed to come from the ark. Anyone who was in the synagogue heard the ark cry, "If only... If only..."

It became too much for the community. They built a new synagogue and started over (Based on a story by David Einhorn, *The Seventh Candle and Other Folk Tales of Eastern Europe* [New York: Ktav Publishing House, Inc. 1968]).

This story is one that tries to define Torah. It teaches that Torah is not something you only study; it must be something you do. Torah is actions. The question it asks as the Torah is carried around the synagogue is, "How do you live Torah?"

TORAH BLESSINGS

When one is called to the Torah one has an *aliyah*. *Aliyah* means "going up." The person receiving an *aliyah* says blessings before and after the reading of the Torah. Originally, and still sometimes, the person who has the *aliyah* also reads the portion of the Torah.

Different synagogues read Torah differently. Traditionally Torah is read on Monday and Thursday mornings and twice on Shabbat (morning and afternoon). Today some synagogues read Torah on Friday night. Traditionally there are three *aliyot* that connect to each Torah reading. On Shabbat morning the tradition calls for seven *aliyot* and a person called the *maftir* who will go on to read the *Haftarah*. On Jewish holidays there can be four, five, or six *aliyot*. Some synagogues read fewer than the traditional number of *aliyot*.

We say a blessing both before and after reading Torah. Very few acts in the Jewish tradition get blessings both before and after. We bless before and after eating. We bless both before and after reading Torah, *Haftarah*, and the Purim *Megillah*. The Talmud connects eating to the other three. It explains that food nourishes our bodies while Torah feeds our souls; that food keeps us alive while Torah plants within us eternal life (*Brakhot* 21a).

> When a person recites the blessings over the Torah, he or she should point his or her heart to the giving of the Torah and experience the moment when God gave us the Holy Torah that is the source of our life. The Torah is God's cherished possession that gives God delight every day (Tur, *Laws of Morning Blessings*, Chapter 47).

> This blessing first says "Who *gave* us the Torah" in the past tense. It then calls God "*Giver* of the Torah" (present tense). Zev Wolf of Zhitomir pointed out this change in tense (*Or ha-Meir*, vol 1:8).

EZRA'S MOMENT

The Temple was in Jerusalem. It was the one place where all Jews went to connect to God. It was a place of community, prayer, and Torah. In the Temple there were three copies of the Torah. In each there was one mistake. They were the oldest and best copies. These were used to check all other Torah scrolls that were written (*Mesekhet Sofrim* 6:4). The king and the priests used to read Torah to the people in the Temple (*Sotah* 7:7–8). It is probable that, in those days, the Temple was the only place where a copy of the Torah could be found.

We don't know when local synagogues got started. We suspect that it happened before the first Temple was destroyed and before the Jewish people were exiled to Babylon. We suspect that the synagogue became more important to the Jewish people during the Babylonian exile. We know that the synagogue remained important once they returned.

One Rosh ha-Shanah after the Jewish people returned from Babylonia, Ezra the Scribe gathered the people in the square by the Water Gate. He took a Torah scroll and climbed on a high wooden tower and read Torah to the people. As part of the ceremony he said words that were very much like "בָּרְכוּ אֶת יי הַמְבֹרָךְ *Barekhu et Adonai ha-M'vorakh* (Praised be the Eternal Who is to be praised)." The people then responded in a way that was very much like "בָּרוּךְ יי הַמְבֹרָךְ לְעוֹלָם וָעֶד *Barukh Adonai ha-M'vorakh l'Olam Va-ed* (Praised be the Eternal Who is to be praised forever and always)." He showed the text to the people in a way that was very much like the way we make *hagbahah* (lifting up the text to the congregation) today (Nehemiah 8).

Ezra had copies of the Torah written. They were taken to every Jewish community and placed in a synagogue in every village and town. On Monday and Thursday Ezra had the elders of the town sit in the gates and use the Torah to judge between the people. On Monday, Thursday, and Saturday Ezra had each community read and teach the Torah in synagogue. This was the moment when the Torah moved out of the Temple and was placed in the hands of every Jew. The Torah was now ours to explain and teach.

> We still follow Ezra's ruling and read the Torah weekly in synagogue. When we do we begin each reading with words very much like those that Ezra used at the Water Gate. We begin *Barekhu et Adonai ha-M'vorakh* (*Bava Kamma* 82a).

The Ezra moment that is described in the Torah and expanded in the Talmud is a moment of radical democratization of the Torah. Before him the Torah was kept by the priests in the Temple. After Ezra every village had a Torah, every village had a chance to use the Torah to judge between people, and every village had the chance to interpret and explore the Torah's meaning. The Torah moved from being a guarded national treasure in a protected shrine to being the hub of every Jewish community. Everyone now had access to Torah. It became a family and community thing. Ask: "How do I make Torah mine?" "How does Torah shape my family and my community experience?" "How is Torah still my national treasure?"

THE DEATHS OF THE MAHARAL

The Torah blessing teaches us that "God has planted within us eternal life." The Talmud makes it clear that Torah is the way that the seed of eternity enters our soul (*Hagigah* 3b). The Maharal, Rabbi Judah Lowe, was a rabbi in Prague in the 1500s. Stories tell that he was the one who made the Golem, an almost-person, out of mud and did many other miracles for the good of the Jewish community. Stories also tell that he knew the secret of eternal life. The Maharal knew that the Angel of Death could not take a person who was studying Torah. As he grew older and older (and he lived eighty-five years) he studied more and more, leaving the Angel of Death no window of opportunity. Still, he did die, and two different stories tell how.

THE PRAGUE VERSION

> The Maharal could smell the Angel of Death and would always study more intently when he approached. Finally the Angel of Death made a plan. He hid in a beautiful dark red rose. Once, when he was studying, his grandson came running up to the Maharal and said, "Grampa, smell this beautiful rose." The Maharal stopped studying, put his book down, and

took the flower from his grandson. He breathed it in deeply, and the Angel of Death sadly completed his mission (J. Funzig in Die Wundermänner im Judischen Volk).

THE POSEN VERSION

Just before the High Holidays the Maharal was studying in the synagogue late into the night. He thought he was alone, but then he saw a man enter and start to sharpen a big knife. The man was looking at a long list of names. Suddenly the Maharal realized that this man was no man. He was the Angel of Death. The list was the list of those who would live and those who would die in the next year. He grabbed the list out of the Angel's hand and ran home. The bottom corner of the list tore off and stayed with the Angel. The Maharal went through the list and was relieved to find that he had gotten all the names of everyone in the community. They would be safe. The Maharal died right after the holidays. He had forgotten to check for his own name (From Knoop's *Sagen und Erzählungen aus der Provinz Posen* [1893], Retold in J. Bergmann's *Die Legenden der Juden*, [1919]).

The question asked by these stories and by the closing Torah *brakhah* is "What is Eternal life?" Judaism has many answers. In our collection we can find resurrection of the dead, reincarnation, a "world to come," and even "the souls return to God." The school of logical positivism gives us the best way to understand these two stories. "The soul lives on in the memories of those who have gone before." Here the stories converge. The Maharal has the capacity to defeat the Angel of Death and therefore live forever. In each story he trades death for a good deed. One is connection to his grandchild, the other is the saving of lives in his community. Because we have both stories, both events helped him to be remembered, to live on in people's memories. The questions for us: "How are we using the Torah to build eternal life?" "When are we building the memories that will give us eternal life?"

BLESSINGS AFTER EACH *ALIYAH*

An *aliyah* comes with opportunities for blessing. Jewish tradition has attached a number of very short blessings that can be said for or by the person who just had an *aliyah*.

END

THE BAR/BAT MITZVAH *BRAKHAH*

In the Midrash we are told that when Jacob and Esau turned thirteen Isaac said the bar mitzvah *brakhah*. He said: בָּרוּךְ שֶׁפְּטָרַנִי מֵעָנְשׁוֹ שֶׁלָּזֶה *Barukh she-P'tarani me'Onsho she-la-Zeh* (Praised be the One Who has freed me from this child's punishment).

The idea of this blessing is that when children turn thirteen they become old enough to be responsible for their own actions. In traditional synagogues parents now say this blessing. However, in many synagogues the *she-heheyanu*, the blessing that celebrates holy moments, is said in addition to or instead of this formula.

SAYING גּוֹמֵל *GOMEL*

גּוֹמֵל *Gomel* is a prayer that is said after having survived a dangerous situation. It is a special thank you to God for having come through the danger. This is based on a verse in the Psalms that says "LET THEM THANK THE ETERNAL FOR GOD'S MERCY AND FOR THE WONDERS DONE FOR PEOPLE" (*Psalms* 107:8). The Talmud requires a person who has survived a serious injury or illness, gone on a dangerous journey, or been released from imprisonment to say a prayer (*Brakhot* 54b). In many synagogues a person who needs to say *gomel* is given an *aliyah* and says the prayer after finishing the closing Torah *brakhah*.

מִי שֶׁבֵּרַךְ *MI SHE-BERAKH*

מִי שֶׁבֵּרַךְ *Mi she-Berakh* is a chance for the congregation to ask God's blessing for the person(s) who just had an *aliyah*. Sometimes this is done in a standard way. If you have an *aliyah* you get a *Mi she-Berakh*. Sometimes if something special is happening in your life—if you have had a baby, if you are getting married, if there is some other honor—the congregation gives you an *aliyah* so that you can be given a *Mi she-Berakh*. More and more, older traditions that use *Mi she-Berakh* as an opportunity to ask God for healing are becoming part of congregational life. Many congregations invite everyone to contribute the names of people in need of healing.

Mi she-Berakh is a moment where a congregation celebrates being a community. It is a chance to celebrate and seek strength with each other.

NOTE: There is no fixed text for *Mi she-Berakh*. Different *siddurim* offer different texts for different situations. It is more an opportunity than a fixed set of words.

> The *Mi she-Berakh* is not a magical incantation. It obligates the *oleh* to give *tzedakah* and to pray personally on behalf of the person for whom the prayer is given. It summons us all to recognize our own utter powerlessness in the face of illness (Danny Landes, *My People's Prayer Book* [Jewish Lights, 1997]).

GOD'S PARTNER

Abraham Joshua Heschel (not the one who made a major impact on American Jewry) was the Rabbi of Apt. He once heard that in a village near his city there was a shopkeeper who was doing miracles. If a person was sick and he asked God's blessing for him or her, that person got better. When he prayed for a person to succeed in business, that person's business improved. No one could figure out why the shopkeeper's prayers seemed to be so effective—there was nothing particularly unusual about him.

Finally, after hearing more and more stories about the miracle-working shopkeeper, Rabbi Abraham went and directly asked him, "Why does God listen to your prayers?" The shopkeeper said, "I don't really know why. Perhaps it is because I trust God.

"Whenever I am distressed, whenever things go wrong, I give away much of what I have to help others. Helping others often helps me. Once I was feeding a poor man when a government official showed up and demanded that I go with him. Because feeding the poor is a *mitzvah* that comes from God, I told the official I could not go until I finished a task for a higher authority. He said 'Okay' and never came back.

"Once I lost almost everything I owned when business turned bad. My wife quoted an old Jewish saying, 'Change your location and change your luck.' She told me to go to another town and find a partner to go into business with me. I left and started to look for a partner, but then I asked myself, 'Why should I trust a human partner when I can ask God to be my partner? I can trust no human partner the way I trust God.' I asked God to be my partner. I went home, managed to borrow some money, and got back into business. Since that day I have kept two cash boxes in my business. I put half the money in one box for me and half the money in the other box for God. God's money I use for *tzedakah*."

When Rabbi Abraham heard this he said, "I understand. When one partner makes a commitment, Jewish law says that the other partner must help to fulfill it. When the shop owner makes a commitment, God must help with it" (Reworked from Rabbi Abraham J. Twerski, *Prayerfully Yours : Creating the Bond Between Man and His Maker* [Shaar Press/Artscroll Mesorah Publications, 2010).

When we ask God for a blessing we commit ourselves to doing all we can to make that blessing come true. Actualizing blessings is part of being God's partner. In our partnership God gives us the resources to make blessings happen, and we point out the blessings that are needed. There are many questions, but there is a simple one: "How are you God's partner?"

וְזֹאת הַתּוֹרָה *V'ZOT HA-TORAH*

הַגְבָּהָה *Hagbahah* is a ceremony that happens during the Torah reading. Sephardic Jews do *hagbahah* before the reading from the Torah. Ashkenazic Jews do *hagbahah* after the reading from the Torah. During *hagbahah* the Torah scroll is held up and the portions that were or are to be read are shown to the congregation.

Hagbahah is the acting out of a story we read about in the book of Neḫemiah. When the Jews came home from the Babylonian Exile they had trouble getting organized and unified. Ezra the Scribe came with a *Sefer Torah* and gathered the people by the Water Gate. The Torah was read from beginning to end, and it became a new beginning for the Jewish people. As part of the ceremony Ezra had the text of the Torah shown to the people. It brought the words of the Torah off the stage and into direct contact with each of the people who were gathered to hear the reading.

Today, when we lift the Torah as part of the *Hagbahah* ceremony, it is a tradition to hold up one of the *tzitziyot* (fringes) on our *tallit* that we then bring to our lips. It is as if we are kissing the very words we have read (or are to read). We also sing a prayer assembled out of a number of biblical verses. These words that begin *V'Zot ha-Torah* connect the words of the Torah to God.

HOW I LEARNED TO STUDY TORAH

There was a ten-year-old boy who refused to study Torah. His parents tried all the usual parent things: yelling, punishing, begging, and crying. None of these worked. When the greatest Hasidic Rebbe of their generation, Aaron of Karlin, visited their little stetl, they brought the problem to him. The Rebbe looked at the little boy, who stood defiantly. His gaze was down, his arms were folded. The Rebbe told the parents, "Leave him here with me for two hours. I'll give him a talking-to that he'll never forget!"

As soon as the parents had left, the Rebbe went up to the little boy and slowly, tenderly, put his arms around him. The boy was stiff at first but then slowly allowed himself to be hugged. He relaxed and was finally squeezed against the breast of the great man. He stood there hearing the Rebbe's heartbeat. Their breath flowed in and out together.

On the way home the parents looked at their little boy. Was there any change? They stopped at the butcher's. The butcher slapped a piece of meat on the counter. The boy said, "That butcher is angry. What happened to him to make him feel that way?"

From then on the boy was somehow more in touch with people, attuned to their feelings, interested in their stories. That week when he heard others discussing the Torah he suddenly realized that the Torah was the stories of people! He became fascinated with them. What made the people act that way?

Immediately he began to read the stories for himself. Within a year his teachers saw him as their most talented student. Once two neighbors were arguing over the purchase of a calf. The

> boy went up to them and said, "There's a way for both of you to get what you want." He showed them a workable compromise. Before long, adult villagers were bringing their quarrels to the boy, and he would point out to them the solutions that had been in their hearts.
>
> Years later, when he was known as the greatest Rebbe of his generation, his disciples would sit around him and ask: "How did you get your deep insight into the Torah?" The boy, now the Rebbe, answered: "I learned everything when the Rabbi, Aaron of Karlin, hugged me" (Retold from a telling by Doug Lipman from *Chosen Tales: Stories Told by Jewish Storytellers*, edited by Peninnah Schram [Jason Aronson, 1995]).

This is a story about stories. It is the Rebbe's heart that interests the boy in stories. Stories connect him to Torah. Torah demands that the boy get involved with people's stories. The story says getting involved with stories is getting involved with people. When the Torah is lifted and shown to the congregation we ask ourselves: "How am I connected to the Torah?" "How are its stories my stories?" "Whose life stories connect me to Torah?"

בִּרְכוֹת הַהַפְטָרָה
HAFTARAH BLESSINGS

הַפְטָרָה *Haftarah* is not "Half Torah." It comes from a Hebrew root that means "completion". The *Haftarah* is a reading from the prophets that is read after the Torah portion on Shabbat and holidays as the "completion" of the Torah reading.

The origins of the *Haftarah* readings are not clear. The oldest story about the *haftarah* is this: Before the story of H̲anukkah happened, before the Jews fought back, Antiochus IV banned many Jewish practices. Among the new rules he created was "No more reading Torah." Jews were good at getting around such orders. Antiochus banned Torah readings, not readings from the prophets. So they created the *haftarah*. They picked passages from the prophets that reminded them of the Torah readings. They read these passages as a replacement for the Torah portion of the week. Later, when they could again read Torah, these passages were kept and added to the weekly readings *(Sefer Abudarham)*.

The reading of the *Haftarah* is very much like the reading of the Torah. There are blessings that are said before and after it. One blessing is said before the reading of the *Haftarah*. Traditionally, four blessings are said after the *Haftarah* reading, though in some Reform congregations they say only one.

The person who reads the *Haftarah* is called the *Maftir*. Traditionally, the *Maftir* also has the last *aliyah* of the Torah reading. The *haftarah* is usually read out of a book (although some congregations have scrolls) and has its own *trope* (melodies used for chanting). In addition to one *haftarah* portion for every Torah portion, there are special *haftarah* readings for Jewish holidays and other special *shabbatot*.

> Five blessings surround the reading of the *haftarah*; one is said before, and four are traditionally said afterwards. The five blessings connect the *haftarah* to the Torah (which has five books). They teach us that the words of the prophets are the equal of the words of the Torah (Abudarham).

THE REAL JEW

Rabbi Mendele Sokolover had a mission. He was looking for a "real Jew." He went on a search for a Jew who fully lived a life of Torah. The rabbi found many good Jews, but he found the person he was looking for in Moshe, the water carrier. A water carrier was a person who was paid a few pennies to draw water out of the well and then carry buckets of water to the houses of the rich. Water carrier was a low- level job from the days before indoor plumbing.

Moshe lived in Sokolov, and when he was not carrying water he could usually be found with a book of Psalms in his hand. When Mendele became the Rabbi of Sokolov he tried to talk to Moshe, but the man said little. One night the rabbi was walking through the streets of the town and he found a party of water carriers, shoemakers, and tailors. There he learned the story of a "true Jew."

Moshe was fed up with his poor life. He was sad to see his wife growing old too fast. He was pained to watch his children walk around in rags and have too little to eat. One night he went into the empty synagogue and prayed to God, asking for help. The next morning he went to work. In the middle of the day he was delivering water when he found a thousand-ruble note in the mud. He picked it up and thanked God. With joy he saw all the things he would be able to buy his family. That evening he came to synagogue for evening prayers and found H̱annale, the widow of another water carrier, crying bitterly. She had lost the thousand rubles the water carriers had collected for her when her husband died.

Moshe did not go into the *shul* to pray. He began screaming at God, "Why did You have to give me H̱annale's rubles? What kind of God are You? I don't want to have anything to do with You anymore." Then Moshe did what he knew he had to do. He found H̱annale and returned the money. At that moment his whole life changed. He said, "I knew that my life would never be different. I knew that my children would always wear used clothing. I knew that there would never be enough food on our table. But I knew how good it felt to be a Jew and to live the Torah." His friends made a party in his honor, and the rabbi joined them (From a story told by Eugene Labovitz in *Time for My Soul: a Treasury of Jewish Stories for Our Holy Days* [Northvale: Jason Aronson, 1996]).

The opening *Haftarah* blessing says "Who chose through Torah, and through Moses, God's servant, and through Israel God's people and through the prophets of truth and justice." This is the story of taking that blessing seriously. We have the story of a man who, against his own best interests, against his dreams, does the right thing. The prophets set justice as the prime Jewish value. He is someone living up to the challenge of the prophets. We finish the *Haftarah* reading and think, "Does my life reflect Prophetic values?" "Do I walk in the footsteps of the Prophets?" "Would I have returned the money?"

INTRODUCTION TO THE *BRAKHOT* AFTER THE *HAFTARAH*

Reading the Torah is a lot like eating. Reading the *Haftarah* is a lot like reading the Torah. We say a blessing before and after eating, and we do the same with Torah (*Brakhot* 21a). Based on the Torah pattern, we say blessings before and after the *Haftarah* (and before and after the Purim *Megillah*, too).

Rabbi B.S. Jacobson wrote in his commentary on the Siddur that the reason that the Rabbis created the blessings after the *Haftarah* was to make clear the differences between Jews and Samaritans. The Samaritans are a group that are a lot like the Jews. They have a Torah and many holidays that are similar to ours but are still very different. Once Jews were in competition with the Samaritans over who were the true Jews. Today there are very few Samaritans, but we still have the full set of five *Haftarah* blessings. These blessings remind us of the central things that Jews believe.

BLESSING ONE (BEFORE THE *HAFTARAH*): This *brakhah* thanks God for the prophets and states that their words are true. Here we state that the truth that came through Moses into the Torah is continued in the teaching of the prophets.

BLESSING TWO: The central theme of this *brakhah* is the statement that God is "The One Whose every word is dependable." This blessing is the follow-up to the "God speaks the truth" theme of the opening *brakhah*.

The next three *brakhot* will list some of the promises made through the prophets on which we can depend.

BLESSING THREE: We can trust that Jerusalem (and the Temple) will be rebuilt. This does not only mean that the State of Israel will be reborn (the way it was) but that "the exile of the Jewish people" will end.

BLESSING FOUR: Next comes the arrival of the Messiah (or the Messianic Age). This is the next step in the redemption.

BLESSING FIVE: The last blessing is about Shabbat. It is the wrap-up. We read the *Haftarah* on Shabbat. Shabbat is also the advance sample of the *Olam ha-Ba*. Through the celebration of Shabbat, through the words of the prophets read on Shabbat we move towards a Messianic future. The Reform, Conservative, and Reconstructionist movements have all made changes in these blessings.

THE CLOTHES THAT WENT TO A WEDDING

Elijah was the prophet who did not die. He flew up to heaven, alive, in a flaming chariot. Legend teaches that he will come back again, helping to bring the Messiah. Legend also teaches that from time to time Elijah comes and visits people, teaching interesting lessons.

Once, dressed like a beggar, Elijah came to join in a wedding. His clothing was torn and dirty. His hair was oily and matted. They threw him out. They thought he was trying to crash the wedding just to eat the free food.

An hour later he returned. This time he was dressed in an expensive suit. He was walking with a fine cane with a golden handle. On his head was a very elegant sable hat. When he entered the room the guests all stood out of respect for this distinguished visitor. The bride and groom came up to him and asked him to join their table. He nodded and sat near them.

The first course was a piece of gefilte fish. The old man picked up his fish and put it in one of his pockets. He added a scoop of horseradish on top of it. When the soup was served, he poured it into another pocket. This time he asked for the salt and

> sprinkled a little of it into the soup pocket, saying, "It needed just a little."
>
> Each time a course was served, this stranger shoved it into one of his pockets. The string beans wound up sticking out of his vest.
>
> Finally, the stranger stood, took his glass of wine, said, "A toast to the bride and groom," and then spilled the wine over his sleeve. When he finished there was complete silence in the room. Many people sat with their mouths open. Elijah let the silence hang while he looked around the room. Then he said, "When I first came here dressed as a beggar you threw me out. When I returned dressed in expensive clothing you welcomed me and showed me respect. It is obvious that you were respecting my clothes, not me. So when you asked me to join in your feast, I let the clothes eat. They were your real guests." Elijah laughed and then disappeared. Left on the chair was his gold-handled cane.

I have known this story for a long time. My telling is probably influenced by hearing Peninnah Schram's telling. She transcribed it in *Tales of Elijah the Prophet (*Northvale: Jason Aronson, 1991). She attributes the story to Bar Ami Segel, *Elijah der Prophet, Cine Studie Zür Judischen Volks—Und Sagenkunde* (Ost und West Berlin, 1904).

The closing *Haftarah* blessings connect the prophets to a redemptive image. Elijah is a prophet who is directly connected to the redemption. That is clearly his role at seder, *Havdalah*, and circumcisions. This particular story is one of many that show Elijah either rewarding good behavior and/or challenging poor behavior. Elijah stands as a symbol that justice can happen, that things that should be stopped can be stopped and things that should be rewarded will be rewarded. Many people have Elijah moments. Mine happened in New York when I left a notebook I needed in a cab and two hours later the cabdriver dropped the notebook back at the hotel. Do you have a personal Elijah story?

ENDING THE TORAH SERVICE

The Torah service ends by revisiting the metaphors we used at the beginning.

- We took out the Torah we started by lifting the Ark that led us through the wilderness.
- We remembered when David brought the Ark up to Jerusalem.
- We visited Mt. Sinai and recalled hearing Torah through Moses and remembered hearing Torah directly from God.
- We had an experience of feeling close to God.

יְהַלְלוּ *Y'HAL'LU*

A call to praise God.

הוֹדוֹ עַל אֶרֶץ *HODO AL ERETZ*

A short *"halleluyah"*—a quick praising of God.

מִזְמוֹר לְדָוִד *MIZMOR L'DAVID (PSALM 29)*

This psalm echoes the words reported in 1 Chronicles 16:28-9 that David sang as he moved the Ark to its permanent place in the Temple (*Ha-Mikra v'ha-Mesorah*).

וּבְנֻחֹה יֹאמַר *U'V'NUKHOH YOMAR*

This paragraph is made up of a number of biblical verses strung together to connect two themes: the return of the Ark (which parallels the return of the Torah to our ark) and the return of the relationship between God and Israel (that is what we hope the reading of Torah will accomplish). עֵץ חַיִּים הִיא *Etz Hayyim Hi* (It is a tree of life) and הֲשִׁיבֵנוּ *Hashiveinu* (Return us) are part of this second part. The Reform Movement skips the first part of this paragraph.

THE TORAH IS A TREE OF LIFE

God hid the tree that gave eternal life to those who ate from it, and in its place God gave us the Torah. We know this because it says "IT IS A TREE OF LIFE TO THOSE WHO HOLD FAST TO IT" (Proverbs 3:18). When a person studies it and sees God's wisdom in it—and God's righteousness and God's just laws and statutes—that person can be immediately induced into a new state of mind.

When a person does this it comes with reward in this world and reward in the next world. We know this because it says "THE ETERNAL COMMANDED US TO OBSERVE ALL THESE LAWS FOR OUR LASTING GOOD AND TO GRANT US LIFE" (*Deuteronomy* 6:24) (*Midrash ha-Gadol, Bereshit* 3:24).

The Tree of Life was planted in the Garden of Eden. When we return the Torah we sing עֵץ חַיִּים הִיא *Etz Hayyim Hi* (It is a Tree of Life...). Here is an obvious connection. That which was given for free in the Garden of Eden can be earned through acts of Torah (study and practice). We are told that Torah can "change our state of mind." It is not just laws and stories. It is a way of seeing and living life. Ask yourself: "Is Torah bringing you closer to eternity?" "Is Torah improving your state of mind?"

ARCHIK'S TORAH

During the Russian Revolution it was often hard to get food. Students at the Chofetz Chayim's yeshiva were starving. One Shabbat afternoon on the way home from services, the Chofetz Chayim ran into Archik. Archik had been a yeshiva student, but he was now a communist and the local commissar.

The Chofetz Chayim said, *Gut Shabbos* to him. He said, "Saturday is like any other day to me." "Good enough, because all days come from God," the Chofetz Chayim answered. Archik smiled, and the two of them talked for a while. Finally the rabbi asked the Bolshevik, "Would you like to hear a good piece of Torah?" The communist said, "No, thank you." "How about a good saying?" "Why not?" was Archik's answer.

The Chofetz Chayim said, "God put the Tree of Life in the middle of the garden and not on a side so that every person can have equal access. Every person can get to the Tree of Life in his own way. Some do it through studying Torah. Some do it through good deeds. Some do it through the strength of their heart. You could get to the Tree of Life, you could win a place in the *Olam ha-Ba* (the next world), by selling us a little food."

After Havdalah, as they were wishing each other *Shavu'ah Tov* (a good week) at the end of Shabbat, a wagon arrived at the yeshiva filled with flour and other foods (Variation of a story from Reb Shalom Shvadron that he heard from Ha-Rav Segal).

This story could easily be called "Communist does a *mitzvah*." It has the simple message that everyone has his own path to Torah—and that will assure him eternity (even if it is only in memory).

In the alternate version Archik is called Moshe, and the dialogue ends: "So listen to me, Moshe. If you take it upon yourself to personally support these forty families, then this is your path to the Tree of Life; because everyone has his path, no matter where he is situated, and this road is yours." Moshe answers, "Rabbi, it's a deal...If everyone were like you, Rabbi, we wouldn't need Bolsheviks in the world!"

As we finish the Torah service we are moving from Torah as an idea, Torah as a body of content, to Torah as action. We are moving toward Torah as redemption. We will get to that in *Hashiveinu*. For the moment, ask yourself: "How is my Torah turning into actions?"

THE SEVEN SHEPHERDS

One Shabbat Rabbi Isaac Luria, the Holy Ari, told his disciples, "If you can keep from saying a word other than the prayers, and if you can keep from laughing, I will call the seven shepherds to read from the Torah." All of the students knew who the shepherds were, and readily agreed. They prayed with great intensity. When it came time to read the Torah, the Ari called Aaron, the first High Priest, for the first *aliyah*. Aaron said the blessings and read from the Torah. Aaron had been a shepherd of sheep and a shepherd of people. Moses was called for the next *aliyah*. He, too, had been a

> shepherd. Abraham, Isaac, Jacob, and Joseph were called for the next four *aliyot*. For the seventh *aliyah* the Holy Ari called King David. He came from the back of the synagogue. He was dancing and jumping and singing. He was filled with spirit and energy. One of the students laughed with joy. It broke the moment. David vanished. The Ari came to the *bimah* and took the final *aliyah*. It was quiet and sad. All knew that the Messiah would have been the *Maftir*, the one to read the *Haftarah* (*Hemdat ha-Yamin, Shabbat* 81a).

When we say חַדֵּשׁ יָמֵינוּ כְּקֶדֶם *Hadesh Yameinu k'Kedem* (Renew our days as of old) we are asking for redemption. It is a call for David's descendent to come back, be the Messiah, and rule over Israel. Israel is then to lead the whole world into peace and prosperity. That's the traditional view. More liberal theology, which speaks of a Messianic Era, makes this a metaphor for getting the world back to its ideal form, or maybe, finally making it all right. This comes at the end of the Torah service, because Torah is going to be our guide to finally making it all right. We sum up the Torah service thinking about the once and future redemption. We ask ourselves, "How is Torah helping us to bring the best possible future?"

CONCLUDING SERVICE

אֵין כֵּאלֹהֵינוּ *EIN KELOHEINU*

אֵין כֵּאלֹהֵינוּ *Ein Keloheinu* is a hymn, a song that is sung near the end of the service. In the traditional pattern (also found in Conservative services) it comes after the מוּסָף *Musaf* (additional) service. Reform synagogues do not have *Musaf,* and they often use *Ein Keloheinu* as a closing hymn. In Sephardic (and H̲asidic) services *Ein Keloheinu* is said every morning. In the Ashkenazic tradition it is said only on Shabbat.[4]

אֵין כֵּאלֹהֵינוּ *EIN KELOHEINU* MATH

It is a *mitzvah* to say one hundred *brakhot* a day. The Shabbat *Amidah* has only seven, while the weekday *Amidah* has eighteen. That leaves us eleven short for each of three services, or a total of thirty-three. The *Musaf* service with its *Amidah* makes up seven of them. We still need twenty-six. Six of them come in the blessings for the "extra," third meal on Shabbat afternoon. The other twenty times are taken from the twenty times we mention God directly in this prayer (four names times five verses). In addition we have בָּרוּךְ *Barukh,* אַתָּה *Attah,* and even אָמֵן *Amen.* Amen comes from the verses that begin אֵין *Ein,* מִי *Mi,* and נוֹדֶה *Nodeh.* (*Rashi's Siddur*)

THE SPICE CONNECTION

The last verse of *Ein Keloheinu* (not usually said in Reform congregations) talks about the spices burned as incense in the Temple. This is followed in the Traditional Siddur by a paragraph from the Talmud that gives the formula for the incense. We are told two interesting things about that incense. First, that by just listing its formula we are given credit for fulfilling the *mitzvah* of burning it (*Darkhei Moshe* on the *Tur* 233). Second, prayers go up to heaven just like incense (*Psalms* 141:2).

[4]Sephardic Jews are Jews who come from countries with dominant Islamic influence. Ashkenzic Jews come from countries with dominant Christian influence. Spain has had both influences. Sephardic comes from the Hebrew word *S'pharad*, which means Spain.

THE TEMPLE

The Traditional Siddur has many passages about the Temple and our desire to have another one. The Reform Siddur has cut out all (or just about all) references to the Temple, stating that we have no desire to have another Temple. The Conservative Movement keeps most of the Temple passages but usually explains them as an historical memory and not the hope for an actual new Temple.

THE INCENSE OFFERING

> Every one of the *Kohanim* (priests) wanted to be the one to give the incense offering in the Temple. The incense offering was burnt over fire, and a cloud of smoke rose up toward the heavens, up to God. No one ever got to do it twice, because everyone wanted to do it. It was believed that offering this giving would make you rich (*Yoma* 26a).
>
> There is a rule in the Torah that the formula for the incense could only be used in the Temple. No one could practice making it. No one could make it for his own use. One family in Jerusalem used to mix all of the spices for the incense in the Temple. They taught the secret to no one. To prove that they were not using the formula to their own advantage, none of them ever wore perfume, not even at their weddings (*Kritot* 5).

In the Torah we learn that God has a sense of smell. When Noah offers a sacrifice, the Torah tells us, "And when the Eternal smelled the pleasing odor, the Eternal said in God's heart, 'I will never again curse the ground because of people, for the imagination of people's heart is evil from youth; neither will I ever again destroy every living creature as I have done' (Genesis 8:21). Based on this passage, the one way we know we get to God is via smell. God's apparent sense of smell translates into the incense burned in the Temple. When we remember the incense, we remember that our prayers can reach God. The story that everyone wants to burn the incense is the story that everyone wanted to reach God. For us, we want our prayers to reach God. We sing *Ein Keloheinu* with its praises, hoping that our prayers will make it to God. Ask: "What do I have to do to have my blessing reach God? What to I have to do to have my blessing reach the God within me?"

עָלֵינוּ *ALEINU*

עָלֵינוּ *Aleinu* is a prayer with history.

- There is a memory that Joshua first said *Aleinu* after the Families of Israel defeated the city of Jericho. When "the walls came tumbling down," Joshua knew that God was The Ruler and the One Who deserves praise (*Kol Bo, Rav Hai Gaon, Sha'arei T'shuvah*, 43).
- There is another memory that Rav, a Babylonian rabbi from the third century, wrote the *Aleinu* or reclaimed *Aleinu* and made it part of the *Musaf* service on Rosh ha-Shanah. There it was used to introduce the theme of God as Ruler and us as subject to God's rule (*Otzar ha-T'fillah, Iyyun T'fillah*).
- In 1171, during the persecution of the Jews of Blois, France, thirty-four Jewish men and seventeen Jewish women falsely accused of ritual murder died as martyrs at the stake. An eyewitness wrote to Rabbi Jacob of Orleans, "Their death was accompanied by a mysterious song resounding through the stillness of the night. It caused the gentiles who heard it from a distance to wonder at the melodious strains, the likes of which had never before been heard." The martyrs had sung *Aleinu* as their dying prayer (*Yosef ha-Kohen, Emek ha-Bakha,"Valley of Tears"*).
- By the 1400s the *Aleinu* had become one of the concluding prayers of every service, probably because of the memory of the way that martyrs used it as a song of faith.
- At the turn of the fifteenth century Pesach Peter, an apostate Jew, spread the lie that part of the *Aleinu* was used to slur Christianity.
- Today *Aleinu* is one of the prayers that is most changed in various editions of the Siddur.

Rabbi Joel Sirkes wrote "*Aleinu* is a theological summary at the end of the service reminding us of God's unity and the ultimate goal of eradicating idolatry."

JOSHUA SAYS *ALEINU*

Joshua's life was filled with close calls. He was an orphan who had no place and was then chosen by Moses to be his assistant. Joshua found a place. Joshua was chosen to lead the battle against Amalek. When Moses raised his hands inviting God's help, Joshua and the Army of Israel won. When Moses let his hands down, Israel lost. When Aaron and H̲ur held up Moses' hands and they stayed in the air, with God's help, Israel was victorious.

When Israel needed spies to check out the Land of Israel, Moses changed Joshua's name. His name had been הוֹשֵׁעַ *Hoshea* (He has saved). It became יְהוֹשֻׁעַ *Yehoshua* (God will save). Moses changed Joshua's name as a prayer: "May God save you from misunderstanding your mission as the spies will misunderstand theirs." When ten of the spies chickened out on their mission, Joshua and Kalev retained faith that with God's help Israel could win.

Almost forty years later Joshua led the Families of Israel into the land of Canaan. He came to Jericho and found it a walled city—just about impossible to conquer. For seven days Israel marched around the city. On the seventh day they blew *shofarot* and shouted. With God's help the walls came crashing down, and Israel was victorious. When the battle was over, when the city was taken, Joshua told the people:

עָלֵינוּ לְשַׁבֵּחַ לַאֲדוֹן הַכֹּל

Aleinu l'Shabei'ah̲ la'Adon ha-Kol

It is our job to praise the Master of All.

Think of *Aleinu* as a victory song. We take Joshua's moment of triumph and move it to express our own sense of triumph. We, too, have victories. God is part of our victories, and our victories should move the world toward God's vision of how we should live. Put yourself back with Joshua. Understand the "walls come tumbling down" moment and ask what memory of yours is closest to that moment. "When do I feel that God helped me succeed?"

THE תִּקּוּן עוֹלָם *TIKKUN OLAM* STORY

In the third paragraph of the *Aleinu* (not found in all Reform Siddurim) we ask God לְתַקֵּן עוֹלָם בְּמַלְכוּת שַׁדַּי *L'Taken Olam b'Malkhut Shaddai* (to fix the world through the Kingdom of the One on High). While this is not the origin of the phrase תִּקּוּן עוֹלָם *tikkun olam*, it is the place where we see its popular usage.

Also think of this as the finale of the service. As in a Broadway show, we string together all of the hits and add a final bit of energy and a twist. We review creation, revelation, and redemption and echo the *Shema* with בַּיּוֹם הַהוּא יִהְיֶה יי אֶחָד וּשְׁמוֹ אֶחָד *Ba-Yom ha-Hu Yih'yeh Adonai Eh̲ad u'Shemo Eh̲ad* (On that day the Eternal shall be One and God's name shall be One.) The story of *tikkun olam* is the Humpty Dumpty of Jewish mysticism. It is where all of us work hard and put God back together again. This story will reveal how "God becomes One."

Close your eyes (or imagine with your eyes open). Imagine everywhere in the cosmos. Imagine every when in the universe. Fill all space and all time with light. Even though we can't see God, we will think of the light as God, because God is everywhere and every when.

God decides that God wants to create the cosmos, the universe, the world, and people, but there is nowhere to do it. If God is everywhere, then anything that God creates would be "toasted" by the light. Remember, no one can get too close to God. No one can see God's face and live.

So watch God do something amazing. God breathes in and leaves a hole inside of the everywhere where there is no God. Think of it as a dark room in the middle of everywhere. Inside that room God creates everything: cosmos, universe, world, and people.

But God now has a problem. God has created people in the one place where there is no God. That doesn't work at all. So imagine this. God places a bunch of empty glass light bulbs in that space. Then slowly, carefully, God begins to breathe a little light back into the containers. Imagine lots of sparks of light flying like fireflies into those light bulbs, bringing the right amount of God close to people.

> Next there is an accident. Imagine the light bulbs shattering. Imagine that a jumble of sparks and broken glass tumble down together. God can do nothing about it. God can't come into the room or there will be too much God there and everything will be toasted.
>
> God can only tell us to take a broom and start sweeping. It is our job to sweep the glass into one pile, and gather the sparks of God's light in another. When all the light is gathered, everything will be great. This is called תִּקּוּן עוֹלָם *tikkun olam,* "repair the every and always." A rabbi named Isaac Luria used this story to explain our job (From the Lurianic creation myth).

This story transfers the responsibility for fixing the world from God to us. God serves as the vision, the inspiration, the source, but all the work is ours. We have to find the pieces and make a whole. It makes being "God's partner" a very active role. We get asked the question "What have I done to fix the world? Recently?"

THE JEWEL

This jewel was the biggest and the best of all the jewels that came out of the mine. The king wanted it from the minute he saw it. It was the best. He had to have it. He said, "If it is the best, if it is the biggest, it is mine!"

The king had first seen the jewel when he was visiting his ruby mine. He saw it lying in a wagon of unpolished stones. He picked it up, put it in his pocket, said, "Mine," and walked out of the mine. He knew it was the biggest and the best. The king didn't need to see anything else.

The king gave the giant ruby to the royal jeweler. He said to him, "Polish it. Make it perfect." The jeweler put the ocular in his eye. He looked at every side of the ruby. He looked it over and over again. Finally, in a soft and shaky, voice he said, "Your Majesty, there is a crack in this stone."

The king said, "So fix it."

The jeweler said, "I am sorry, Your Majesty, but it cannot be done."

The king went and got another royal jeweler. This one put in his ocular. This one also looked and looked. After a long time this one said, "Your Majesty, the best thing we can do is cut the big stone into three beautiful smaller stones. Each one of the three will be wonderful."

The king said, "Then it will not be the biggest or the best." The king went and got a new royal jeweler. The king got a lot of new royal jewelers because not one of them knew how to fix a crack in a large and beautiful ruby.

The king left the ruby on the table. One day a visitor came to the palace. He said, "Your Majesty, may I look at your stone?" The king gave permission. The visitor took out his ocular and looked and looked. After a long time he said, "I can make your stone into something beautiful."

The king asked, "Will it be big? Will it be beautiful? Will it be perfect?"

The visitor said, "Yes. Yes. Yes." He took the stone and went into the workshop. Everywhere in the palace you could hear the grinding and the polishing. It took three days.

The visitor came before the king with the jewel under a black cloth. The king asked, "Is it still big?" The visitor nodded. "Is it still beautiful?" The visitor nodded. "Is it perfect?" The visitor nodded. Then the king asked, "How did you get rid of the crack?"

The visitor said, "The crack is still here, Your Majesty."

The king started to say, "But, but, but, but..." when the visitor pulled the cloth off the ruby. Everyone in the palace gasped. The stone was huge. It was beautiful. And at the center of the stone was now carved a wonderful rose. The crack had become a stem.

The king opened his mouth and said, "Wow!" Then the king did something unusual. He stopped talking. He just looked and looked at the jewel. Later he rewarded the jeweler. He showed everyone who came to the palace his jewel with a rose. At the end of the story the king told everyone, "I learned the most important lesson of my life that day."

> Things in the kingdom were much better from that day on (A story of the Maggid of Dubnow).

This story is the classic *tikkun olam* story. It is about finding the perfection in a flaw. It is about fixing. When we say *Aleinu* we face the cracked jewel that is the world we live in. We are looking for the possibility of the rose. We are looking for a way to make the kingdom much better. Ask yourself "What is my vision of redemption?" "How well do I see the fixes that are needed?"

קַדִּישׁ *KADDISH*

When the Babylonians destroyed Jerusalem and carried away all the survivors as prisoners, the Jews started *yeshivot* (Torah schools) in Babylon. Later, when Ezra and Ne<u>h</u>emiah organized the return to the Land of Israel, they started new *yeshivot*. No matter what difficulties they faced, no matter how sad they were, Jews gathered to study the Torah and fit it into their lives. The קַדִּישׁ *Kaddish* started out as a prayer said at the end of study sessions. It said "God is great" and "we can find the strength to go on" (*Sotah* 49a).

The *Kaddish* is said seven times a day because of Psalms 119:164: "SEVEN TIMES A DAY I WILL PRAISE YOU." There are five kinds of *Kaddishim*: (1) *<u>H</u>atzi Kaddish,* which divides one part of a service from another. (2) *Kaddish Shalem,* said at the end of the *Amidah.* (3) *Kaddish Yatom,* the mourner's *Kaddish.* (4) *Kaddish D'Rabbanan*, the Rabbis' *Kaddish*, said at the end of a study session. (5) *Kaddish Le'it-<u>h</u>adeta,* said after a burial or after finishing a book of the Talmud.

Even though *Kaddish* is said for many other purposes, it became most famous as a prayer said by mourners. Rabbi Isaac Luria taught, "When *Kaddish Yatom* is said for eleven months by mourners, it helps to move a soul from *Gehinom* (purgatory) to *Gan Eden* (paradise). When *Kaddish* is said on a *Yahrzeit* it helps to lift a soul to higher levels of paradise."

The *Kaddish* is made up of ten expressions of praise. It is also a prayer that needs a *minyan*, a community of ten. In the *Zohar* we are taught (*A<u>h</u>arei Mot*), "The person for whom *Kaddish* is being said gets credit for gathering ten Jews." We are also told there, "The words of the *Kaddish* make God feel better."

DREAM *KADDISH*

An old woman was in her bedroom in Prague. The angel of death entered and got ready to take her. She said, "Not yet." He said, "What's wrong?" She said, "I was the maid for the rabbi, and the community takes good care of me, but

> I need someone to say *Kaddish* for me." The angel asked, "Do you have a relative?" The woman answered, "I have a great-grandson I have never met. He lives in Germany." "That can be arranged," said the angel.
>
> That night the woman died. The people of Prague found her with a big smile on her face. That night Joseph, her great-grandson, had a dream. In that dream an old woman in white appeared. She put his face in her hands and said, "I am your great-grandmother. Say *Kaddish* for me. There is no one else to do it but you."
>
> Joseph woke in the morning. He barely remembered the old woman who lived in Prague. He had nothing to do with his family any more. He had nothing to do with the Jewish people either. He went to his dresser and took out his bar mitzvah *tallit*. He had not thought about it in years. He took it and started to walk.
>
> He walked and walked through the city, through the forest, past fields—not knowing where he was going, but knowing where he should go. He came to a small Jewish village and made his way to the synagogue. He told his story to the *shamash*, the spiritual custodian of the *shul*. The *shamash* taught him the words of the *Kaddish*. He said it every day for eleven months.
>
> When the year was over many things had changed. Joseph had sold his apartment in the city and moved to this village. He became part of the community. He met a woman, and they were ready to get married. In saying *Kaddish* Joseph found his way back to his people (Based on "Amen" in *Ze Zidovskeho Ghetta* by A. Hoffman and R. Heuerova, found in *Jewish Tales from Eastern Europe*, Nadia Grosser Nagarajan).

While *Kaddish* is thought of as a kindness to the deceased, it is also a transformative act for the person saying it. *Kaddish* heals and *Kaddish* clarifies. Much of this truth is not in the words, but in the ongoing practice. The words themselves are a simple statement of praise. But, the daily/weekly performance of an act of memory and reflection makes its impact felt. It is traditional for mourners to stand and for the congregation to remain seated. For a number of different reasons some congregations have everyone stand for *Kaddish*. In my synagogue the mourners stand, and the person next to the mourner stands and puts an arm around the mourner. No one says *Kaddish* alone. There are places in the *Kaddish* where everyone joins in, adding a louder voice to the solo performance of the mourner (if it is a solo performance). *Kaddish* can't be said alone. It takes a *minyan*. The very act of mourning binds one to the community that responds to you.

A TALE OF RABBI AKIVA

Rabbi Akiva was walking through a cemetery. He saw a naked man, covered in soot, carrying a huge bundle of wood on his head. The man was running with the load. He was shouting the Aramaic version of "I'm late. I'm late. If I don't finish they will make it worse." Rabbi Akiva asked the man, "Is there anything I can do to help? If you are poor, can I buy you out of this debt to these masters who are way too demanding?" The man said, "You are talking to a dead man. I am in *Gehinom*, the place one waits before going on to the Garden of Eden. I will be here forever. Every night they boil me in oil using the wood I collected."

Rabbi Akiva asked, "What is your name?" The man answered, "Akiva." Rabbi Akiva asked further, "What was your crime? What will help you to move on?" The man answered, "I was a tax collector, and I took bribes from the rich and taxed the poor to death to make it up. They told me that my only way out of *Gehinom* was for a child of mine to say the *Kaddish*. I need that child to count as one of my good deeds." In those days one said the *Kaddish* only at the end of Torah study. It was not a mourner's prayer. The person with the best Torah insight led it.

Rabbi Akiva left Akiva and went looking for the child. He found a son. The son was living as a non–Jew. He did not know even one Hebrew letter. The Jewish community had abandoned him. Rabbi Akiva began to teach him, but the son's heart was not in his studies. Akiva tried all his best teacher tricks—nothing worked.

Rabbi Akiva prayed to God and asked for the child's heart to be opened. Slowly the lessons went better. Once when Rabbi

> Akiva brought the son to a Torah study, the son was picked to lead the *Kaddish*. When the prayer was over, Akiva went to the Garden of Eden.
>
> That night Rabbi Akiva had a dream. In the dream he heard Akiva's voice: "You saved me from *Gehinom*. May your soul go quickly to the Garden of Eden in its time." In his dream Akiva said, "Eternal, Your Name lasts forever, Your memory is for all generations" (*Psalms* 102:13). This is when the mourner's *Kaddish* began (*Maḥzor Vitry*).

This post-Talmudic story is the classic statement of the motivation behind the mourners' *Kaddish*. While a lot of contemporary teaching argues that the *Kaddish* is "a prayer for the living" and just "a praising of God," the tradition connects it to the soul of the departed. We are acting to be one of our beloved's good deeds. We have a role in moving the soul from *Gehinom* to *Gan Eden*. When my Uncle Seymour died a Muslim cab driver took me from O'Hare Airport to my aunt's house. The driver taught me (from his version of the Koran) that when a good deed you do causes other good deeds, each derivative good deed is added to your total. Likewise, any bad deed that engenders more bad deeds is deducted from your score. Good deeds can keep growing. I've never forgotten that cab ride. When we say the *Kaddish* as mourners we ask, "Am I becoming a good deed?"

אֲדוֹן עוֹלָם *ADON OLAM*

אֲדוֹן עוֹלָם *Adon Olam* is a song that is sometimes sung at the beginning of services, often sung at the end of services, and sung at Moroccan Jewish weddings. It is a song that talks about God.

There are a number of *midrashim* that tell the story of Abraham discovering that there was only one God by looking at nature and by thinking about the world. In the Talmud we are told that Abraham was the first one to call God אֲדוֹן *Adon* (Master) (*Brakhot* 7b/*Genesis* 15.8) When we sing *Adon Olam* we are like Abraham discovering God in the world, God in our experience, and figuring out things about God through thinking. In the same Talmudic passage we are told that Daniel's prayers were answered only because of his connection as a descendent of Abraham. We, too, come from Abraham.

It is unsure who wrote *Adon Olam*. Various opinions include Rabban Yo<u>h</u>anan ben Zakkai, Rabbi Sherira Gaon or his son Rabbi <u>H</u>ai Gaon, and Solomon Ibn Gabirol. Our best guess, however, is that it started out as an evening prayer. The last verse, which talks about going to sleep and waking up safely—because God is with us—gives it away.

THE GREAT GARDEN

A ruler planted an amazing garden. In the middle of the garden the ruler had an amazing maze built. Each visitor received a letter from the ruler that said "Enter by the door of the maze and seek the center. There you will find what you have been seeking your whole life."

Many entered and became lost. They found the maze too hard, and they discovered enough beautiful places along the way that they gave up. Most people just enjoyed the hedge, the benches, and the flowers. They gave up their quest. Many of them cried out, "This is too hard. Why did you hide our hearts' desire in the center of a difficult maze?"

> Then they heard the ruler call out from the center, "It is only by seeking and wandering that you can be prepared to find me. The seeking is a necessary part of the finding." Then they realized that finding the ruler, being close to the ruler, was the thing they desired most (Drawn from *Chassidic Stories Retold*, edited by Edith Samuel).

Adon Olam is about the "wow factor." It tells the story of being transformed by the radical experience of the reality of God. You can turn God into any kind of "higher power" you want. But *Adon Olam* puts God at the center. God is the Ruler we were always seeking. If God doesn't work for you, enjoy singing with energy, but ask, "What am I seeking at the center of the maze of my life?"

קַבָּלַת שַׁבָּת KABBALAT SHABBAT

קַבָּלַת שַׁבָּת KABBALAT SHABBAT

On Friday night we have a very short service that is unlike any other service. It happens just before the evening service, and it is called *Kabbalat Shabbat*, "The Welcoming of Shabbat." It has three parts:

- six psalms and a poem(Psalms 95–99 and 29)
- the song לְכָה דוֹדִי *Lekha Dodi*
- a Shabbat psalm, plus another (Psalms 92–93)

This service goes back to the Israeli city of Tzfat, where it was created in the sixteenth century.

THE TALMUD

In the Talmud we are told that Rabbi Hanina would put on his best clothes and go outside to watch the sunset on *Erev Shabbat* (Friday night). He would sing "Come and let us go out and welcome Shabbat the Queen." Rabbi Yannai would do exactly the same thing except he would sing to Shabbat ,"Come, O bride, come, O bride!"

THE CITY OF TZFAT

In 1492 Columbus discovered America, and King Ferdinand and Queen Isabella declared the Spanish Inquisition. Jews began leaving Spain, Italy and other places in Europe because they were not allowed to practice their religion and live in peace. One of the places they gathered was the city of Tzfat. The city became a magnet for Kabbalists, Jewish mystics. These scholars turned the Talmudic description of Rabbi Hanina and Rabbi Yannai going out to welcome Shabbat into a service.

לְכָה דוֹדִי *LEKHA DODI*

Rabbi Shlomo ha-Levy, a Kabbalist from Tzfat, wrote a song to use at this service. It is לְכָה דוֹדִי *Lekha Dodi*.

Some things to know about *Lekha Dodi*:

- It has eight verses and spells out Shlomo ha-Levy's name in the first letter of each verse.
- It calls Shabbat both a Queen and a Bride.
- It talks about three things: Shabbat, Jerusalem, and the Redemption. (The Redemption is when God finally helps us to fix the world and make it into a place that is good for everyone.)

SHABBAT THE BRIDE

In the Midrash we are told this story. Shabbat went crying to God, saying, "I am all alone." She explained, "Every other day of the week has its own partner. Sunday has Monday. Tuesday has Wednesday. Thursday has Friday. I am the only own who is alone." God said to her, "Don't worry. The Families of Israel will be your partner" (*Genesis Rabbah* 11:8).

The idea of Shabbat as a bride comes from this story. Question: "How can the community of Israel and a day of the week be partners?"

Ahad ha-Am was a Zionist thinker who helped the modern state of Israel come to be. He taught, "More than Israel has kept Shabbat, Shabbat has kept Israel."

MORE ON *LEKHA DODI*

Verses one and two talk about Shabbat. Verses three to eight talk about Jerusalem being rebuilt. Verse eight adds the Messiah to this story. Verse nine brings us back to Shabbat.

There is a teaching in the Talmud: "Three things give us an advance sense of what the *Olam ha-Ba* (world to come) are like. They are Shabbat, sunshine, and wonderful smells" (*Brakhot* 57b).

One really big idea about Shabbat is that in its *shalom*, things that have been far apart can come back together again. Remember, *shalom* really means "whole" or "together."

When we make Shabbat at home, families that have drifted away from each other in the week's business can have a new sense of *shalom*, coming close again. Especially if two family members have been arguing, Shabbat is a perfect way to feel *shalom* again.

We are taught that the same is true of God and Israel. At times we can be far apart. When we welcome the Shabbat Queen into our house and our community, we are really inviting God in.

We are told in the Talmud that God often avoids places with sadness but comes close to a person who is in the middle of the joy of doing a *mitzvah* (*Shabbat* 30b).

SHABBAT STARTS WITH A SIGH

Rabbi Hanokh of Alexander told this story. "When I first became a rabbi this happened in my synagogue. A butcher was working and working. He didn't stop on Friday afternoon to get ready for Shabbat. He kept on chopping and chopping meat. Suddenly he realized that it might already be Shabbat. He was afraid that he had broken the Torah's rule and been working on the Sabbath. He ran directly to the synagogue. He didn't even take off his bloody apron. He burst through the doors and heard the first words of *Lekha Dodi*. He had just made it. He sighed a big sigh of relief. At that moment the sigh that came out of his mouth was the sigh of all the Jews who were in Egypt. They sighed to God out of their bondage. They, too, stopped their labor when Shabbat came (Martin Buber, *Tales of the Hasidim, Later Masters*).

At the end of *Lekha Dodi*, during the last verse, we turn toward the door and bow. This is the actual moment we welcome the Queen Shabbat. This story is rooted in a *midrash* (Exodus Rabbah 1:28) that Moses talked Pharaoh into letting Israel keep Shabbat while they were slaves. It was their first taste of freedom. Shabbat has two basic themes (rooted in the two sets of the Ten Commandments): that God rested on the seventh day and that God took us out of Egypt. This story connects those two themes into a single sigh. This is the sigh of the week ending and Shabbat beginning. The question: "When does your Shabbat sigh come?"

REBUILDING JERUSALEM

Lekha Dodi talks about the rebuilding of Jerusalem. Today we have a wonderful modern city of Jerusalem, but that is not the Jerusalem that is being talked about. This Jerusalem is an idea. It is a hope for the future.

The first set of the Ten Commandments was carved by God's own hand on two tablets of stone. When Moses saw the Golden Calf these tablets fell and broke. Israel did not leave the broken pieces sitting in the desert. They were stored in the Ark of the Covenant along with the second set of tablets that Moses carved with his hand.

Years later, on the same day as when the tablets were shattered, the walls of Jerusalem were broken by the Romans.

A teacher named the *S'fat Emet* taught a lesson about the connection between these two breaks. He taught, "Both of these breaks need to be healed. These pieces need to be put together again. When the pieces are put back together and these objects made whole, it will be a time of dancing and celebration. Israel will come out of exile. We will again be worthy to have the original Ten Commandments. It will be a time of joy."

THE SHABBAT SEDER

On Friday night there is a very short service that we do at our dinner table. It can include:

- Lighting of candles. Some families do this at the table; some families light candles quietly at the very beginning of Shabbat.
- *Shalom Aleikhem,* a song that welcomes angels to our home.
- Family blessings. Parents bless children. Husbands and wives recite wishes for each other.
- *Kiddush*, the prayer over wine that makes Shabbat holy.
- Washing of hands.
- *Ha-Motzi*, a blessing over bread to begin the meal.

שָׁלוֹם עֲלֵיכֶם *SHALOM ALEIKHEM*

שָׁלוֹם עֲלֵיכֶם *SHALOM ALEIKHEM*

שָׁלוֹם עֲלֵיכֶם *Shalom Aleikhem* is the song we use to welcome Shabbat into our home. It is based on two Talmudic stories that tell us that angels enter our home at the beginning of Shabbat. This song welcomes the angels, invites them in, asks them for blessing, and then bids them farewell.

Shalom Aleikhem can be a big family singing opportunity. It is the perfect change for the kind of loud singing that links people together. It is also the kind of song for which people link arms and sway. While we ask angels to bless us with *shalom* our singing can actually build *Shabbat Shalom*.

ANGELS

The angels you find in the Bible, the Talmud, the Midrash, and other Jewish works are not like those you find in movies and on television. Many movies show that angels are dead people that have gone to heaven. The Jewish tradition believes that angels are special creations of God. One of the angels' jobs is to sing praises to God. Another one of their jobs is to run errands for God. The Hebrew word for angels is מַלְאָךְ *mal'akh,* "messenger." A third job is to carry prayers from people to God. Angels also play a role in judging people.

In the *Zohar* we are taught that angels are packets of God's energy. It is as if God sends a small piece of God off to do a mission. When the angels are doing something on earth they can sometimes be in human form (*Zohar,* 1:34a, 8 la, 101a; *Pardes Rimmonim.* sect. 24, ch. 11). One image in the *Bahir,* a Kabbalistic book, is that angels are chariots carrying our prayers to God.

THE SHABBAT ANGELS

Two angels visit Jewish homes every Friday night. When they arrive at the house they check to see if the Shabbat candles are lit, if the table is set, if there is a sense of שְׁלוֹם-בַּיִת

> *sh'lom bayit* (family peace). They want to know if Shabbat has been made in this home.
>
> If there is a feeling of Shabbat in the house, the good angel says, "May this family have a Shabbat like this every week!" and the evil angel is forced to say, "Amen."
>
> But, if there is no feeling of Shabbat in the house, the evil angel says, "May this family have a Shabbat like this every week!" and the good angel is forced to say, "Amen" (*Shabbat* 119b).

This particular story always bothered me. It sort of says "If you don't make Shabbat, you will be cursed to never make Shabbat." But that is not the story's intent. It is suggesting that celebrating one Shabbat can lead to celebrating the next. Ask: "So what was last Shabbat like?"

בּוֹאֲכֶם לְשָׁלוֹם *BO'AKHEM L'SHALOM*

In the first verse we talk about מַלְאֲכֵי הַשָּׁרֵת *Mal'akhei ha-Shareit* (ministering angels). In the other three verses we talk about מַלְאֲכֵי הַשָּׁלוֹם *Mal'akhei ha-Shalom* (angels of peace).

Rabbi Isaac of Komarna explained that each verse actually speaks to two different sets of angels. *Mal'akhei ha-Sharet* refers to the angels who work in heaven and directly serve God, *Mal'akhei ha-Shalom* to the angels who do the Shabbat visit in every home (*Ateret Tiferet*).

The lesson here is that Shabbat is so important that it gets its own category of angels: Angels of Peace just for Shabbat. Ask yourself: "When Shabbat comes, do I feel the angels?"

THE OTHER SHABBAT ANGELS STORY

In the Talmud is a second, very short story about the Shabbat angels.

> If a person prays on *Erev Shabbat* (Friday night), two angels walk with him, place their hands on his head, and say, "God will forgive you for whatever you have done wrong" (*Shabbat* 119b).

That is the Shabbat angels story I like. It says that Shabbat is healing. It can be life-changing. Celebrating Shabbat can make a difference in your life. It is not only an end but a means. Ask again: "So what was your last Shabbat like?"

קִדּוּשׁ *KIDDUSH*

The קִדּוּשׁ *Kiddush* is a prayer that welcomes the holiness of Shabbat or a holiday.

The *Kiddush* is actually made up of two *brakhot.*

- One is the *brakhah* that is said over the wine, grape juice or other liquid (other than water).
- The other is a *brakhah* over Shabbat (or other holiday).

You can't hold Shabbat in your hand. You can't taste it or smell it, see it or hear it. Shabbat is not concrete. We say a *brakhah* over wine that we can smell, taste, and see, that we can hold in our hand, and we add the Shabbat part to it.

The Talmud tells us that we have to say the wine *brakhah* before the *brakhah* for Shabbat. The Talmud compares the wine *brakhah* to a friend we see every day and the *brakhah* over Shabbat to a queen. One might want to say hello to a queen first and then realize that a friend is in the room, but that would be rude. The Talmud wants us to celebrate the everyday first and then look at the special. That is why the wine *brakhah* comes before the *brakhah* for Shabbat.

The *brakhah* over Shabbat teaches two big ideas:

- We celebrate Shabbat because God created the world and then rested.
- We celebrate Shabbat because we were slaves in Egypt and God liberated us.

The Ten Commandments appear twice in the Torah. In each set there is a different reason for Shabbat. In Exodus (20.7–11) we are told to celebrate Shabbat because God rested on the seventh day of creation. In Deuteronomy (5.12-15) we are told to celebrate Shabbat because God took us out of Egypt. Both of these reasons are part of the *Kiddush.*

Kiddush means "holy." Holy means having a special relationship with God. The final message of the *Kiddush* is that Shabbat can help to make us holy.

SHIMON AND REUBEN SEE MUD

This is a story about miracles. The *Kiddush* is a prayer that is about recognizing God's miracles. It is about remembering creation, and it is about remembering the Exodus from Egypt.

> Six hundred thousand Jews escaped from Egypt. Two of them were Shimon and Reuven. When the Reed Sea divided 599,998 Jews were filled with wonder. They saw the water stop flowing. They saw dry land emerge. As they watched, huge flows of water froze into solid walls. This was a miracle.
>
> Shimon and Reuben were looking at their feet. Shimon complained, "For years I had to work with mud. I had to go down into the mud and get my feet dirty. I took the mud and made it into bricks. This is some freedom. Here I am, still in the mud."
>
> Reuben agreed. "We have to walk too far. If God wanted to do a miracle, we could have been lifted back to Canaan. But instead we have to walk. Walking through mud is much harder, and my feet hurt."
>
> Everyone else walked along with their mouths open, totally amazed at how God had stopped nature and made a miracle. For Shimon and Reuven there were no miracles, there was just mud (*Exodus Rabbah* 24:1).

Kiddush does mean "holiness," but it is about defining time as different. Making a moment different is connected to the miraculous. It is recognizing God's presence—God's presence in creation and God's presence in our liberation. *Kiddush* is the proclamation of a moment. We ask: "Where is God at the moment?"

בִּרְכַּת הַמָּזוֹן *BIRKAT HA-MAZON*

בִּרְכַּת הַמָּזוֹן *BIRKAT HA-MAZON*

בִּרְכַּת הַמָּזוֹן *Birkat ha-Mazon* means "the blessing of the food," and it is said after eating. It is sometimes called, "the grace after eating."

Some things to know about *Birkat ha-Mazon* are:

- It should be said at the table where you ate.
- When three or more people say it together, it begins with an invitation and response that is very much like the *Barekhu.*
- There are actually four blessings in *Birkat ha-Mazon* (and extra pieces that one does on Shabbat and holidays), but we are only going to look at the first paragraph.
- Each paragraph tells a story, and when you put them together they retell the history of the Jewish people.

Here are the four stories:

1. Moses wrote the *brakhah* "The One Who Feeds all" when God first fed Israel with manna.
2. Joshua wrote the *brakhah* "For the land and for the food" when the people of Israel first entered the Promised Land.
3. David and Solomon wrote the *brakhah*: "The One Who in kindness Rebuilds Jerusalem." David wrote "On Israel Your people and on Jerusalem Your city." Solomon wrote "And on Your great and holy house."
4. The last *brakhah*, "The One Who is good and does good," was written after a small miracle made things slightly better after the defeat of Bar Kokhba. A moment of major Jewish sadness showed one good thing (*Brakhot* 48a).

When we say *Birkat ha-Mazon* we turn every table into a place of worship.

ABOUT MANNA

Israel spent forty years in the desert. God made manna rain down six days a week. Manna was the special food that fed the Families of Israel in the desert. God made twice as much manna fall on Fridays. God let no manna fall on Shabbat.

The two *hallot* on the Friday night table remind us of the double portion of manna that was stockpiled for Shabbat.

Rabbi Shimon Bar Yohai's students asked, "Why did God make manna fall daily rather than falling only once a year and providing a year's worth?"

He told this story: Once there was a king who gave his son an allowance big enough to last a whole year. Therefore, the prince came to visit his father only once a year to pick up his money. The king got lonely so he changed the plan. He switched the annual allowance to a daily allowance and got to see his son every day (*Yoma* 76a).

Rabbi Shimon bar Yohai taught that each day the manna fell was a new chance to get close to God. *Birkat ha-Mazon* turns each meal into a reliving of the Jewish experience. We ask: "What stories are part of this eating experience?"

A VISIT TO HEAVEN AND HELL

A very righteous man died. The angels offered him a choice between heaven and hell. He said, "I've never been there. How can I choose?" The angels offered him a visit to each. First he was taken to a banquet hall loaded with food. It was the ultimate feast. Out came sad, very skinny people who walked to the tables filled with food and just stood there. They could not eat because on one hand was tied a very long fork and on the other a very long spoon. The people could not reach their mouths with the utensils. This was hell.

Then he was taken to a second hall, also loaded with food. Out came happy people, well-fed people who were singing and dancing. They walked to the tables. On their hands were tied

> the same huge spoons and forks. When they reached the tables they picked up the food in their giant silverware and lifted it to their neighbors' mouths. When the rabbi was offered his choice again, he chose hell. He said, "I know the secret of how to turn it into heaven" (A Jewish folktale).

The first blessing in *Birkat ha-Mazon* ends with the idea that "God feeds everyone." This story makes it clear that for God to feed all, we have to feed each other. Ask simply, "Who needs food? Am I part of the solution?"

ABRAHAM'S TWO *MITZVOT*

The Midrash tells two different stories that connect Abraham to *Birkat ha-Mazon*.

> Abraham had a tent with four doors, one pointing in each direction. That way no one looking for hospitality would ever have to look for a way in. He would feed them and offer them a place to stay.
>
> After dinner Abraham would invite his guests to join him in thanking God for the food and shelter that God had provided. Abraham tried to teach them that even though he was sharing food with them it really came from God. In this way Abraham was the first person to say a *Birkat ha-Mazon* (*Genesis Rabbah* 48:9. 49:7, 39:21).

We are back at Max Kadushin's *Worship and Ethics*. Abraham embodies the duality. First he performs the *mitzvah* of feeding, an echo of God's feeding people. Second, he performs *Kiruv*, bringing people closer to God. *Birkat ha-Mazon* is about both. We ask: "Do I share my food?" "Do I help people to get closer to God?"

THE TWELVE LOAVES OF HALLAH

> In 1492 many Jews had to leave Spain because of the Spanish Inquisition. Two of them were Esperanza and her husband Jacobo. When they left Spain they decided to go home. They went to the Land of Israel and settled in the

city of Tzfat, the place that was becoming the new center for Kabbalah. Jacobo was just a tailor. He set up a shop. On his first Shabbat he went to the synagogue. This Shabbat was the rabbi's sixtieth birthday, and he gave a sermon about the twelve loaves of shew bread that the tribes put in the Temple before each Shabbat. Jacobo did not understand much of the sermon, but he did understand clearly that the rabbi said, "God liked the smell of the bread."

When he told Esperanza about the sermon she came up with an idea. She said, "I will bake twelve loaves of *pan de Dios* (the bread of God), and we will offer them as a gift of thanksgiving." When Shabbat was over she began to bake. In the middle of the night Jacobo brought them to the synagogue and left them in the ark. He said a prayer thanking God for the good things that had happened to them, and then he went home.

A little while later the *shammes*, the man who worked for the synagogue, came in to start to get things ready for the service. He cried to God while he worked. He said, "I have not been paid in many weeks." He yelled at God, "I am doing Your work, taking care of Your house, and my family is hungry. You need to do something." When he started to clean the ark he found the *h̲allot* and thanked God for the help.

Thirty years went by. Every week Esperanza baked *h̲allah*. Every week Jacobo brought it to the synagogue and thanked God. And every week God gave the *shammes* and his family food. On the rabbi's ninetieth birthday he decided to give another sermon on the shew bread. He stayed late on Saturday night, using the library at the back of the sanctuary to do research. When Jacobo came in he listened to the tailor's prayer and then yelled at him, "Fool! People do not feed God." When the two of them heard the *shammes* coming, they hid. When the *shammes* took the *h̲allot* out of the ark, the rabbi called him a thief, saying, "That food belongs to God."

The three men were yelling at one another when the door opened. In walked the Holy Ari, the great Kabbalist, and who "God sent me here to tell you the following. People can really share what they have with God, and with their help God really is הַזָּן אֶת הַכֹּל *ha-Zan et ha-Kol,* the One Who feeds all. Remember, your hands are the hands of God."

Here is another story about the duality of *Birkat ha-Mazon*. It brings us to feed others, and it brings us closer to God.

This is a story I first heard from Rabbi Arthur Green when I was a college student involved in Boston University Hillel. This retelling of the story is my own, based on what I remember of his telling. The story has beem credited to Shlomo Carlebach but the best source for the story is *Mimekor Yisrael,* which defines its sources as anonymous but it is first found in *Ma'asiyot Nora'im ve Nifla'ikm.*

הַבְדָּלָה *HAVDALAH*

הַבְדָּלָה *Havdalah* is a way of ending Shabbat. It is a ceremony that uses a candle, a cup of wine, and a spice. It many ways, we end Shabbat the same way we begin it.

INTRODUCTION

First we say a collection of verses from five different places in the Bible. These verses talk about "cup" and "light." They describe the symbols that will be used in this service. At the same time, these verses talk about the time in the future when God will help us fix and perfect the world. The end of Shabbat is a time when we hope for the best possible future.

WINE

Wine is used welcome Shabbat. The blessing over wine is also used to organize the ending of Shabbat. Every time we use wine it is a celebration. It is traditional to fill the cup to overflowing and spill a little bit as we lift it (*Eruvim* 65a). The Rama said, "The wine shows that we are blessed" (Chp. 291, 1).

SPICE

There is a tradition that on Shabbat we are given a נְשָׁמָה יְתֵרָה *n'shamah y'terah* (an extra soul). We smell spices at the end of Shabbat to give us a boost when that extra soul is taken from us. Their smell refreshes us (Abudarham).

FIRE

In the Torah we are told that one should not create fire on Shabbat. In the Talmud (*Pesahim* 53b) we are taught that God showed Adam and Eve how to create fire after the first Shabbat was over. God gave them fire as a tool. At the end of Shabbat we celebrate that gift by creating fire and saying a blessing over it.

HAVDALAH

The last blessing in the service is a blessing over distinctions. The Midrash teaches that Adam and Eve learned about distinctions during the first *Havdalah*. They saw shadow and light, and they saw the difference between holy and ordinary. We use the end of Shabbat to learn the same lesson.

ADAM AND EVE RECEIVE FIRE

Adam and Eve spent their first Shabbat in the Garden of Eden. They knew that when the day was over, when night came, they would have to leave the garden. As it began to get dark they got scared. The darker it got, the more their fear grew. Adam was scared that the serpent would return and bite him in the heel. God told Adam to pick up two rocks. One rock was darkness. The other was the shadow of death. Adam banged the two rocks together, and out came a spark. The spark lit a fire, the fire lit a torch, and the torch was held high in the air, showing Adam and Eve where to go as they left the garden. Together they prayed, בָּרוּךְ אַתָּה יי אֱלֹהֵינוּ מֶלֶךְ הָעוֹלָם בּוֹרֵא מְאוֹרֵי הָאֵשׁ *Barukh Attah Adonai Eloheinu Melekh ha-Olam Borei m'Orei ha-Esh*, thanking God for the creation of fire. Then, as they watched the shadows flicker, they realized that God made a world with *Havdalah* in it. They knew that fire could not be created on Shabbat, but now it could. They thanked God for all the distinctions, ending בָּרוּךְ אַתָּה יי הַמַּבְדִּיל בֵּין קֹדֶשׁ לְחוֹל *Barukh Attah Adonai ha-Mavdil Bein Kodesh l'Hol*. This was the first *Havdalah*. The next day Adam and Eve began to use the fire to cook, to keep warm, and as a tool (From *Pirkei d'Rabbi Eliezer* 20 and various sources cited in Louis Ginzburg, *Legends of the Jews*).

AN ELIJAH STORY

This story starts with a poor Jewish man who cries out to God. The man, though poor, was always good to other people. Elijah, dressed as an Arab merchant, came to

> him and gave him two coins. The two coins built themselves into a fortune. The man became rich and forgot about others. He got lost in his new wealth. The Arab merchant appeared before the man again and demanded the return of his two coins. When Elijah is paid back the man's fortune collapsed. Again he was poor but returned to his kindness. The man again cried out to God. This time Elijah appeared before him dressed as Elijah and said, "I will make you rich again if you promise not to change the way you treat other people" (Drawn from Louis Ginzburg, *Legends of the Jews*).

The tradition teaches that Shabbat is a foretaste of the World-to-Come. It is a moment when we have re-experienced the Garden of Eden. It is a time when the Messiah is closer. This is why *Havdalah* has an Elijah connection. Elijah never died. He went up to heaven alive in a fiery chariot. The memory goes that he is coming back to announce the coming of the Messiah. In the meantime, Elijah is a trickster, appearing and disappearing, rewarding the good and punishing the wicked. This story puts us back in the real world. Shabbat has ended. But, redemption is still possible. The question here, "How can I take Shabbat and its sense of hope into my week?"

בְּרָכוֹת *BRAKHOT*

WHAT IS A *BRAKHAH*?

There are two kinds of Jewish prayers.

One kind just pours out of our hearts. These are personal words that are made up on the spot. The other kind you find in the Siddur or other books. These are the prayers that Jews share. At the heart of most of these book prayers is the word *Barukh*.

בָּרוּךְ *Barukh* is a Hebrew word that is very hard to translate. Sometimes it is translates as "bless" and sometimes as "praise." Neither tells the whole story.

A *brakhah* is a prayer that either begins or ends with a sentence that starts with the word *barukh*. The word *brakhah* actually means three different things.

- A *brakhah* is a gift from God. A person can say, "I have been blessed with good health" or "I have been blessed with a wonderful family."
- A *brakhah* is a "thank you" to God for a gift that we have received. That is why we say prayers like "Praised are You Who gives strength to those who are tired."
- A *brakhah* is a request for a gift from God. In every morning service Jews say, "Grant us peace… the One Who blesses Israel with peace."

In order to really mean a *brakhah* in our hearts we need to:

- notice the gifts that we have been given.
- believe that God is the source of those gifts.
- believe that it is important to thank God (if this is a "thank you" *brakhah*) and that it makes a difference if we ask God for help (if this is a "please give us a gift" *brakhah*).

A *brakhah* is not just words. It is a connection to God.

BENJAMIN THE SHEPHERD

The Rabbis of the Talmud got into a big debate over something a shepherd named Benjamin did.

Benjamin took a loaf of bread and cut it in half. He then put meat in the middle and began to eat and enjoy the sandwich. In his joy at eating his lunch Benjamin called out, "This is a great sandwich. Praised be the God Who created it."

Some of the rabbis thought that Benjamin had said a wonderful prayer because it was based on true feelings. Two of the rabbis, Rabbi Yosi and Rav, thought that there were big problems because he didn't use the same six words that begin most *brakhot*.

A *brakhah* is said both for the person speaking it and for others who may be listening. A *brakhah* is both a way of thanking God and a way of teaching others about the things that God does. The problem with Benjamin's prayer is that when he said "Praised be the God who created it," he didn't name the God. People hearing it could fill in the name of their own pagan god. Or worse, they could think that Benjamin was praising himself for making the sandwich. That made it problematic.

After Benjamin the Rabbis made it a rule that all *brakhot* should use the six words:

בָּרוּךְ אַתָּה יי אֱלֹהֵינוּ מֶלֶךְ הָעוֹלָם

Barukh Attah Adonai Eloheinu Melekh ha-Olam.

This formula names our God as the One God of the Cosmos (*Brakhot* 40b).

PRAYERS TELL THE TRUTH

The Rabbis of the Talmud, the ones who shaped the prayers we now say, believed that it was important for every prayer to tell the absolute truth. Here is the example they give.

There is one *brakhah* we say over "fruit that grows from trees." There is another *brakhah* we say over "fruit that grows in the ground." In the Talmud they teach that it is okay if you say the "fruit from the ground" *brakhah* over fruit that grows on a tree, because that *brakhah* is still a true statement. It is not okay to say "the fruit of the tree" *brakhah* over things that grow in the ground. That is not a true statement. Fruit that grows on trees also grows in the ground. But fruit that grows in the ground does not always grow on trees. Every time we say a *brakhah* it is our job to be a witness and testify to the things that God does.

To be a good witness we must observe all the different kinds of things that God creates, and our testimony must always be true and accurate. Saying *brakhot* makes us look closely at the world and learn how it works. This helps us to appreciate the ordinary miracles that sustain us every day.

MISHNAH BRAKHOT, CHAPTER 6

> Maimonides, a famous Jewish teacher, wrote: "Anyone who eats any food or enjoys anything without saying a *brakhah* is a thief." What do you think he meant?
>
> Maimonides began his book *Mishneh Torah* by writing, "The basic principle of all principles, the foundation of all science, is knowing that One God created everything." Maimonides explains that our job is to examine the world and come to know and love The Creator through the creation.
>
> Our job is to appreciate everything that God created and thank God for it. When we fail to notice and learn, when we do not say thank you, we are "stealing" and not paying the "rent" on the things that God gave us (Maimonides, *Mishneh Torah, Introduction to Book of Knowledge*).

We have already established that blessings are acts of appreciation and the recognition of the Divine presence. This chapter of the *Mishneh Torah* makes it clear that *brakhot* must be true statements.

MOSES SEES THE AFTERWARD OF GOD

This Moses story begins with Jacob. Only part of this story can be found in the Torah. Much of it comes from different places in the Midrash.

> Jacob left home on an adventure. Partially he was running away from his brother, who was ready to kill him.

He had pulled a very bad trick on Esau. Partially he was out looking for a wife. Clearly, he was on his own for the first time. As sundown came he found a place to camp for the night. He took a stone, put it under his head as a pillow, and fell asleep. What then followed was one of the great dreams of all times. In his dream Jacob saw a ladder that went from earth into the heavens. Angels were traveling up the ladder, and angels were traveling down the ladder. The next thing that happened was that God spoke with Jacob and told him, "I will always be with you."

The meaning of dreams is never clear. Every dream has many interpretations, and this one was no exception. Many scholars have said many things about this dream. But this much is clear: Jacob woke up in the morning and said, "God was in this place, and I, I hadn't noticed." The ladder showed him that people have many ways of connecting to God.

Moses also had to run away from home. He left Egypt and went to a country named Midian, There he, too, found a wife, Zipporah. He began work as a shepherd for her father. One day he had taken his sheep way into the wilderness to find a good place to graze. It was here in the wilderness, near a mountain that would later be called Sinai, that he had his vision of getting close to God. He was awake when he saw a bush burning, a bush that burned and burned and yet was not burned up. It was then that God spoke to Moses.

God wondered for a long time about how to sound. God didn't want to sound too powerful, for a loud voice might scare Moses into running away. God didn't want to sound too soft, or Moses wouldn't have the right respect. God came up with an idea. God spoke to Moses using his father's voice. Moses thought his father had come into the desert and asked, "Is that you, Father?" God answered, "I am not your father, but the God of your father" and began to speak. Moses hid his eyes because he was afraid to look at God.

Years later Moses led the Jewish people to Mount Sinai the way he had once led his sheep there. Many things happened. God spoke words of Torah to everyone gathered there. Moses went up the mountain and received the Ten Commandments.

> The Jewish people made a Golden Calf, and God got really angry. So did Moses. God and Moses calmed each other down. Then Moses said to God, "I want to see Your face. I want to know what You look like." Things had changed from that first moment at the mountain when Moses was afraid. God said, "You cannot see My face and live." Moses said, "Please."
>
> God said, "I will let you hide your face in the rock and cover you with My hand. I will go past you. When I have gone by, I will take away my My hand, and you will see my 'afterwards.'" And that is what God did. Many people think that God showed Moses God's "back," but if you read the Hebrew carefully, it says "afterward." Moses saw the wake of God, the differences made because God was there.
>
> We are like Jacob and Moses. We want to get close to God, but that is not easy. We have to realize that God is where we are, because we often forget that. And we have to learn that while we cannot see God, we can see God's afterward. We can see the things God does.
>
> A *brakhah* is a way of saying God is in this place. A *brakhah* is a way of saying, "I noticed what God did, and I am thankful" (Your author's assemblage of lots of parts of the Jewish tradition).

A *brakhah* is a way of saying "God has been here." What's the last thing that God did for you?

MITZVAH BRAKHOT

Being a Jew is trying to:

- learn about and love God.
- become the best people we can be.
- make the world into the best possible place for everyone.

The Torah is the guidebook that God gave the Jewish people. It gives us ways to learn about God, it teaches us lessons about becoming the best people we can be, and it directs us to work on making the world better.

When you study the Torah you learn that it has 613 ways of living that bring us close to God and help us to live the way God wants us to live.

Some of these are holiday celebrations like Passover, Sukkot, and Shabbat. Some of these are good things to do like loving your neighbor, giving *tzedakah*, and helping people to get well. And some of these ways to live are things not to do. These include not murdering, not embarrassing, and not hating another person in our heart.

We call these ways of living, *mitzvot*. In Yiddish the word *mitzvah* is understood to mean "good deed." That is not exactly the meaning that is found in the Torah. Most English translations of the Torah and the Siddur translate *mitzvah* as "commandment." These are things that God has told us to do and that God has told us not to do.

Some (but not all) *mitzvot* have *brakhot*. These *brakhot* help us to remember that the reason we are doing these things is to get closer to God. There are *brakhot* for putting on a *tallit*, lighting candles, studying Torah, and sitting in a *sukkah*.

A *mitzvah brakhah* is different from an ordinary *brakhah*. We add a few more words to the beginning. We add: אֲשֶׁר קִדְּשָׁנוּ בְּמִצְוֹתָיו וְצִוָּנוּ *Asher Kid'shanu b'Mitzvotav v'Tzivanu.*

It says that the when we do a *mitzvah* it is a connection to the holy. This *brakhah* with extra words reminds us that the thing we are doing is a chance to experience holiness.

THE HISTORY OF MITZVOT

It is hard to be a parent. God learned that with Adam and Eve. God wanted people to be good to themselves and good to each other, so God gave them just one rule.[5] It should have been enough. This one *mitzvah* was "No idols." This was a big rule. It wasn't just "Don't carve things out of wood and stone." "No idols" meant "Don't ever think that you are God." It also meant "Don't think that you can make up your own gods who will tell you what you want to hear." And most of all "No idols" meant "Don't think that you can decide that right is what you feel like doing." Even if you are angry at someone, you cannot hit him. Even if someone cheated you, you cannot cheat the person back. Fighting is never the way to solve anything. You can't steal something no matter how much you want it. "No idols" meant that there is One God Who created everyone and Who wants us to treat everyone the right way.

The "No idols" *mitzvah* didn't work. The world turned into a pretty bad place. People stole. People hurt. People did what they wanted and didn't care about anyone else. Adam and Eve's descendents were unhappy, and God was really angry. God decided to start over. That is where the flood came in. It was time for the Parent to add some new rules. This time God gave Noah and his family six more rules. God kept the (1) "No idols" *mitzvah* and added (2) be good to your family, (3) no killing, (4) no stealing, (5) no cursing out God, (6) no being cruel to animals, and (7) set up courts to fix things when you are angry at each other. God hoped that by His being more specific people would act better. It didn't work. Even with seven *mitzvot,* they still hurt, killed, stole, and more or less did what they wanted. The world wasn't much better.

God decided to try a third way of parenting. God went for an experiment. God picked one small family, Abram's family, and said, "We are going to make a deal. I will work with you (in private lessons), and when we figure it out you will teach everyone else." So God gave the Families of Israel lots of rules,

[5]There were actually two other rules. "Be fruitful and multiply:" This wasn't counted because it was given to all life and not just people. And "Don't eat the fruit from the tree in the middle of the garden:" This also doesn't count because it was particular to just the people living in the garden. God gave them only one mitzvah that is still on the list.

613 *mitzvot*. Some of these were things to do. Some were things not to do. Some were rules about how to treat each other. Some were ways of looking at our actions—the way one looks at a wardrobe in a mirror—and learning how to improve them. Israel got the Torah, which had holidays and stories, things to do every day, and a large collections of "Do this" or "Don't do this" things. The idea was that God gave them the gift of not just a couple of rules but a whole way of living that would help them to make themselves into better people and help them teach others how to be better, too. All of this is just a huge version of "No idols" that works on getting us past the moments when "how we feel" gets in the way of "what we know we should do."

Therefore, it is hard to be a Jew. Torah comes with a lot of things to do and not do. But being a Jew also offers a path to becoming happy by letting the best you emerge and join with others to make a much better world (From all over the *Midrash*).

The Torah is a gift from God. It contains 613 mitzvot. Of these, 365 are positive. That means they are rules that we are supposed to do. There is one positive *mitzvah* for every day in the year (though we are supposed to do a lot more than one every day). There are 248 negative *mitzvot*. These are *mitzvot* that say "do not do." There are also 248 bones in our body.

The big idea is this: *Mitzvot* are the ways we are supposed to shape ourselves—down to the bone—every single day. They are chances to come to know God. They are ways of becoming better people. They are ways of making the world better.

THE FLYING LETTERS

Once there were two towns. One was rich, and one was poor. The rich town had a wonderful, beautiful synagogue. It had stained-glass windows. It had polished wooden pews. And it had its own *Sefer Torah* (Torah scroll). A *Sefer Torah* is very expensive.

The other town was very poor. It could not afford a beautiful synagogue. In this town people gathered in a small room at the back of a store to pray. This town was so small that they could not afford a *Sefer Torah*. They could not afford to pay a scribe to spend nine months copying every letter by hand. What the poor town did was to take two wooden rollers and stretch parchment between them. It was an empty Torah. But, they hoped one day to have enough money to turn it into a real Torah. Sometimes they would open the empty scroll and pretend that it was filled with words while one of the members read the portion out of a book.

In the rich town almost no one came to services. At first they had services every day. Then, when no one showed up, they began to hold services only once a week, on Shabbat. When it became hard to get a *minyan* (a group of ten Jews) on Shabbat they started holding services only once a month. Eventually the beautiful synagogue was locked, closed, and empty every day except for Rosh ha-Shanah and Yom Kippur.

In the poor town people loved to come together. There was a service every morning and every night. Every Shabbat the whole town showed up and made it a real gathering. In this poor town this little dark room with wooden benches became filled with the light of friendship and community. Even though the room was not beautiful, it became a wonderful place to be.

People in the rich town began to get selfish. They stopped thinking of their neighbors as being like family. If someone was sick, fewer and fewer people visited or brought food. If someone died, almost no one stopped by to comfort the family that was left behind. If someone was poor, there was no point in expecting help. In the rich town everyone took care of number one. This was true in business, and it was true at school. It was true when their children played games, and it was true of the way they talked about each other.

The poor town was like one big family. Everyone knew what other people needed and tried to help. If someone was sick, chicken soup arrived. If someone was in mourning, her house was filled with people comforting them. If someone had a bad business time, his neighbors helped in many ways. The poor town was poor, but it was rich in the love that went from neighbor to neighbor.

> On the night before the night before Yom Kippur the Torah reader of the rich synagogue opened the lock and tried to make sure that the Torah was rolled to the right place. The synagogue was dark and quiet. When he opened the ark door hundreds of Hebrew letters flew out of the ark and surrounded him. It was like being attacked by a swarm of bees. He brushed them away and shut the ark door. He ran home and even forgot to lock the synagogue door. He didn't tell anyone what had happened. He was sure he was dreaming.
>
> On the night before the night before Yom Kippur a couple of men were walking home from evening prayers. They looked up and were sure that they saw a swarm of Hebrew letters fly across the face of the moon, looking like a swarm of bats. But they told each other it must have been bats, because Hebrew letters don't fly.
>
> In the middle of morning services the congregation of the rich town took out their *Sefer Torah* and opened it to begin to read. They had a big shock. Their scroll was empty. No words. No letters. All of the Torah was now missing from their scroll. At almost the same moment the families of the poor town had a shock, too. When they opened their empty scroll to pretend to read they found it filled with words and letters. It had become a complete Torah (From a story by David Einhorn, *The Flying Letters,* the story "The Seventh Candle").

I love this final story. I found it in an out-of-print book by David Einhorn, then heard my friend Rabbi Ed Feinstein tell it. It has always symbolized for me the difference a Jewish life can make. It is the perfect "doing *mitzvot* can change your life" story. Each time we take a small action and notice God in it, each time we define our actions as sacred, each time we notice God's afterwards, we move letters into our *Sefer Torah.* The last question, also the first: "What did you add to your Torah today?"

STORY INDEX